A Final Reckoning

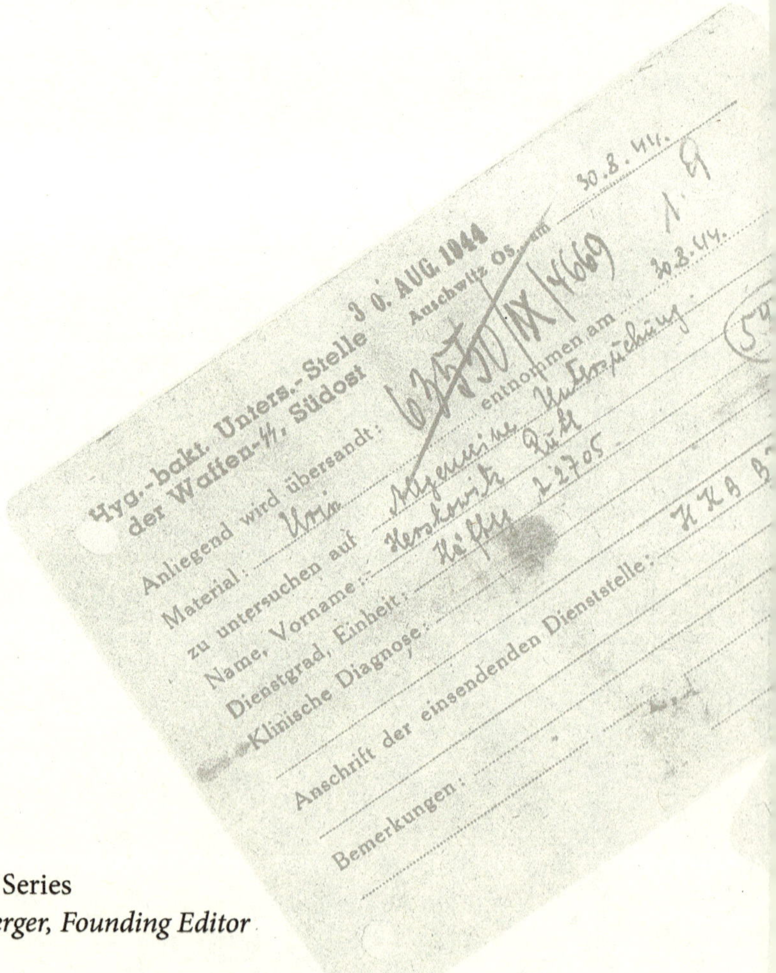
Hyg.-bakt. Unters.-Stelle
der Waffen-SS, Südost
30. AUG. 1944
Auschwitz OS.
Anliegend wird übersandt:
Material:
entnommen am
zu untersuchen auf
Name, Vorname:
Dienstgrad, Einheit:
Klinische Diagnose:
Anschrift der einsendenden Dienststelle:
Bemerkungen:

Judaic Studies Series
Leon J. Weinberger, Founding Editor

The University of Alabama Press • Tuscaloosa

A Final Reckoning

A Hannover Family's Life and Death in the Shoah

RUTH GUTMANN

Foreword by Kenneth Waltzer

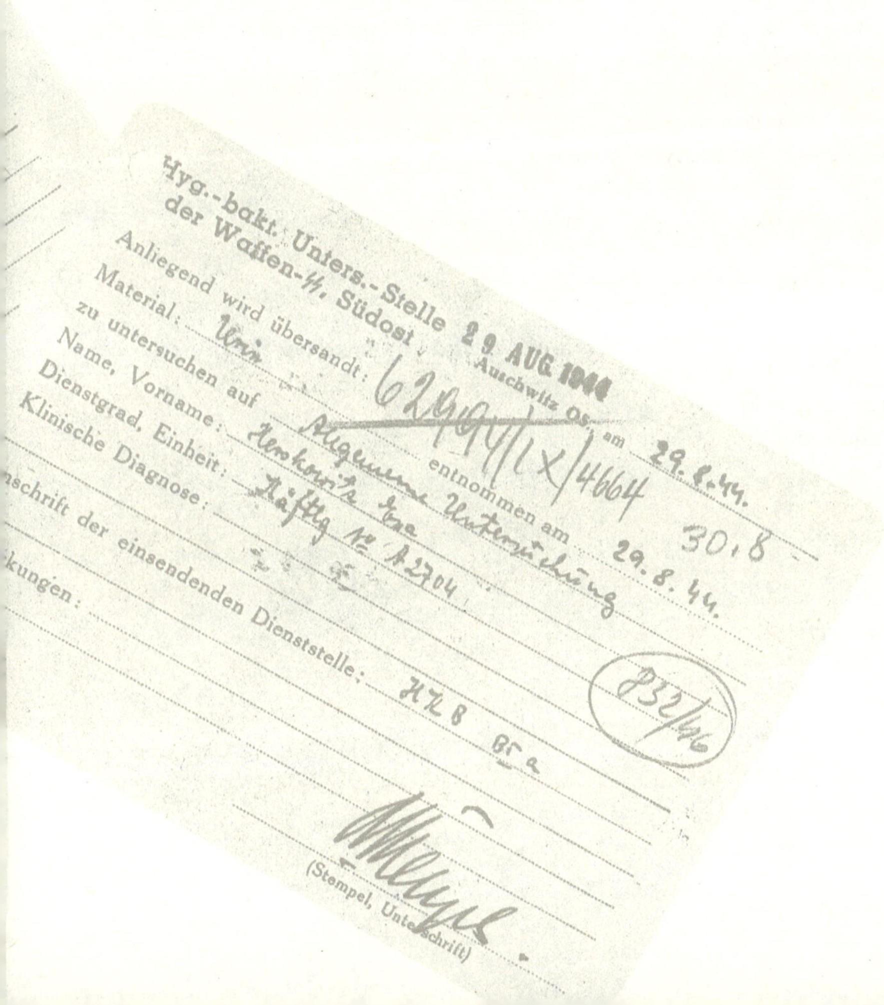
Hyg.-bakt. Unters.-Stelle der Waffen-SS, Südost
29 AUG 1944 Auschwitz O/S
Anliegend wird übersandt: 62994/IX/4664 am 29.8.44.
Material: Urin entnommen am 29.8.44. 30.8
zu untersuchen auf Allgemeine Untersuchung
Name, Vorname: Herskowitz Ilse
Dienstgrad, Einheit: Häftling Nr. A 2704
Klinische Diagnose:
Anschrift der einsendenden Dienststelle: HKB BIIa
Bemerkungen:
(Stempel, Unterschrift)

The University of Alabama Press
Tuscaloosa, Alabama 35487-0380
uapress.ua.edu

Hardcover edition published 2013.
Paperback edition published 2020.
eBook edition published 2013.

Typeface: Minion and Cambria

Cover images: Ruth Gutmann three days after Liberation, May 3, 1945
(courtesy of the author); twins Eva and Ruth in front of the Swedish sanatorium
where Ruth was recovering, 1946 (courtesy of the author);
laboratory slips signed by Dr. Josef Mengele, dated August 30, 1944
(courtesy of Gedenkstätte Auschwitz)
Cover design: Michele Myatt Quinn

All photographs are courtesy of the author unless otherwise noted.

Paperback ISBN: 978-0-8173-5993-5

A previous edition of this book has been catalogued by the Library of Congress.

ISBN: 978-0-8173-1809-3 (cloth)
E-ISBN: 978-0-8173-8718-1

Contents

Foreword

Ruth Gutmann's memoir is a distinctive work in several ways. It is a book of memory—clearly the young Ruth's memoir—especially focused on her ruminations about her father; it is also a book of critical memory and sophisticated reflection, informed by study. Early on, we hear the voice of a young girl, pushed about by incomprehensible forces; subsequently, we hear the considered tones of an intelligent woman who has wrestled difficult matters into thoughtful perspective across a lifetime. Ruth is especially interested in her father, Samuel Herskovits, his biography, and state of mind and actions; he was the leading Jewish community official in Hannover, and she loved him but brooded over whether he was perhaps guilty of cooperating with the Nazis in deporting the city's Jews. The mature Ruth stresses the man's powerlessness and inability to do anything but dutifully comply with the Gestapo's demands. She also shows ambivalent feelings about him for his love of Germany and German culture and for his failure to protect his daughters by timely family emigration before the war.

Ruth Herskovits, one of two female twins, was born in Hannover in March 1928, in a German Jewish family with Hungarian roots. After the pogrom—*Kristallnacht*—of 1938, Ruth and her twin sister, Eva, were sent by their parents on a *Kindertransport* to Holland. Shortly after the twins' departure, their mother died following a minor operation. The girls had just finished elementary school when the Nazis occupied Holland in May 1940. Samuel brought them home to Hannover in November 1941. The girls now lived with their father, stepmother, and stepsister in the Jewish Community House, which a Nazi law to evict all Jews from the houses of German citizens caused to be converted into one of the sixteen Jewish dwellings for Hannover's remaining Jews. Their father had completed his preparations to emigrate to Cuba with his family. But their permission to leave Germany was "postponed" and never restored, and next, they were moved to the Jewish Horticultural School at Ahlem, where the Gestapo gathered the city's Jews for deportations between 1941 and 1943. Then, when nearly all of Hannover's Jews were deported, the city was *Judenrein*, and all remaining Jewish communities in the cities of Nazi Germany were dissolved, the Herskovits family was sent to Terezin in June 1943 and, from there, to Auschwitz-Birkenau in May 1944.

At Birkenau, the twin girls attracted Josef Mengele's interest: They were photographed for the Nazi doctor, and he examined them, but they were spared involvement in further experimentation. Instead they survived as adolescents in the women's camp at Birkenau, and then in several other camps, where they worked for Telefunken when they were not traveling, among them Reichenbach, Porta Westfalica, Beendorf, and Wandsbek. After the war, Count Folke Bernadotte and the Danish Red Cross brought them to Denmark and Sweden to convalesce. Both girls later came to the United States. Here, Eva could not escape the terrible burdens of pain and self-reproach she carried from her traumatic experiences. Ruth, who also struggled with such burdens, endured.

Ruth writes sympathetically about the plight and dilemmas that officials such as her father faced—they could not comprehend the full potential of Nazism or foresee until very late all the threatening possibilities. They were powerless when they did see and without real meaningful choices. Samuel sent his daughters out—an elder sister went to England—but any efforts he explored to move the family as a whole were simply unavailing. Besides, the Nazis needed the Jewish community official and, Ruth concludes, no doubt would not ever have let him go. Meanwhile, the Nazis ordered lists to be made and "resettled" Hannover's Jews eastward to Riga even before the Wannsee Conference, while German Jews from other cities were deported to Minsk and Lodz in addition to Riga. Later the so-called *Prominente* were sent to Terezin. Samuel Herskovits registered the properties, (most likely) made up the lists, and facilitated the deportations.

As well as her father's story, Ruth also explores and assesses her own and her sister Eva's experiences in Hannover, Holland, at Terezin and Birkenau, and after liberation and since. The chapters on Terezin, Birkenau, and the several subsequent camps, and on life after the camps, are as strong as any camp memoirs I've read, casting light on her own and her sister's story(ies)—the girls got contiguous tattoos, Eva A-2704 and Ruth A-2705, at Birkenau. She also offers thoughtful witness about the internal functioning of the camps, the hierarchy of prisoner functionaries therein, and the elements of everyday life under conditions beyond extremity. All family members were initially placed in the Czech family camp, but the stepmother was selected for work—they knew not where—and the twin girls were taken out; Samuel suffered the fate of other prisoners who were mostly elderly, remaining in the nearly empty camp, and then he was gassed. Eva tried with bravado but without success to intercede with Mengele and thereafter never forgave herself for her father's death. Ruth reports she was disappointed in her father's inability to protect them and her own inability to protect him. Ruth made her peace with the past and, in the memoir, makes peace with the man and his role.

Ruth's final chapter, an afterword, also adds a distinctive touch. Here she argues convincingly against some despairing judgments the great Italian survivor-writer Primo Levi offered in his powerful final book of essays, *The Drowned and the Saved*, published not long before his suicide. Ruth's reflections should be read by all students of human experience in the camps. She says she learned not to judge too harshly the prisoners who inhabited the gray zone of the camp at Auschwitz-Birkenau. These prisoners were not all the same—some carried the moral standards of the outside world into the hell they inhabited and acted appropriately, and others succumbed and were degraded. She notes that Primo Levi, even while he cautioned against judging, tended to judge these figures despite his insistence that it was inappropriate to do so. In this memoir, so deeply rooted in her own struggles then and since, survivor Ruth Gutmann offers a plea for greater understanding and wisdom in contemplating the situations and relative powerlessness of ghetto and prisoner functionaries during the Holocaust and cautions us against (too hasty) judgment. It is with no little special authority of her own, rooted in experience and reflection, that she insists Levi fell victim to his despair, shame, and displaced rage at the end, while she offers us a memoir of traumatic experience that remains balanced, sensitive, and considered throughout.

Kenneth Waltzer
Professor and Director of Jewish Studies
Michigan State University

Acknowledgments

Whenever I think of the friends and acquaintances whose friendship and help I want to recall, Dr. Marlis Buchholz and the MA thesis she published in 1987, *Die Hannoverschen Judenhäuser: Zur Situation der Juden in der Zeit der Ghettoisierung und Verfolgung 1941–1945* (The Houses for the Jews in Hannover: The Situation of the Jews at the Time of the Ghettoization and Persecution 1941–1945), are foremost in my mind. Her book has not been translated into English, but its German words deeply affected me. It described the frightful situation that greeted my twin, Eva, and me when we returned from Holland to Hannover.

Marlis helped me to remember my experiences of these and many associated events. She also opened the door to the Historische Seminar of the University of Hannover (now Gottfried Wilhelm Leipnitz University). I shall always be indebted to Marlis for her hospitality and that of her friends, the Family Riebe, and for the opportunity to participate in seminars about Ahlem and in general to learn German Jewish history from Professors Hans-Dieter Schmid, Claus and Katja Füllberg-Stolberg, and my subsequent translator, Dr. Bernhard Strebel.

This English edition, written years before it was translated into German, came to be with the encouragement of my children and grandchildren, Sam Gutmann and Hannah Sherak and her sons, Raffi and Ben. Their confidence in my abilities would have been flattering if I had not realized that it was my persistence they trusted.

I want to thank the University of Alabama Press for assigning Joan Matthews, a first-rate copy editor, who helped me with both her technical knowledge and her sensitivity to the subject. This was especially surprising because we readers have been given to understand that copyediting and proofreading are no longer economically feasible.

My special thanks go to Dr. Thomas Bardelle, a historian who was at the time an archivist of the Hauptarchiv in Hannover, for enabling me to read the files of my father, Samuel Herskovits, and to reprint several documents.

I am indebted to the Lower Saxony State Archive, the Main Archive of Hannover, for access to my father's file and the information I obtained. The file's designation is NLA HStAH Hann 210 Acc 2004/023, Nr. 1541.

I am also grateful for the prompt permission we obtained from Dr. Wojciech Plosa, the head of the archive of the Gedenkstätte (Memorial site) Auschwitz to copy Eva's and my laboratory slips, signed by Dr. Josef Mengele, in my memoir.

Last but not least, I am grateful to the country of Sweden that sent Count Folke Bernadotte to negotiate the release of thousands of barely surviving prisoners from many countries that the Nazis had held for several years. Eva and I had the good fortune to be among them. Finally I dedicate this memoir to my husband, Alfred, who never fails to find the perspective that I am sometimes in danger of losing.

Time Line

1905 Samuel Herskovits emigrates to Germany, and attends a business school.

1909 Samuel is employed as a clerk in the Office of the Jewish Community of Hannover.

1914 World War I

Samuel enlists in Austro-Hungarian Army and is stationed in Theresienstadt.

1915 Samuel's mother and stepfather flee from Hungary and live with him until 1925.

1920 Samuel marries Helene Kiss in Hungary. They settle in Hannover.

1922 Margarete (Grete) is born.

1924 Samuel is named *Gemeindesekretär* (executive secretary) of the Jewish community; the family moves to the top-floor apartment of Lützowstrasse 3, the community's office and school.

1925 Fraternal twins, Karl Franz and Francisca Klara, are born.

1927 Two-year-old Karl dies in a children's hospital.

1928 A second set of fraternal twins, Eva and Ruth, are born.

1933 Hitler, leader of the National Socialists, becomes Chancellor of Germany.

1934 The law of "Restoration of Professions" is passed. Jewish professionals are fired in all of Germany. Anti-Semitism worsens.

1935 A Jewish elementary school opens in the family's house. The Nuremberg Racial Laws are passed.

1937 Samuel is arrested for allegedly breaking foreign currency laws.

1938 Approximately 17,000 Polish Jews are deported from Germany. November 9–10: The major pogrom known as *Kristallnacht* occurs.

1939 January 4: Eva and Ruth travel on the *Kindertransport* to Holland.

March 16: Helene dies at age 44 after a minor operation.

May: Margarete emigrates to England.

June: Samuel marries Mania Münzer. She has a 13-year-old daughter, Lotte.

1939 September 1: Hitler marches into Poland. England declares war.

1940 Hitler's armies invade and defeat France, Holland, Belgium, Norway, etc.

September: Klara is taken from a Catholic home in Bavaria and "euthanized."

1941 June 22: Hitler attacks the Soviet Union. Last year for Jews to leave.

German Einsatzgruppen massacre Jews, Russians, and Partisans by the thousands.

Samuel asks for help to emigrate "to any country whatsoever."

Eva and Ruth return to Hannover hoping to go to Cuba. Their plan fails.

1943 July: All remaining German Jews have now been deported.

1944 Samuel, Mania, Lotte, Eva, and Ruth are sent to Theresienstadt, then to Auschwitz, where Samuel is gassed.

July: Mania is selected for work and is sent to Stutthof near Danzig. She is said to have died in February 1945.

Lotte and her son, Danny, are deported from Theresienstadt to Auschwitz. Both are gassed in September. Lotte was not yet 19; Danny was 1 year old.

1945 April 30: Hitler commits suicide. Germany surrenders.

May 1: After being shipped to a half-dozen camps, Ruth and Eva are liberated.

1945 The Nuremberg Tribunal.

Prologue

> And now, beloved Little Ones and dearest Gretel, we wish you the very best for the approaching High Holy Days. May an eternal peace of justice and mutual understanding arrive for you and all humanity so that true redemption may make its entrance in the world. When that legendary age arrives, peoples of the most diverse faiths, conceptions, and opinions will join together for the sole purpose of mutual help and support. Human and other powers of nature and art will serve only the ends of peace, and humanity will strive for one aim: to attain and preserve the palm of peace. Amen.
>
> —September 10, 1939,
> original in German

Father ended his New Year's greetings to the three of us with that fervent wish for our and all humanity's redemption. World War II had started the week before. Hitler had been in power for six years, during which many of his provocations pointed to the war to come. Life had steadily worsened for the Jews of Germany. Father had succeeded in sending his oldest daughter to England and his twins to Holland. Eva and I had only recently learned that we had lost our mother. He remained in Germany although he, too, had a permit to immigrate to England. His remarriage in June 1939 to Mania Münzer, who had no permit, made it impossible for him to leave Germany. But his most serious problem we learned about in a second letter he wrote us only days after his holiday wishes. I am not sure that, at the time, even Grete fully understood what he hinted at: The Gestapo might not permit him to leave Hannover.

His ability, nonetheless, to evoke for us a world of such all-encompassing peace and perfection had long amazed me. Now I see it as Father's way of expressing himself: This wish is, after all, only one of a pair. Father has spared us what he is seeing as the first half: It is no less than an apocalypse, the result of the recent outbreak of World War II. Whether this New Year's wish was his inspiration or a description of a promised messianic age, it is a stern reminder that I did not know him long or well enough. My focus in writing about him can, at best, be a narrow and at times childish one. What I shall say of him here will not do him full justice and may, at times, even be unjust. Father speaks of the "powers of nature and art" but makes no mention of God. Yet I think that he was guided that day by his faith in God and in his often-expressed conviction that "ultimately all is for the best." His faith had been instilled in him by his mother when he was a very young child. We knew of Father's deep respect for Jewish learning, which he had acquired at the ultra-Orthodox Sofer (Schreiber) Yeshiva in Bratislava, where he spent so much of his youth. He told us of having gained an understanding of Jewish life that those not similarly schooled in the Talmud lacked. I feel that he held fast to his faith and that it guided him during the few years that remained to him.

His conviction that "ultimately all is for the best" is the more remarkable because, on a practical level, quite early in the Nazi regime, Father's work as a Jewish official brought him face-to-face with the ever-increasing irrationality of the demands the new German regime made of the Jewish community and officials like him. After working with German civil servants during the Weimar Republic of the prior decade, he will have encountered the changed attitudes of some of the same officials when he had to deal with them after Hitler's accession to power.

Despite our parents' efforts to protect us from these political developments, my twin, Eva, and I were aware of their worries, and our older sister, Grete, had on occasion even been taken into Mother's confidence. Even as adults, Eva and I were to see some of our experiences, no matter how innocuous, through the prism of those early Nazi years. At the time, while our mother wanted to leave Germany, Father's answer to her concerns was an ever-greater caution and a seemingly endless adaptability to what confronted him. I am not sure why Father was so reluctant to immigrate to Palestine. He was a man who did not share his thinking, which left us to focus on his actions to try to understand his reasoning. Some years after my mother died, Father assured me that she had been a very intelligent woman. It was the time when deportations were being prepared, and while I was very pleased to hear him praise her, I think he may have been recalling that she was correct in having urged him to leave. Sadly, it was too late for his realization.

In February 1941, Father made another effort to leave Germany and wrote to Grete in England to urge our relatives to help him leave. When Eva and I returned from Holland to join the family for the trip to Cuba, we believed that our papers were waiting for us. But apart from a small number of individuals who were able to leave, the German authorities no longer permitted Jews to emigrate. Our family had received permission to emigrate, but on January 5, 1942, the form was stamped "Emigration currently not possible" and put in the inactive file. While we did not know it, it was the time of the Wannsee Conference when the highest Nazi officials got together in Berlin, and formalized the preparations for the Holocaust that had been under way for the last six months.

Over the years I have thought of describing the three years that followed our final failure to leave Germany. My first attempts to record what I remembered of our family's life during the Nazi years go back to the 1970s. The loss of my twin sister, Eva, with whom I had shared so much, made me fear that I had lost the last thread that connected me to our experiences and to our even more distant childhood.

Like dreams, memories can become plans. They came to me quite unbidden, as images of people that I could hardly recognize, or as sounds and events, for which I had to find the words to help me tell the story of that time.

What I relate here cannot be free of the distortions of hindsight. Every passing day with its reflections on the past becomes an addition *to* that past. I needed first to strip away the protective layer I had gradually created to shield me from the memories that sometimes threatened to overwhelm me. I wanted to record as truthfully as I could the images and voices that have continued to accompany my daily life. Some of these I have loved because they reminded me of the joys and soothing daily routines of childhood. But there were images and thoughts that, because they were so disturbing, prevented me from enjoying being in the here and now with my own family. At times this caused me to imagine threats from which I had to protect my children—threats that other parents might never have known existed. While I fought against the hold such irrational fears had on me and wanted neither to admit their existence nor to give in to them, my past experiences made it difficult for me to believe in a future for myself. Unavoidably, this also cast a shadow on the childhood of the children, and burdened their father. In spite of this, the hopes that I nurtured for my children were as ambitious as those of any other parent.

It was raising our children in this country in very different political circumstances and expectations that helped me realize that some of those old apprehensions of "what might happen" were spilling over into the present. Once the children were older, I began to read histories in both English and German to learn about the events that had caused us and so many others so much grief, and to gain some understanding of their causes. I wanted to encourage our children to pursue their interests and dreams, independent of what they had learned of their parents' past, and strove hard not to damage their joie de vivre.

My reading helped me to understand my parents' perspective and how the history of the lives of the German Jews of earlier times had influenced later generations. It taught me that Germany's small Jewish population never achieved full legal standing in Germany. There were, during the first few years of the nineteenth century, brief periods of legal equality in the German states that were influenced, and in some cases created, by the Napoleonic regimes. However, these new laws were soon canceled when those regimes came to an end. The gradual emancipation of the Jews that had begun during the eighteenth century was both ambiguous and partial, being contingent on what was called Jewish "moral regeneration," as that problematic term was understood in discussion among the Protestant clergy and educated German classes. The ancient accusation of deicide, which clung to the Jewish people for centuries, championed both by Voltaire and the English Deists, resonated in Germany also. Life for the Jews became somewhat easier if they assimilated or actually converted to Christianity. In later years, however, assimilation became a "solution" whose high price evoked strong disapproval in the Jewish community, while it in no way improved acceptance of German Jewry among the German population.

Starting in the early nineteenth century and even earlier, the German Jews, less than 1 percent of the German population, contributed more than their share to many areas of intellectual life in German society. In their own fields they created the *Wissenschaft des Judentums* (Science of Judaism) and sponsored a series of journals. Among other subjects, these were devoted to encourage the self-improvement of the Jews to be worthy neighbors of the Christian population. They established Reform and Neoconservative branches with their own seminaries, and built beautiful synagogues. For the first time, influenced by Moses Mendelssohn and his translations, they studied the Old Testament and their own religion, as a religion, rather than interpreting the Mosaic laws to understand why the ancient rabbis disagreed with one another or had allowed some actions and forbidden others. And in the spirit of their own Enlightenment (Haskala), and the demands of German states in charge of Jewish affairs, rabbis were required to have a secular education in addition to their Jewish learning. Rabbi Nathan Adler, a rabbi in Hannover, received the first doctorate in philosophy in 1828. A scholarly and practical man, who worked hard to improve the lot of the Jews in his communities, by 1845 he had been called to become Chief Rabbi of Great Britain.[1]

The Jews were not accepted in most of the many civic organizations that constituted the backbone of the governments of the German states. Their solution was to create their own cultural, philanthropic, and educational organizations while failing to perceive that this continued their isolation from the larger society. According to David Sorkin's study of the period, they were in effect creating "a subculture," a new ghetto, for themselves. This early period of Jewish life and its consequences are well worth studying.[2]

In Hannover, a Jewish Law was passed in 1842. This seems to have served to raise the legal standing for Jewish life and may have been influenced by Hannover's connection to England. Until that time, some members of the Jewish community who lived as *Schutzjuden* (protected Jews) of the state were the only ones with rights approaching those of the larger society. Their contributions to the state were largely economic and financial and were at times indispensable. But like an unstoppable, hurtful refrain, "contemporary Jewry," according to Sorkin, "was assumed to be the bearer of an immorality of the Old Testament unchanged by time."[3] There were influential German historians, such as J. G. Droysen, who denied the connection between the Old and New Testaments and claimed Hellenism as the root for the New Testament, omitting the Old Testament entirely.[4]

During the last three decades of the nineteenth century, new concepts of racial anti-Semitism were born in Germany as well as in Austria. These resulted in several anti-Semitic outbreaks and were to feed the prejudices of the future.

Ironically, during a time when the German Jews worked hard to achieve better conditions for their specific endeavors and life in general, they did not feel obliged to extend their sympathy to the Eastern Jews who came as refugees to Germany in 1881, fleeing murderous pogroms in Russia. It seems that the German Jews no longer shared a lifestyle and manner of speech with these refugees and were insecure enough to fear that the likely disapproval of German society would badly reflect on them.

The First World War, aside from heavy losses, spawned the accusation that the German Jews had not fought in large enough numbers and had not sacrificed themselves for their fatherland to the same extent as German men. A "Jew Census" was ordered, but the results were not released. Instead of too few Jews fighting for Germany, it was found that their numbers far exceeded their percentage in the population. By the end of the war, twelve thousand young German Jewish men had given their lives for their country.

When the Nazis came to power in 1933, their newly written laws quickly destroyed what democracy there had been during the turbulent Weimar Republic of the 1920s. Jewish scientists, judges, and lawyers were the first to be dismissed from their positions.

Because of our father's position as executive secretary in the Jewish community, it became his task to work with the Jewish department of the local Gestapo. They asked that he establish a precise inventory of the Jews of Hannover and surroundings, and their precise "degree of Jewishness." Two years later, further "refinements" were added to the request for information. This new work must have disturbed Father and perhaps even served as a warning of the possible intentions that were inherent in such demands by the Gestapo. I do not know what he thought about it, or what conclusions the leaders of the Jewish community drew from these measures. Then the Nuremberg Laws of September 15, 1935, were announced, and their impact was immediate. These new laws, among them severe restrictions and rules how Jews had to conduct their lives, caused many Jews who had the opportunity and means to flee the country. Jews, Social Democrats, and Communists, who had been politically active in opposition to the National Socialists, were never able to join forces. These natural allies opposed each other almost as much as they opposed their common enemy, the Nazis. Some managed to flee but were killed by Nazi thugs in whatever countries they had found refuge. Others were incarcerated, and some were tortured to death in Dachau, one of the earliest concentration camps established in Germany.

This was the background of our childhood. I do not know if our parents had any means of comparing the uncertainties of that time with their own earlier experience in Austria-Hungary. It was easy to understand that our mother wanted to leave Germany since her parents and five siblings had fled from Hungary after the failed revolution of Bela Kun in the early 1920s. Because he was a Jew, it was feared that the Jewish population would have to suffer for Kun's failure. A sister and a brother of Mother's left Hungary first and went to Palestine and then helped their parents and remaining siblings join them. Father, on the other hand, seems not to have expected life to become unlivable in Germany. He knew Jewish history, and Jews, on the whole, knew how to deal with adversity; they were used to pervasive anti-Semitism. But many Jews were meanwhile leaving

Hannover, and those that remained often did so because they were unable to find a refuge elsewhere in Europe (which would not have helped for long), or on another continent.

It is striking that these prior centuries that I have touched on shared one quality: the insecurity of Jewish life. This was the case even when, on the whole, the Jews seemed to be doing quite well. Any crime, or no more than a minor misstep that someone was accused of, elicited just one question in a Jewish mind: "Is that perpetrator Jewish?"

Freely choosing one's political beliefs can stand for many other freedoms: When the early Zionist movement was beginning to make an impact in Germany and Austria, possibly offering a solution of the difficulties Jews were encountering in many European countries (Herzl was a Hungarian-born Austrian), German Jews, by and large, withheld their support, fearing that approval of Herzl's ideas would cast doubt on their German patriotism and result in an increase of anti-Semitism in Germany.

There is no question then that living in the United States allowed me, a Jewish survivor from Germany, to breathe freely and be less fearful. But soon old worries in a new guise made their appearance.

On May 11, 1960, Adolf Eichmann was kidnapped in Argentina, and nine days later shipped to Israel for trial. A friend of ours, Dr. Jacob Robinson, was the legal adviser to the Israeli delegation to the UN. He was an international lawyer who had also been involved in the Nuremberg Tribunal. After Eichmann's capture, it fell to Dr. Robinson to write a brief defending this procedure.

Only sometime later did I realize that the rather abstract brief he asked me to type for him, which had as its subject the law of the sea, was connected to Eichmann's kidnapping!

After Hannah Arendt issued her report on the Eichmann trial, there was a lot of discussion in the Jewish community here and in Israel about the fairness of her assessments. I am not certain the Germans were all that upset by her assertions, for example, of the guilt of the Jewish *Sonderkommando* (Jewish prisoners who were forced to work in the crematoria of Auschwitz and other killing centers). According to Dr. Robinson's rebuttal, her assertions were badly flawed and legally incorrect.[5] The Jewish *Sonderkommando* worked with the bodies; the SS and their Ukrainian helpers did the actual gassing.

My own concerns were given new grounds with Hannah Arendt's assertions that the Jewish officials in Germany should have known better than to work for the Gestapo—that they were never sworn to secrecy and that they did the bidding of the Gestapo essentially voluntarily. Reading just a single page demonstrates how language can be used: Untruth is mixed with truth, producing an overall effect of some very serious accusations.[6]

Certain themes were pervasive. Hannah Arendt's report forced me to confront the question of how my father fit into the group of German Jewish officials she called a *Judenrat*, a term that is usually applied to Jewish ghetto officials who were essentially captives of the Nazis in charge of the Polish and Baltic states ghettos. Regardless of this callous name, the sad truth is that in most German cities the Jews did lose all authority and had to obey the Gestapo's orders. Still I did find Jewish historians, such as Isaiah Trunk, who were both intelligent and empathetic enough to trace and analyze the dilemmas of such Jewish officials, whether they were in the cities of Germany or the ghettos of Poland.[7] Recently German historians, especially Beate Meyer in great detail, have studied the Jewish officials and confirmed the untenable position they were caught in.[8]

Since I first wrote this memoir, I got access to some of the documents in my father's file in the main archive of the state of Lower Saxony. I was able to read some of the documents in that voluminous file, mostly pertaining to our aborted emigration to Cuba in 1941. There were even Nazi documents giving us permission to leave. Some of Father's dates do not match those found on earlier documents or indeed as recalled by me. If these documents prove anything, it is that documents, or their authors, are no more infallible than memoirists.

Despite inevitable discrepancies between memory and document, or among documents themselves, nothing in my writing has sprung purely from my imagination. The "he must have" phrases I had to resort to tend to be logical extensions of events. It was my twin sister, Eva, who had a wonderfully dramatic style. I never could compete with her.

I have not given up hope that this report might persuade historians and survivors to try harder than heretofore to understand the suffering borne by Jewish officials such as my father. Surely they, too, were victims. I was long held captive by these intractable problems and have spent decades of my life wrestling with these questions and what must have been my father's dilemmas. I have tried to look at them from every angle. I have tried to learn all I could about the immediate pre-Hitler period, and the Jewish community's expectation that my father's work would help it restore its financial health. That is why I wrote chapter 11, "Then and Now," and expressed my disagreement with Primo Levi in the afterword about his often harsh judgment of his fellow prisoners. I do not believe that the concentration camp was a laboratory in which to study human behavior, even though some prisoners behaved worse than others. That is true in the world at large as well, and as inexplicable.

A Final Reckoning

1

Early Years

When I look back, I am never alone. Eva, my twin sister, is always beside me. A big curl on top of her head moves with the song she is singing to herself, and I, sitting on a small stool next to her, rock to its rhythm. She is holding my favorite doll in her arms, and I pull it away from her. She lets out a loud wail. The door opens a crack, and a head with thick chestnut brown hair and dark eyes appears. Grete, our big sister, a tall eleven-year-old, wants to know why we are making so much noise. We have disturbed her in her homework. Drying her hands on her apron, Mother comes in from the kitchen. She, too, looks cross and gives Eva another doll to play with. "You should play together and share your toys," she pleads. Her plea was quite familiar; five-year-olds should really be more sensible! Eva's lower lip trembles, and she begins to cry. I tighten my grip around my doll.

The rain has stopped. Mother has sent Eva and me to play in our backyard. Worms have appeared between the cobblestones. The school bell rings, ending the children's religious instruction. Soon they will come running into the yard to enjoy their release from the classroom. They won't even notice if they step on those worms. I do not like to see them, trampled and squirming on the ground. With a twig I scoop up as many as I can find and carry each one to safety by the fence.

It is evening. Father has come upstairs from his office. The lamp with the green metal shade has been lit and pulled low over the kitchen table. Mother has made some cream of wheat for us and puts a little sugar on each spoonful before feeding us. Grete is doing her homework. Mother hands Father a mug with coffee and milk. He cuts a thick slice of dark bread and dunks it in his coffee. "Have some bread," he urges us. "There is nothing better. It is the staff of life." His head disappears behind the newspaper. When he has finished, he folds his paper and asks Grete about school. He reminds us that it is bedtime. Eva and I beg for a little longer to finish a board game we are playing. Eva is smiling. She is about to win. I am fighting my tears. Father takes us to give us our bath and then carries us, warmly wrapped in large white bath sheets, one in each arm, through the drafty vestibule to our beds. Mother comes in to say good night to us. She brings us two white flannel caps to put on and warns us not to take them off until our hair is dry. With a sigh, she sits down on a chair by our beds. She says a short evening prayer, and word for word, we repeat the Hebrew sounds. She switches off the light and quietly closes the door behind her. I take off my cap. I love to stroke its soft nap as I suck my thumb and drift off to sleep.

What little I know of my parents' past I gathered from snatches of their conversations and the stories they told us. I was still small and had just begun to read when the Nuremberg Laws of 1935 significantly changed life for German Jewry. Our parents returned from casting their vote. They wore large badges imprinted with the word *Ja*. It was an involuntary agreement with the new government of the Nazis, perhaps the enabling law of 1934. They now seemed frequently preoccupied; they had little time and ease to tell us about their youth.

Samuel Herskovits, whom we, like most German children, called Vati, was born in Felsoszük, one of a cluster of villages in Transylvania, near Klausenburg, now Cluj, and part of Romania. Father's family came from the Szatmar region. They were strictly Orthodox, Chasidic Jews, who were, and probably are to this day, anti-Zionist. This was not a political conviction but a religious one. In the simplest of terms: Only the Messiah could lead the Jews to Israel.

At that time, Transylvania belonged to the Austro-Hungarian Empire. Felsoszük was a place so small, I needed the help of a librarian to find it on the map. Although Father's birth date was March 3, 1883, his birth certificate reads 1881. In the nineteenth century, Jewish boys were often forcibly converted at the time of conscription, so that religious Jews felt doubly threatened by possible military service of their sons. They tried to protect them by predating the boy's birth date in the town's register. This, they hoped, would make him appear frail for his age, and help delay or even prevent his military service.

Samu, as he signed his letters to his mother, was the only surviving child of a farmer and his second, younger wife. The farm had a distillery, and Father boasted of being able to drink large quantities of alcohol without ill effect. He was proud of his wine-making skills and annually produced the raisin wine for Passover. When Father was in a good mood, he showed us how the Chasidim danced around their rabbi at holiday celebrations. Circling around an imaginary center, he would clap his hands above his head, snap his fingers, and chant tunes with a lot of "*Oy yoy yoy*" in them. It all must have evoked old memories of his childhood. It is only now that I am beginning to get a picture of what were the dimensions of my father's Orthodox Jewish youth. The yeshiva that Father attended was led by the Sofer (Schreiber) family. Surprisingly, its founder was a German Jew (Moyshe Schreiber, 1762–1869) from Frankfurt who gradually moved east. He left many texts that dealt with the proper observation of the laws, but did not publish them as that would have been considered immodest. He was regarded as the founder of ultra-Orthodoxy. Today's Haredim in Jerusalem are said to be guided in their unbending religious way of life by the Sofers' teaching. Remarkably, at the time of World War II, the yeshiva managed to flee Bratislava and continue its work in Jerusalem.[1]

An older half-brother, Akos, went to America around the turn of the century; according to a document of Father's, he may have taken the proceeds of their deceased father's farm with him. Father's half-sister, Millie, and her family, who lived in Romania, were in all likelihood victims of the Nazis. Several cousins who were part of the Herskovits clan and whose names Father recalled for Grete's family tree, we have not tried to account for. Our family name may have been rare in Germany, but it was quite common in Transylvania. Father recalled only one of his grandmothers, and his memory of her was that she, like one of the hens in their barnyard, was blind in one eye. And so grandmother and hen had the same nickname, but what that nickname was has been lost to posterity. Father confessed to us that he had been a very mischievous boy who would climb the nearest tree to escape his strict mother's anger. He was once thrown off a horse that he was trying to ride, and on the way down, his nose was injured by one of the horse's hooves. He had those scars for the rest of his life. In a 1941 document that Father completed when he made his final attempt to emigrate with us to Cuba, he wrote that he lost his father "52 years ago." That would mean that he was either six or eight years old, depending on which birth date was the real one. The family tree, prepared by Grete with Father's help in 1937 or 1938, shows, however, that his father, Moses Herskovits, died in 1895, when Father was officially fourteen. I had always understood that his departure from home to attend the Sofer Yeshiva some distance away in Pressburg (Bratislava) coincided with the loss of his father at around age thirteen. Regrettably, some of the documents I got to see after Hannover opened its main state archives in 2000 clarified less than I had hoped.

Even so, I understand that Father's teenage years were spent at the yeshiva. Before he was twenty-one, he had earned his "Moreno Rav," a rabbinical degree. Indigent yeshiva students like my father had to depend on the local community for their upkeep. Father never forgot how tired he and his friends were of the yellow pea soup they were served day after day by the wives in the kitchens of the charitable Kehilla (community) elders. Eventually they took their revenge: They smeared quantities of cooked peas on the synagogue seats of the husbands of those charitable women. The men's reaction is not recorded.

Orthodox Jews were not just discouraged but actually forbidden by the yeshiva to pursue secular studies. A student curious about the world had to study everything except the scriptures in secret. To pursue secular subjects, according to a classmate of Father's whom Grete met fifty years later in London, Father would climb over the yeshiva's wall, returning by the same route hours later. Precisely what courses he was able to take, or who his teachers were, his former classmate did not know. But he loved mathematics and classical German literature and often helped Grete with her studies.

After he earned his rabbinical degree, Father decided that he lacked the wish or conviction to practice the minutiae of his faith. Even less did he want to preach to others how to practice their faith. It is apparent from his letters to our grandmother Cillie that he shielded her, a deeply, even fanatically, religious woman, from knowing these feelings. He decided to go to Germany because he admired what he had managed to learn of German culture. In Hamburg he attended a *Handelshochschule* (business school). He supported himself by working for a cigar maker called Rosenduft, whose name I recall because we children thought it so hilarious, as were the rhymes talented Grete made with it. In 1909, at the age of twenty-six, Father earned a business degree (*Diplom Kaufmann*) and found work as a clerk in the office of the Jewish community in Hannover. That Jewish community must have been quite different from those he had known as a youngster. I can only imagine what gifts he had to draw on to understand and find his way in a new environment that had few similarities with his old home.

It was in connection with the stories of Father's youth that we first heard the Latin term *numerus clausus*, which essentially imposed a quota on the number of Jews to be admitted to a university. While this regulation was first formalized in Hungary after World War I, the problem was not unknown in other places at earlier times. Thus as a Jew, Father seems to have been unable to obtain a proper university education in his homeland, even aside from the religious scruples of his elders, but he had high hopes that his daughters would not be similarly hampered. Thus his final messages sent to Grete in England via the Red Cross in 1942 were good wishes for her impending nursing exams and inquiries about their results. Only the grandchildren he never knew would realize his dream of a freely chosen field of study at a university.

Father never tired of telling us that he got his job because of his excellent penmanship. Persistent and patient practice, he said, had made the difference. His handwriting was certainly both ornate and legible, and when I visited the state archives in Hannover, I instantly picked out the documents he had completed by hand some sixty years earlier.

During World War I, he was drafted into the Austro-Hungarian Empire's army and stationed in the garrison town of Theresienstadt. There, too, he may have worked in an office, for he saw no frontline service. I recall a picture of that time, which has not survived. He was almost unrecognizable: He had grown a beard and was quite emaciated. Since there was no kosher food, he told us, he had lived on little besides bread and apples. Kosher food, unlike some other Jewish laws and rituals, was not something he would ever give up. A quarter of a century later he was to renew his acquaintance with Theresienstadt—and the hunger he had known there earlier.

In November 1920, Father married Helene Kiss. I do not know where or how they met. His mother had remarried just before the start of World War I, and she and her second husband, a watchmaker called Farkas, lived with him in Hannover during those years. She longed to see her son married also and recommended a wife for him. He traveled to Hungary to visit the young woman, who lived in a small village. He was on his way to meet her when she was pointed out to him: His prospective bride was busy drowning a litter of newborn kittens. He decided not even to introduce himself to her. He would make his own choice. When we were told this story, we always wondered how we would have turned out if our mother had been that other woman, a woman who drowned kittens!

Mother, called Nuszi (Nooshi) rather than Helene by her family and Mutti by us, was born in Transylvania also, in a town called Turcz. I cannot imagine that she would have been capable of drowning a kitten. I watched how she reacted to the last, unexpected reflex movements of a carp she had just brought home from the market and unwrapped on the kitchen table. She called Father on the telephone to please come upstairs and help her. He would deliver the coup de grâce; she couldn't do it.

She grew up in Dej, the daughter of a wine dealer who had five daughters and two sons. Her father was a rigidly observant Jew, while her mother, Charlotte, was both tolerant of different views and well educated for a woman reared in the second half of the nineteenth century. We know that our maternal grandmother's maiden name was Hartmann and that she was the younger of two sisters. She was a lovely and musical young woman who played the violin. She must have been proud of her musical talent to pose with her violin in a family photograph. Their father, Franz Hartmann, had been a country lawyer with a wicked sense of humor. Years later, when my husband and I visited our mother's youngest sister in Tel Aviv, she regaled us with stories of the practical jokes our great-grandfather had played: When he saw the peasant girls carry fresh eggs in their aprons to market, he would untie their apron strings with the expected disastrous consequences. But she added reassuringly, he always paid for the damage he caused. His wife, Clara Mendelsohn, adopted young orphaned girls, rearing them until they were to be married and providing them with the customary dowry. One of these little girls stands next to her adoptive mother in that family photograph.

In the early 1920s, after the Jewish Communist Bela Kun's aborted revolution in Hungary, our mother's siblings and parents, fearing an anti-Semitic backlash, left their homeland and went to Palestine. Grandmother Charlotte's only worry, documented in a letter to her faraway children in Hannover, was the fate of her older son, Ludwig. He had completed his medical studies in Hungary and left with them, but he found the climate in Palestine unbearable. He returned to Europe and settled in Prague, where he worked for a pharmaceutical company. Ludwig's return to Central Europe sealed his and his family's fate. Sometime after the Nazi takeover of Czechoslovakia in 1939, Ludwig, his wife, and their two children fled to Hungary, where they succeeded in surviving Hitler's war. Grandmother Charlotte lived long enough to learn of Eva's and my survival but, sadly, also of Ludwig's and his family's death at the hands of the invading Soviet Russians in 1945.

The Jewish Community of Hannover

After Edwin Oppler had completed our beautiful synagogue in 1870, the Jewish community asked the Jewish architect to build a *Predigthalle* (memorial hall) for the Jewish cemetery and a *Gemeindehaus* (community house). The latter, a three-story building constructed, like the synagogue, of the yellow-brown glazed brick traditionally used in Lower Saxony, was completed in 1875. Oppler's drawings show that the Jewish community originally intended to use the building as a school, a plan apparently not approved by the city government. The stairwell led to a big backyard, where two small brick buildings housed three toilets each for both school kids and office staff. There was no greenery except for an acacia tree that smelled sweetly when it bloomed. The front entrance of the building had a heavy wooden portal, which was asymmetrically placed. It had a decorative brick arch whose apex touched the window of the school library on the second floor. Here the children of our Jewish community got their religious instruction, and Jewish youth organizations and political clubs held their often contentious, noisy meetings later in the afternoons. Father, the *Gemeindesekretär* (literally: community secretary, but better described as executive secretary), had his office several steps above ground level to the right of the entrance. His and his secretary's desks stood at right angles to the last of four large windows, and the wall behind them contained a safe and built-in, floor-to-ceiling dark brown, polished wooden file cabinets with vertical roll-up doors. Shields of white porcelain labeled the contents of the files. Father and his secretary, Fräulein Arnstein, were always busy; and at the front of the office, with a lamp with a glass shade suspended over his desk, the bookkeeper with the large shiny pate was poring over huge ledgers with columns of numbers. Right inside the entrance a rectangular area, separated by wooden railings, contained a couple of benches and served as a small waiting room. Here the visitors or petitioners could discuss their questions with Father without being overheard or disturbing the office staff. We were not allowed to enter the office unless we had a good excuse, such as having a "painful" wood splinter in a finger. Then Father would get up from his desk, come to us in the waiting area, and swiftly, blowing on the "injured" finger to lessen the pain, remove the culprit. And we would put on our roller skates and return to our play.

A door opposite the windows led to the conference room (*Sitzungssaal*), which was furnished with heavy oak tables and matching, carved oak chairs. It was used for evening meetings of the governing board of the community, called the *Vorstand*, at which Father functioned as recording secretary. For many years, the Welfare Office was across from Father's office, and beyond the glass-walled vestibule with its porter's lodge, Herr Levisohn, the cemetery administrator and Hebrew teacher, had his office. Father had been promoted to executive secretary of the Jewish community in 1924 when his predecessor, Jakob Hoffmann, died. Jakob Hoffmann had been the first person to hold the position of secretary. It was then that Father, his young wife, and two-year-old daughter Margarete, called

Grete, moved into the private apartment on the third floor of Lützowstrasse 3. Dr. Lesser Knoller, the retired head of the Teachers Seminary, and his wife had befriended our parents, and like so many educated German Jews, the Knollers were admirers of Goethe's *Faust*. They had persuaded our parents to give their oldest daughter the name Margarete. In 1924, fraternal twins, Karl Franz and Franziska Klara, were born, and a second set of fraternal twins, Eva and I, in 1928.

Only rarely did I hear my parents speak of the difficulties they were likely to have faced during those early years of their marriage: rampant inflation, the unsettled political situation, and Father's increasing responsibilities. After fleeing Austria-Hungary at the start of World War I, our father's mother and her second husband were still living with Father. They stayed with the newlyweds until they left for Jerusalem in 1925. There they lived near our mother's parents in an old neighborhood called Siebenbürger Häuser (Transylvanian houses), and the two grandmothers, despite their different, even opposite, temperaments and views, became good friends. Grandmother Cillie survived three husbands; she died in 1941. In accordance with her wishes, she was buried on Mount Olive.

After Father's parents left, Karlchen, a healthy boy during his first year of life, fell ill with typhus, it was said, of which several cases were making the rounds in Hannover at the time. Mother wondered if a careless nanny had allowed him to drink some of his bathwater. He spent a whole year in the children's hospital, only to catch a series of childhood diseases before dying after months of terrible suffering. He was just two years old, and to this day I think of my own children at that age—lovable, impressionable little human beings full of feelings. It was that moment their pediatrician, Dr. Huneus, chose to finally reveal to our parents, who had been wondering about her erratic behavior, that Karlchen's twin sister, Klärchen, had been injured during her high forceps delivery. She was brain damaged and would never be able to speak. Our parents rarely touched on these events, except to say that I looked a little like Karlchen. But even as a small child I felt that our mother's occasional sad demeanor was due to these losses. When Eva and I were one year old, our parents decided to board Klärchen with a Christian family on the island of Norderney. It was explained to us that they feared Eva and I would imitate Klärchen's less than rational behavior. Norderney was a popular vacation resort where the Jewish community of Hannover maintained a children's convalescent home. From that time on, our parents annually took us on vacation to Norderney so that we could visit Klärchen.

Hannover's Jewish community, much like others in Germany, provided a sturdy framework for the spiritual and physical well-being of its members. Unlike some communities in other cities, Hannover's community had determined that its membership would include both Orthodox and Reform factions, and it followed liturgical customs that honored that decision. Despite that decision, we did have a mixed choir, a somewhat unorthodox choice—but no organ. The Eastern Jews, many of whom may have lived in Hannover since the early years of the twentieth century, were not eligible to vote in community elections until sometime in the thirties. They held their own services near our synagogue, but on High Holy Days would come in to hear the cantor.

In general, for some members of the Jewish community there was little need, and for others there were few opportunities, to interact with the surrounding Christian society. Several old age homes, a hospital, a day care center, and an orphanage served the social needs of the Jewish community. This impressive array of institutions was supported by several foundations that had been established by members of earlier generations whose descendants had emigrated from Germany to settle in the United States. All these institutions were maintained by a charitable community that never exceeded five thousand to six thousand members. After Hitler came to power in 1933 and deprived many of our members of their livelihood, the Jewish community provided opportunities for retraining, and men (and some women), who had been established professionals, became manual laborers, skilled craftsmen, and even gardeners in the nearby Jewish Horticultural School at Ahlem. When that adaptation to the persecution by the National Socialists proved fruitless, the Jewish community established an office to help its members emigrate. Since all Germans of Jewish descent and faith were excluded as creators, performers, or audiences from all cultural pursuits in German society, a nationwide organization, the *Kulturbund*, was established. Traveling Jewish artists gave concerts, performed plays, and lectured in the various Jewish communities. In addition, Hannover itself had a *Kulturkreis* (cultural circle), an organization that employed local Jewish artists who did their share to provide cultural fare by performing plays and concerts, and giving readings, for members of the local and nearby Jewish communities.

The Jewish community, like similar organizations, had lost its resources in the inflation that followed World War I. Father's first task as its executive secretary had been to document the financial status of individual members of the congregation. Under German law, he became the Jewish community's first tax officer and as such was considered a public employee. Since Germany had no separation of Church and State, the Jewish communities were taxed by the State and a percentage of this Church tax was returned to them, as to other religiously affiliated organizations, for the activities of the congregation. Thus, sworn to secrecy, Father had access to the files of the State's Office of Finance (*Finanzamt*). Instead of using estimates as had been the custom, the community was able to base its tax assessments on factual information of the members' income. In August 1934, at Father's twenty-fifth anniversary celebration, *Kommerzienrat* (Councillor) Joseph Berliner, head of the Jewish community and a retired industrialist himself, singled out this task of Father's for special praise—because with skill and absolute discretion, he had managed to overcome the understandable resistance of his community to this new development. According to the report in the *Jüdische Nachrichtenblatt*—the local Jewish newspaper and primary source for our community's news—Kommerzienrat Berliner stressed Father's absolute reliability and exceptional memory for detail.

Perhaps it was Father's discretion that helped restrain his sharp wit, and to deal daily, patiently, with the varied needs and demands of the members of our community. He must also have been aware that some members of the community he was serving so conscientiously regarded him with the suspicion they reserved for Eastern Jews generally. While his discretion was thus well advised, it had other consequences as well. When our mother or one of us children asked Father a question about his work, he explained that his title of *Gemeindesekretär* meant that he was trusted with keeping the secrets of the members of our community. There were to be ample occasions when he chose to make use of that explanation.

His own needs, shaped in the rural society of his youth, were very simple. And although he insisted on the same unpretentious customs in his family life, he was surprisingly tolerant of the very different values espoused by some of the members of our community. There were those who were able to live extremely comfortable lives, in villas on grounds that had fish ponds in which trout were being kept, and there were others who, going from Jewish door to Jewish door, sold shoelaces and other sundries. Wealthy members of the community were not pleased when the new tax assessment was instituted in the 1920s, and some canceled their membership in the community. Even so, most did not refuse to help when, after Hitler's rise to power, many families lost their livelihood as men and women were expelled from their professions and businessmen lost their businesses.

Father's sympathy for and private support of families in need not only exceeded his duties as secretary of the community, but also exceeded his own financial resources. Frequently when poor individuals came to him, he helped them himself, rather than "shaming" them by a referral to the Welfare Office. As he remarked years later in a letter to Grete, the Welfare Office did not treat those asking for help with sufficient sympathy just when they were most in need of it.

Probably related to Father's generosity was Mother's extreme frugality. Many of her and all of our own clothes were made at home during the monthly visits of a professional seamstress, who taught Mother the secrets of her trade. A wool cloth coat she had worn for nineteen years was turned inside out and resewn to be worn some more. The memory of Father's generosity and her frugality has accompanied my life both in keeping or in breaking their rules. When I was nine or ten, I was allowed to draw pictures of the designs Eva and I liked, and Mother and the seamstress did their best to reproduce them for us.

While this was uncommon for men at the time, Father took an active part in our upbringing and daily care. Father often bathed us and put us to bed, handling us with real tact, but I recall that he also spanked Eva when she was out of bounds or otherwise made him angry. When I cried with sympathy for her, he told me I cried for fear of being next. I said nothing, but did not agree. Nightly he checked that we were comfortable and warm. In the morning he got us up, served us hot chocolate milk, from which he would remove every last trace of skin, and buttered our fresh breakfast rolls, which were daily delivered to our door. We were ready for school before Mother even woke up.

Father never stopped learning. From the typewriter repairman he learned the workings of typewriters and how to repair them. This was to stand him in good stead when, because of the racial laws, it became first difficult and later impossible to employ Christian workers, and he was able to fix both his own typewriter and the machines used in his office. Father also continued to study foreign languages. During the 1930s he concentrated on English. In the early 1940s, until we were deported, he studied Italian. He must have realized that he would have no more opportunity to use his English, or he feared being seen with an English grammar book. But he still had his music and quite a few of the texts were in Italian. He also studied and vocalized the nineteenth-century liturgical works of Sulzer and Lewandowski—some of which were familiar to us from our synagogue Services—and he taught himself the lieder of Schubert, Brahms, Grieg, and Wolf.

It was the summer of 1933. We were sitting in our compartment in the train that was taking us home from our fifth annual vacation in Norderney. To our chagrin, we learned that this visit would have to be our last. Bernhard Rust, the minister of education and popular culture, himself a Hannoveranian, after a visit to Norderney, issued a decree forbidding Jews the use of beaches and spas. These places were among the first to be made *Judenrein* (cleansed of Jews).[2] Our father assured us that there were many other beautiful places we could visit. We were to have other opportunities to observe his facility for finding a "remedy" for the ever-increasing restrictions and prohibitions that were to circumscribe our life because of what had now become a major problem: We were Jews.

1933–1935

Sometimes on our walks with Father, we used to go to a sweetshop on Theodorstrasse, which was owned by the Brechner family. Frau Brechner, a small, gray-haired woman, opened the door to her store, which was located slightly below street level. She was pleased to see us. She gave Father a playful hug and, in the German custom, pinched our cheeks to the point of pain. She asked that he sing something for her. More pleased with our reception than we were, Father laughed and obliged with a short Yiddish song. Then he purchased one of those large pound-size tins of green eucalyptus candy that he kept in his office. The sticky candy with the pungent taste helped him fight his frequent sore throats, and he never stopped recommending them to us. He knew we preferred Frau Brechner's marzipan *Kartoffeln* (potatoes), small, fragrant, cocoa-dusted balls. For Chanukah we bought her tiny green and yellow candy that we used as chips when we played the traditional dreidel game at Chanukah.

We were just leaving the Brechners' shop after one of these shopping expeditions when, in rapid succession, we heard strange popping sounds. These were interspersed by intervals of total silence. We asked Father what it might be, but he only gripped our hands a little tighter and told us to hurry to get home. As soon as our heavy front door closed behind us, he explained to Eva and me that some people were quarreling and fighting on the street. Soon enough we learned that these street fights and shootings were, in fact, *Parteikämpfe*—fights among different political parties during the election campaign that preceded Hitler's accession to power. Many of these fights had been instigated by local Nazi storm troopers (the SA).

Other sights and sounds became familiar, regular occurrences. From the window of our *Kinderzimmer* (children's room), I watched columns of these SA men in khaki uniforms, black swastikas on white circles on their bright red armbands, flags aloft, marching on Goethestrasse. In perfect unison they sang the "Horst Wessel Lied" and other Nazi songs. Traffic came to a standstill. Long after those marchers had disappeared, the rhythmic sound of their jack boots on the pavement seemed to reverberate in our room. If Eva and I were on our roller skates or scooters when the SA marched by, we instinctively hurried inside. Once in a while we even sought shelter in Father's office. He would get up from his desk and meet us in the waiting area. He offered us one of his eucalyptus candies and encouraged us to go back to our play.

Our father must have loved his life in Hannover; he loved the German language and the country. He had made a life for himself and for his family by his own efforts, and he would not listen to his wife, who wanted to join her parents and five siblings in Palestine. Our parents had many discussions about the direction our lives should take, and Mother did not always suffer defeat gladly or in silence. Even when I was quite small, I was certain that there was profound disagreement between them. I watched them, trying to understand what they were saying to each other in that strange Hungarian language they spoke. Mother's face was masklike in her effort to remain calm. Behind his steel-framed glasses, Father's dark eyes appeared even darker. Suddenly, with a flourish, he'd sing a passage from a Hungarian song and repeat it in a higher key. The low-ceilinged kitchen could barely contain his voice. Mother looked pained. Then, with his thumb and index finger, he extracted the small tuner he always carried from his vest pocket. He adjusted it and checked his pitch. That ended their conversation.

Father may have been reluctant to start over again in another country. While his rabbinical knowledge and vocal musical skills could well have been usable abroad, his experience as executive secretary of the Jewish community would not have been as portable. Such thoughts may well have been on his mind, but they were not expressed until the summer of 1939 when time had essentially run out.

And yet Father was keenly aware of the world of politics. When the *Hannoversche Tageblatt* printed a picture of a smiling Franklin Delano Roosevelt in his open convertible—perhaps on the way to his inauguration—Father showed it to me with the words: "He will help us because he will counterbalance what is happening here." To please him, I had started to look at the daily paper. At five or six, I could not have grasped the hope or even certainty Father was expressing. But that picture and Father's optimism have remained with me. What then held him back from going to Palestine? Whatever the cause of his disagreement with our mother, it must have decisively influenced his thinking.

The one disagreement of our parents that we children could plainly see concerned the keeping of the Sabbath. Father had left the ultra-Orthodoxy in which he had been brought up. It seems that Palestine and freedom from the looming threats of the Nazi regime could not make up for his loss of freedom from the requirements of the ultra-Orthodox practices of his family that would be expected of him in Palestine.

Father helped other families with their immigration to Palestine. Many were poor Eastern Jews with large families. Sometimes their creditors appeared at the railroad station to claim payment or to prevent their departure. Frequently it was Father who prevented altercations by promising to liquidate such debts so that the family could leave. Once the creditor who became Father's opponent was a Jewish boxer! Sometimes the emigrants would leave some unsold merchandise with him from the stores they had to liquidate before their departure. Once he came home with a large box of woolen gloves. When we opened the box, they were for the left hand only, and he joined in our laughter when we saw the "present" he had received. Regularly he visited the wealthier members of the congregation to ask them for funds to help poor families emigrate. Many responded generously, well beyond their regular taxes and their other contributions to the Jewish community.

Mother was often pensive. She missed her family, and their regular correspondence could not make up for their separation. In 1935, in Jerusalem, while he officiated at a Sabbath service, Mother's father collapsed and died. For weeks Father managed to keep this news from Mother. When she finally learned of her father's death, she was overwhelmed by grief. I had never seen her so distraught, her features swollen beyond recognition. She had not seen her father since her marriage. And because she was told so late of his death, she could not observe the weeklong shiva, the customary period of mourning.

Unlike Father, who did not read novels and for whom literature seemed to stop with the German classics to which he counted his beloved Heine, Mother read avidly. She liked nineteenth-century French novels and kept volumes of Balzac's *Human Comedy* on her bedside table. She also read the stories by Jewish writers such as Mendele Mocher Sforim, Scholem Aleichem, and I. L. Peretz. Her reading may have helped her cope with her difficult life, but if she learned to be philosophical or even resigned, I saw these attitudes instantly undone when her unhappiness got the upper hand.

Father loved music, especially vocal music, which he studied assiduously. In the 1920s he took singing lessons with a teacher he called "the good Hans Emge." Years later from liner notes of a lieder album by the baritone Gerhard Huesch, I learned that Huesch, a well-known lieder singer from Hannover, had been a pupil of the same Hans Emge, whom he praised as an exceptional voice teacher. As Father recalled in a letter to Grete in 1940, Emge taught him to "treat his voice as if it were fine silk." We children became familiar with the names and voices of many of the famous singers of the time. While we did not have a radio in the 1930s—perhaps a precaution of Father's to avoid being accused of listening to forbidden foreign broadcasts—he never tired of winding up the gramophone. We would listen to recordings of arias and lieder, sung by Tauber, Schlusnus, Caruso, Scotti, Kipnis, Galli-Curci, Alpar, Gigli, Schmidt, and others. Father taught us the liturgy, mostly composed by Sulzer and Lewandowski, sung in our synagogue. To demonstrate the art of the cantor, he played recordings of Sirota and Rosenblatt. I think that Father's singing at the weekly Sabbath service and the annual cycle of holidays, for which he practiced diligently, was a blend of the art of the cantor and the heart of the chazzan. While some of the Eastern Jewish members of the congregation had their own services in several small Stibl (Yiddish for a small room), they would come to the synagogue to listen to Father after the end of their own, shorter services. Father taught us Hebrew and Yiddish songs and encouraged us to harmonize and sing in rounds. He was delighted when he discovered that Eva, who had a lovely and strong voice, easily scaled the high C.

On many Sunday afternoons in summer, we walked to a *Schrebergarten*—named after its inventor in the nineteenth century—a cultivated plot outside city limits owned or rented by our friends the Kaunitz family. For us children it was a long walk, and we amused ourselves by running our hands along the interminable green hedges that bordered the road. If we dallied too much, Father urged us along by promising us ice cream, which he bought us from street vendors who scooped it into small boat-shaped biscuits.

The Kaunitz family and their friends were of Austrian and Czech origin. They and their circle were comfortably situated businesspeople who owned several menswear and hat shops. In the shade of a large chestnut tree the men played cards, usually *Skat*, while the women did their sewing or embroidery. Mother brought along hard-boiled eggs and sandwiches, in the hope that the fresh air would stimulate our appetite. With the Kaunitzes' three sons and other youngsters, we picked raspberries and other fruit. Somehow I felt special sympathy for Frau Fraenkel, the blind grandmother of Family Hahn, and would take her around the garden and tell her about the flowering shrubs that bordered the paths we were walking on. Eva and I collected caterpillars in a small glass jar and never gave up hope that we would find butterflies the next day. Before we went home, Herr Kaunitz shared the ripe corn—which he called *Kukurutz*—with his friends.

We were probably one of the few families in Hannover to consider green peppers and corn a treat. Generally in Germany corn was thought fit for animal feed only. This was not the only instance in which our family's ways were slightly "eccentric," traceable to Hungarian customs. At times we children felt "different," a feeling reinforced by our mother's slightly accented speech and uncertain use of the difficult rules for the articles *der, die, das* of German grammar.

Our parents' own foreign background may have made it easier for them to understand and sympathize with the Eastern Jews of our community. Most of them were among the poorer members of the congregation. Almost invariably they belonged to the Orthodox membership of the community that observed all Jewish laws strictly. Many German Jews looked askance at the foreign ways of the *Ostjuden* (Eastern Jews). It was not uncommon to hear the surely spurious charge that it was the Eastern Jews who, by their demeanor and obvious "otherness," had helped to intensify, if not indeed introduce, anti-Semitism. These opinions and prejudices of their parents were often reflected in the behavior of some of the older boys who attended the Jewish afternoon school in our house. They belonged to clubs and organizations such as Agudah, Mizrahi, Habonim, or Hashomer Hatzair, whose political and religious orientation ran the gamut from right to left. Sharp differences of opinion among these young people sometimes led to physical clashes. Often Father had to go upstairs to tone them down and, if possible, to make peace. One of the young fellows he encountered during that period was Hershel Grynzpan, about whom we were all to hear more in a couple of years.

A man of strong opinions, which, at least at home, he rarely hesitated to express, Father had many friends among members of the congregation, especially those who appreciated those characteristics. But we children were aware that there were those who strenuously opposed him. We did not understand the meaning or subject of the disagreements he had with some of the functionaries of the community, but his thinking was clearly different from that of some of his colleagues. We often heard his frustration with the inadequacies of the Welfare Office, and the office charged with helping members emigrate seems to have been similarly deficient.

School

When Eva and I were five, we each received a brand-new Hebrew prayer book (a *sidur*). For once we were not asked to share a possession. Then we were introduced to Herr Levisohn, an elderly, kindly teacher, who was also the reader of the Thora at the Sabbath services and the administrator of the Jewish cemeteries. With great patience he taught us the rudiments of Hebrew. Soon we were able to read the morning and evening prayers that our mother had been saying with us almost since we began to talk. Once the Jewish Day School was established in 1935, Jewish studies became part of our curriculum.

Eva managed to amuse Father in many ways. We were allowed to watch the many Jewish weddings at which he officiated in the conference room next to his office. We knew the crucial prayer the husband would have to repeat. Once, when a prospective husband seemed rather slow, or as the grown-ups would later have it, reluctant, to repeat the words spoken by Father—"*Hare at mekudeshes li . . .*" (Behold thou art consecrated to me [by this ring])—Eva, always impatient, piped up with the next word. Later she was scolded although it was quite plain to us that Father was actually proud of her quick mind.

At first, in the fall of 1934, Father had enrolled us in the local elementary school. Our first-grade teacher was the same Fräulein Firnhaber who six years earlier had taught our sister Grete. We each got the traditional *Zuckertüte* (a large colorfully decorated cone-shaped bag filled with sweets), a leather satchel, and a lunch bag. On the way back, Father took us to the photographer. As in all our pictures, Eva's face is grave, and I smile. And as always, the sleeves of her blouse are too short for her long arms. Eva and I sat in one of the last rows of the classroom. That first day the classroom looked enormous to me, and the teacher was a tiny figure in the distance. We began learning to read and write, and Fräulein Firnhaber gave us dictation exercises. One day when Mother called for us, I was very upset. We had had to write the sentence: "*Alle Kinder rufen Heil Hitler*" (All children call out Heil Hitler). I had managed to spell his name "Hilter." It was inexcusable and resulted in an "F." Mutti dried my tears and promised not to tell Father. From then on, I often sat with her in the kitchen and practiced my reading and writing. While she was deftly removing the last bits of fat from the entrails of a chicken—in order to utilize it all to the fullest—she would glance at the words that gave me trouble and encourage me to try again.

My schoolbooks and the newspapers I tried to read contained many pictures of blond, pigtailed little girls who curtsied when they greeted Hitler. And wherever he went, they handed him bunches of flowers. Sometimes I wished I were one of them. But my hair was brown and short, and I felt guilty when I tried to imagine what it would be like not to be Jewish.

To imagine oneself "outside" one's family was very disloyal, and I told no one of these thoughts. I heard Father talk with scorn of those who attempted to save themselves by leaving the Jewish community. "Hitler has done one good thing," he would say. "He showed us Jews that neither baptism nor assimilation will make people feel differently about us. Neither is the answer to our problem." *What* the answer was, he did not say. This was all the more puzzling since, unlike Mother, he was not a Zionist. Such questions remained dormant in me for many years before I learned that the answer lies in the mutual acceptance of the different beliefs and attributes of people. But I have not ceased to wonder at what I understood as Father's acceptance of the inevitability of our Jewish fate and the suffering it imposed on us.

At the end of our first school year, our parents told Eva and me that we would not be able to return to the *Volksschule*, the local elementary school, in the fall. We were to be enrolled in a recently organized Jewish day school on the first and second floors of our house instead. Many of our teachers had advanced degrees; they taught us because they had lost their jobs in the German secondary and high school systems. Others, like Werner Weinberg,[3] were just starting their teaching careers. We had small classes and made good progress. But going to school in the same house in which we lived and where Father had his office had its distinct drawbacks. When we were in fifth grade and had failed to behave "perfectly," Herr Wigdorowitch, our teacher, routinely threatened that he would go straight to Father's office to report our misdeeds. And sometimes he did just that. In general, I was more obedient than Eva in school. She had trouble waiting her turn and blurted out the answers to arithmetic problems when she grew impatient with a slower classmate. Perhaps because she was easily bored, Eva did not enjoy her schoolwork as much as I. This was reflected in her grades, which tended to be somewhat lower than mine. Once when our teacher met Father in the stairwell and complained about Eva, I happened to be standing one flight above them and, unseen by them, overheard Father's response: "Eva is intelligent, Ruth is diligent." It hurt me, although I thought he made the distinction to defend Eva.

The Three of Us

It was a general practice in our family to assign talents to us children: Eva could sing and Ruth could draw. We would not have dreamt of switching talents or roles or, even less imaginable, invading each other's territory. Grete, who played the piano, was said to be in a class by herself. I accepted this judgment I think because she was our "big sister," and that was how we—sometimes boastfully—referred to her when we spoke to our friends. If our parents had visitors, Grete was asked to play the piano for them. Reluctantly she complied. When Eva was asked to sing, she went into the adjacent *Herrenzimmer* (the study), where she felt safe and invisible, and her clear, high voice easily penetrated the dividing door to the *Speisezimmer* (dining room), where our parents' guests were being entertained. I did not mind showing my drawings, and these were duly admired.

Grete was always playing the piano. Her lessons had begun when she was six, but the combination of schoolwork and piano practice was considered too stressful, and the piano was discontinued until she was nine. I enjoyed listening to her, crouched under the grand piano in the dining room. Brahms's Intermezzi were my special favorites. They evoked a pleasantly pensive mood in me, which I was able to re-create by just humming one of the melodies. At one of the congregation's cultural events, organized by the local Jewish cultural organization (the *Kulturkreis*), Eva and I, dressed in the obligatory pink crepe paper dresses, with Grete at the piano, sang Brahms lovely lullaby: "Die Blümelein sie schlafen" (The flowers are sleeping).

Grete could continue her studies at the local Schiller Lyceum, whose director, Herr Dr. Plath, gave proof of uncommon courage: He wore an SDP (Social-Democratic Party) button on his lapel at a time when this could be a challenging gesture in a one-party state, and the majority chose to display Nazi insignia. Occasionally he had a friendly conversation with Father. Father forbade Grete to tarry after school, and one day when she disobeyed that rule, our parents suffered agonies until she returned home. Since she was tall for her age and six years our senior, our parents seemed to expect her to act like a mature adult. From that time on, Father's first question to Mother upon coming upstairs from his office was: "Where is our big girl?" It was the first Hungarian phrase I understood.

On walks we were continually admonished to be well behaved and not to call attention to ourselves. If we played outdoors in the very small front garden, or roller-skated on the sidewalk, we were frequently subjected to verbal taunts. "We are proud to be Jews," we usually answered when kids across the street called us "Jew pigs." Our parents told us to play in the backyard instead and to be very careful: "Pretend that you did not hear and do not answer back." But the backyard was not paved, and we could use neither our skates nor the scooter.

Of course, we knew that we were not pigs or any of the other things we and other Jews were being called. To have it pounded into us by the newspaper, by signs on walls, stores, and park benches, that we were both ugly and evil, not to be trusted and not wanted, created a constant need to oppose at least silently the assertions made by the surrounding society. If, as sometimes happened, a Jew should indeed be found to have broken a law, it was an extremely painful event because in our childish reasoning it threatened to weaken our resolve to disbelieve the image that had been created of us. Our parents must have feared much more serious consequences. These tensions also complicated our parents' relations with us. They feared that we might be indiscreet in casual contact with non-Jews—although only Grete had such contacts in school—and chose not to discuss their feelings toward the National Socialist regime with us. Consequently they did not sufficiently criticize the evil intent and nature of those who maligned us. Father, especially, sought more than anything to shield us, but that effort resulted more often than not in a lack of candor with us.

Shortly after Hitler came to power—this was spoken of as the *Umbruch*—Jews were forbidden to employ non-Jewish household help under the age of forty-five. We lost our longtime sleep-in maid. While an older woman came faithfully every week to do the laundry and heavier cleaning, Mother found it difficult to adjust to these changed conditions. She frequently complained of overwork. The porter who had looked after the offices and the heating of the house also had to leave. Father now serviced the heating system himself and insisted that shoveling coal was excellent exercise for him.

Because Grete's piano practice and schoolwork were deemed too important to interrupt, Eva and I were recruited to help Mother with the dishes. We had to take turns drying them and bickered a lot because we could never remember whose turn it was. I could see that this only upset Mother more. But I could not understand her reaction when we happened to break a dish while drying it. It was not particularly costly porcelain. But it came natural to her to express herself with a great deal of drama, even exaggeration. She would throw up her arms in despair, exclaiming: "What have I done to deserve such clumsy children?" I felt true sympathy for her most of the time and tried to help, but these exclamations made me very unhappy. Her question confirmed my conviction that if anything painful happened to me, it was the deserved consequence of some evil action or thought of mine.

These outbursts and her complaints of overwork were probably expressions of what she felt about a whole constellation of blows that fate had dealt her. Despite Father's attempts to humor or reassure her that "all will be well," she was often brooding. At other times, as I watched my parents converse in Hungarian, I would see a beautiful open smile transform Mother's serious features. I could not understand what they were saying, nor did I know what remark of Father's made her smile. I did not mind. It was enough to see her smile. I was happy.

If I wanted to be close to Mother, I had to seek her out in her domain. I would go to her in the kitchen and offer to help with her baking and other tasks. She might be busy making several kinds of fancy tortes for one of our obligatory birthday parties. My interest in her work earned me her praise and the prediction that I would make a good homemaker when I grew up. Eva, who was often feuding with Mother, took less interest in her activities, and thus deprived herself of the closeness and warmth I felt.

Our rivalry for our father's approval was intense long before we went to school. When Eva and I quarreled, he was judge and jury not only of our behavior but of our intentions. Frequently he seemed to rule in her favor, perhaps because he knew that she was physically weaker than I. And I felt miserable if he decided that it was I who had started our fight. Although he occasionally allowed that both of us might be at fault, my conscience was rarely clear because I was well aware of the feelings of jealousy that frequently overcame me. And because I did not have Eva's quicksilver mind and was slow with words, I was all the quicker with my fists.

Sometimes Grete would enter the fray to try and reestablish quiet—if not peace. Eva and I, instantly united, insisted that we had not fought at all and offered some lame excuse. We had our own private peace-making routine: We never went to sleep before saying to each other, "Let's be friends again." We always agreed. Eva would put her long skinny arms around me, and reconciled, we went to sleep.

Grete was more successful when she instituted reading aloud to us. On Saturday afternoons when our parents took their well-deserved rest, she was charged with keeping us occupied and quiet. She must have been studying Molière in school because she decided that he would do just fine for Eva and me. She sat us down on two low stools in the living room and from a thin Reklam booklet read a German translation of *Le Malade Imaginaire*. We laughed so hard, it woke our parents.

There was no dispute among us who was Father's favorite. It was and remained Grete. Although it was for the purpose of practice, their English conversations shut out Mother and Eva and me. When I heard Father and Grete discuss some point in her reading or schoolwork, I tried hard to understand their conversation. My solution was to read her books, which I slipped under my more innocuous *Nesthäckchen* (the term for the youngest child in a family; a popular children's book series by a German Jewish author). Many times Grete would notice and confiscate her book. Once I managed to read quite undisturbed Schiller's play *Kabale und Liebe* (*Cabals and Love*)—the title was irresistible. I gobbled up other, equally unsuitable, works. But always, halfway through the book when my curiosity and anxiety got the upper hand, I would turn to its last pages to learn how it ended. And so I cried long before the story had reached the point to warrant my sympathy and unhappiness. Reading about the Crusades of the Middle Ages and visualizing their effect on the hapless Jewish communities of that time was a horrifying experience for me. It was impossible to make sense of the stories of the Spanish Inquisition or, for that matter, of the blood libel for which the Jews were persecuted for centuries. These stories convinced me that the lives of Jews were ineluctably different from the rest of humanity. But while I read enough to become quite frightened by this history, the time never came for me to join Father and Grete in their conversations.

I had long enjoyed drawing and made my first acquaintance with the visual arts when Father gave me a Max Liebermann biography, a book that was among the gifts he received at his anniversary celebration in 1934. Liebermann, an assimilated well-to-do Berlin Jew, was one of Germany's best-known but "unconventional" painters who had helped develop German impressionism. One of Liebermann's drawings appealed to me especially because it depicted the last two lines of a dramatic Goethe ballad: "*Halb zog sie ihn, halb sank er hin und ward nicht mehr gesehn.*" (Loosely translated, the demise of a fisherman who succumbs to the lures of a mermaid who drags him down to a watery grave.) Liebermann promptly became my favorite painter—not surprising, since he was the only one I knew. In 1997, to my delight, a beautiful self-portrait of Liebermann, dating to the year 1926, was loaned by its German owner to the Fogg Museum in Cambridge. For several years I regularly "visited" the portrait, which hung across from a self-portrait by Max Beckmann in evening clothes. I sat there comparing those two very different painters. Both had suffered under the Nazis, but otherwise they did not have much in common. Eventually the Liebermann portrait had to be returned to its owner. And I could no longer care that much for the room of the Fogg Museum where Max Beckmann now presides.

Father became *erster Kantor* (first cantor) following the emigration of *Oberkantor* Alter to South Africa. The Board of the Jewish community had decided that the title *Oberkantor* was not suitable for Father in combination with his title of "secretary." I knew this, having read a letter of my father's correspondence still in the typewriter on his desk. (It wasn't the last time my curiosity got the better of me.) A young assistant cantor, Dr. Isaac Vanderwalde, joined our community. Dr. Vanderwalde also taught in our school. He officiated at Eva and Bob's wedding in 1948, and mine and Alfred's in 1949.

Eva and I began to attend choir rehearsals with our father. Eventually we were allowed to sing in the mixed choir. After Sabbath services, we, together with the other members of the choir, made our way down the steep stairs of the turrets that flanked the entrance to our synagogue. Quickly, Eva and I slipped into the large, now empty, sanctuary. We were headed for the small room all the way up front to the right of the ark where Father stored his robe and cap. The room also held the built-in safe to which all silver ornaments were returned after services. When he felt that the service had gone well and he had sung well, Father was in high spirits and greeted us with a big smile. He called us his *Puppen* (dolls), and we helped him put his cap and robe away. Meanwhile he was exchanging stories with Herr Roberg, the Torah reader and beadle of the congregation. A good-humored, rather small man with a pointed beard, he bustled in and out of the dressing room, opened the safe, and carefully replaced the Torah crowns with their ringing bells and shields, and the pointers that had been used to read the Torah. Occasionally a tarrying member of the congregation looked in to shake Father's hand with a "*Yeashir kochacho!*" (Literally, "May your strength increase"; the customary Hebrew phrase for "thank you" for your service on such occasions.)

Our regular Saturday afternoon services and activities, as well as the Chanukah and Purim theatricals organized by our rabbi, Dr. Emil Schorsch, became an important part of our lives. Dr. Schorsch had for years made it his goal to provide the youth of our community with both spiritual and cultural stimulation. (His son, Ismar, now retired, became chancellor of the Jewish Theological Seminary in New York. I recall visiting the family in Hannover when Ismar was born.) There were few other diversions in the 1930s. We did not go to movies or concerts. We were ten in 1938 when we saw our first and only movie in Germany—Shirley Temple's *Recruit Willy Winkie* (originally *Wee Willie Winkie* in English). Except for Sunday afternoon walks with Grete to D'ell Asta, an ice cream parlor on Goethestrasse where we were treated to delicious pineapple sorbet, we never went to a café and never ate a meal in a restaurant. Our parents may have avoided such activities for their own reasons; the pervasive anti-Semitism, expressed on large signs that read *Juden unerwünscht* (Jews not wanted) on many establishments in the city, and the display boxes on street corners that equated Jews with pickpockets and rapists, had to be a crucial factor.

It was indeed impossible to ignore those wood-framed glass cases on nearby streets that displayed the *Stürmer*. The German populace was being encouraged to enjoy reading Julius Streicher's rag, published exclusively for the purpose of fostering hate and untruths about the "dangerous and obscene Jews." The caricatures of Jews almost defied description. Their noses resembled beaks, out of proportion to the rest of their facial features except for their lips, which were thick and curled outward. Their tiny eyes squinted slyly. No member of our family or friends, no one I had ever seen, looked remotely like those pictures. Probably to counteract those distorted images of Jews all around us, Father told us of Jews in other countries of whom we could be proud: Hore-Belisha was secretary of war in the British government; Leon Blum was prime minister of France. Interestingly, he avoided mention of the long list of Jews who, before Hitler's rise to power, had played a variety of significant roles in government, industry, and the arts in our own country. Perhaps if he had reminded himself of the evident deterioration of Jewish life in Germany, he might have come to a different conclusion about our ability to continue our life there. Perhaps it was too painful for him, and might have compelled him to agree with our mother, who wanted, above all else, to leave.

Even now, having lived in the United States for more than half a century, I find that the absurdities of the political beliefs and the threatening atmosphere of the environment of the 1930s in which Jewish families were living are painful to remember, let alone describe.

Religion

I often worried about my parents' very different ideas of what constituted proper religious observance, and it hurt me to see them disagree. Our mother took a strict, Orthodox view while Father gave us many opportunities to observe his more liberal attitudes. Because his primary means for relaxation was his music, and even though this greatly distressed our mother, on Friday nights he occasionally went into his study to listen to his records. Over the years I came to understand that Father's practices were the result of his interpretation of the meaning of Judaism, while Mother's piety, though based on her deep love for her pious father, was also an admixture of old custom and even older superstition. And although I feared God's wrath for my real and imagined misdeeds, I began to realize that God often failed to notice, or to care about, my good or bad actions. But that did not ease my bad conscience.

We were returning from synagogue one Saturday morning when we were stopped by a shabbily dressed, poor Jew who had arrived too late Friday evening to find shelter. Like so many other Jews at that time, he was probably a traveling salesman. Usually such men came to our house just before the start of the Sabbath, and while Father was dressing to go to synagogue, he would quickly write out a voucher for a room at a small Jewish hotel in our neighborhood. This man looked desperate. We did not know where he had spent the night. Father asked him to accompany us home. He unlocked his office, showed the man where cash was kept in the safe, and told him what amount to take. Since as Orthodox Jews we did not touch money on the Sabbath, we were amazed by his action. We asked Father for an explanation. He told us that it was really quite simple: His obligation to help this man, or in general, to save a life, was greater than his obligation to obey the law to observe the Sabbath. This man had needed his help. At that time men and women were picked up on the streets of Germany if there was any suspicion that they were *Landstreicher*, i.e., homeless persons. Prison sentences could be the result with eventual incarceration in a concentration camp. Father's statement that his action was intended to "save a life" has to be understood with that background in mind.

The historian Raul Hilberg asserts that the Nazi government itself did not know in 1933 how they were going to proceed against the Jews. "No bureaucrat in 1933 could have predicted what kind of measures would be taken in 1938, nor was it possible in 1938 to foretell the configuration of the undertaking in 1942."[4] Even so he criticizes the German Jewish officials to have been unable to foresee that the Nazi laws and prohibitions that followed one upon the other would lead to the Jewish people's eventual murder. He decries the time-tested methods they used, such as trying to appease the Nazis by answering (and later even anticipating) their demands for information. But these Jewish men may no more have had the capacity to imagine the enormity of what lay ahead than the Nazi bureaucrats themselves who made these demands on the Jewish officials. I have tried not to let these assertions by Hilberg and others color my personal recollections of the effects of the Nuremberg Laws on our lives and especially on the life of our father. Looked at from this distance, a large shadow had certainly begun to darken our lives.

It did not take very long for the consequences of the "definitions" of who was a non-Aryan and affected by the new restrictive ordinances of the Nuremberg Laws to be felt. For Father, it was a time of increasing pressures. The Gestapo, for whom he had at least three euphemisms such as *Die Behörde* (the authorities) or simply *Die Schlägerstrasse* or *die Südstadt* (the street in Hannover or its neighborhood, South Hannover, where their offices were located), requested that he supply information on all the Jews of Hannover who were members of the Jewish community. He had to furnish proof that, after a certain date, those married to non-Jews no longer belonged to the Jewish community or took part in religious instructions. This was, I had always surmised, in their interest, and in many cases saved their and their children's lives at the time. This was true for a limited period only. A German historian, who studied and wrote about the Gestapo, has since assured me that the Germans had made plans to eventually free Germany of "half-breeds" as well. Of course, "that was the plan if the Nazis would have won the war."

Matters became much more complicated when several generations were involved, and the so-called Aryan partner of a marriage had divorced his Jewish spouse. Even though they had children together who were brought up as Aryans, the Jewish spouse lost all her rights and was invariably deported.

At first, much of it must have amounted to legal hairsplitting. When a couple wished to get married, for example, proof of pure Jewish ancestry on both sides had to be furnished. This could be difficult to obtain. But without such evidence, they would not be allowed to marry. Frequently these tasks were continued during long evening hours at Gestapo headquarters in the Schlägerstrasse. When Father returned home later and later, our mother was unable to hide her anxiety from us. Grete waited up with her while she sent Eva and me to bed. Even though Grete eventually came to join us, we could not sleep because we knew that Father had not yet come home. Eva tossed in her bed, sobbing. Though we might not cry, Grete and I shared her fear that some evil had befallen him. After a while, Eva would get out of bed. Barefoot, dressed only in her nightgown, she stood on the dark, stone staircase and called out disconsolately: "Vati, Vati, do please come home!"

These were the years when German Jews still sought accommodation with the Nazi regime. This search for accommodation may have had different reasons: Even in the face of the belligerence of the new regime, there were those who thought they could prove their absolute loyalty to, and belief in, the rightness of the new Nazi regime in Germany. Many did not know that accommodation would be impossible. Others lacked the means to find another land that would assure their safety. Some ignorance may have been choice or self-deception. Or at the very least, it was an understandable inability to comprehend the full dimensions of the evil represented by Nazism. Some Jews may even have become inured to the successive anti-Jewish measures that had begun by restricting some aspects of their lives and eventually dictated every moment of them. All the while, not unlike earlier times in their history, the Jews hoped to avert new blows by proving their usefulness and upright citizenship. While each new law inflicted fresh pain, it also catalyzed their resolve to hold out, to make do with what was left. Some of the newly promulgated laws actually created the illusion that the German government intended to continue to "tolerate" its Jewish citizens albeit under much reduced circumstances. So the Jews ignored the absurdities, and tried not to see the threats implicit in each pronouncement of the regime. Those who realized that the Nazis' unrelenting hatred of the Jews was more than an intensification of endemic German anti-Semitism fled—if they were fortunate to still have enough funds, and to have found a country that had not yet been infected by the German virus and opened its doors to them, offering them the opportunity to make a new start.

If Father understood this, his very pronounced reticence resulted in not confiding even in his wife. If Mother had been better informed, her demand that the family go to Palestine would have been even more insistent and better founded. Though Father did not speak of these matters to Mother, I believe that she saw that his fears for the future of the Jewish community and his own family weighed heavily on him. And so, despite Father's silence, as her own worries intensified, her demands that he "do something" increased, and their differences widened. The atmosphere in our house became charged with her sighs and—not always silent—rebuke.

In the spring of 1936, our father fell ill. Removed from us children, he spent almost four weeks in our dining room, and aside from Mother, only the doctor and his secretary were allowed to see him. We were told that Father had an abscess in his throat, which he refused to have lanced. This was one explanation. But behind it in the recesses of my memories there lurks another: Father was suffering from mental exhaustion and this was caused by overwork—was it a result of those Nuremberg Laws? Those laws meant that the very existence and whereabouts of every single Jew, half-Jew, or quarter-Jew was now documented in every city, town, and hamlet of Germany. Because of his position, it fell to Father to work with the Gestapo to achieve that goal in Hannover. It was at that time that we first heard Father mention names such as Vinzent Olejnik and Christian Heinrichsmeier, who were Gestapo officials in charge of the specific Jewish department, with whom he had to work during those long evenings.

That summer we went to Siusi (Seis) in the Dolomites, and Father recovered his health. He climbed mountains—a new source of anxiety for both Mother and Eva—and he seemed cheerful and fulfilled. He took us on a long walk, and when we children got tired and hungry, Father stopped with us at a small wayside inn. He treated us to cake and mineral water dispensed by a siphon, a new experience for us. Refreshed and happy, we came home and told Mother of our adventure. When Mother heard our story, she threw up her hands. To her chagrin, Father had forgotten that it was Tisha b'Av, a day of fasting, to commemorate two different anniversaries of destruction of the temple in Jerusalem. (A rabbinic ruling permits the commemoration of several events of that nature on the same day.) How, she seemed to ask, could he not remember such an important fast day! Mother's unhappiness cast a shadow on what had been a wonderful afternoon for us.

It was also the summer of the Berlin Olympic Games, and Father bought the *Berliner Illustrierte* to show us the pictures and read the stories of the various competitions. The irony of the reluctant applause by the racial purists for the record-breaking victories of Jesse Owens was not lost on us. He became an instant hero of ours—as did the boxers Max Baer and Joe Louis a short time later.

In August 1937, we spent four weeks in Buochs, a village nestled in one of the many bays of Lake Lucerne. While we were agreed that the mountains of that region in Switzerland could not compare with our beloved Dolomites, we did enjoy the swimming lessons Father gave us and the trips by boat on the lake. Our parents took us on a special outing by funicular rail and cable car to a pasture at the foot of the Titlis, high above the resort village of Engelberg. Father and Grete visited a boarding school at Baix-les-Bain near Lake Geneva, where she took an entrance exam.

On one of our outings we went to Lucerne, where Father visited a member of the congregation, Herr Thalheimer, who had always been very helpful when Father asked him for assistance for indigent families who wanted to emigrate. He lived in a beautiful house from which one had a good view of the town and lake. Meanwhile Mother took us shopping. She bought us identical red raincoats and purchased some raw silk, from which she planned to make us dresses. Finally we went to a kosher butcher store, where she bought us delicious bologna—we called it "pink salami"—a treat since in Germany we were only rarely able to get kosher meats. While we were waiting for Father in that butcher store, Mother was shocked when she watched the butcher's sales help clean chickens for their customers: The precious giblets were thrown out!

In Zurich, Father visited a bank where he held an account in trust for his mother in Palestine. They informed him that a deposit had been received from abroad, but would not tell him its source. Father was greatly disturbed by this news but, true to his usual custom, did not tell his wife what he had heard. He feared entrapment by the Gestapo. Jews were often accused and convicted of the very serious crime of currency smuggling (*Devisenschiebung*). Because of these laws, the account was registered with the authorities in Hannover. Mother must have noticed that something was upsetting Father and was left to wonder at his worried demeanor.

We returned to Hannover. Father went to the authorities—probably the Finanzamt, from whom he had his permission to maintain the funds for his mother—to report what he had learned regarding the newly arrived funds in his account. Our mother was still totally ignorant of these events. Quite likely this was true for the German authorities also.

On October 27, 1937, just as Eva and I were getting ready to go to the birthday party of Ellen Neumann, a school friend of ours who lived in nearby Linden, several policemen arrived at our apartment. They came to arrest Father. Our parents nevertheless decided to send us to the party. We were warned not to tell anyone what had happened at home.

Mother engaged Dr. Georg Fraenkel, a well-respected Jewish lawyer. Gradually she was learning what Father had so carefully withheld. I can see her to this day, bent low by a painful attack of sciatica, carrying bags full of documents to the lawyer's office in her effort to bring about Father's release. Grete, Eva, and I tried hard not to fight. We missed our father terribly and did not want to cause Mutti more grief. Friday nights and Saturdays his absence was almost palpable. In synagogue two other men took over for Father, and at home Mother said the blessings over wine and bread. Except for Frau Rothenberg, the old peddler who came weekly to us for her support, no one was allowed to sit in Father's chair at the head of the kitchen table—and she only sat there because Mother wouldn't tell her not to. Periodically Father was allowed to write us; his first letter sounded a note of reassurance:

> Hannover, 29. X. 1937
> Dear Mommy [*Liebes Muttchen*]:
> You would not believe how comfortable it is here. A small, simple but very clean room with a bed no worse than what I have at home. I have to see to it that the room is clean, but as you know a bit of housework has never been a cause of despair for me. If you and our dear little ones could be with me—of course in honorable circumstances only—I could live like this for 100 years. The guards are quite kind, they know how

> to teach people who lacked a proper upbringing at home how to behave. They have to have a lot of patience because it sometimes seems as if the inhabitants here think it is the guards whose fault it is that they have to be here . . .
>
> Tell the children to be good . . . and not to be sad. They need not feel any kind of shame about this—their Daddy is as decent a human being as their schoolmates' . . . At night it is extremely quiet here so that I get ample sleep. Getting a rest is really good for me. Please give my regards to all who inquire about me. Many kisses for you and the children from your loving Daddy. Now I shall begin my evening prayers . . .

And at the end of November, after more than a month of imprisonment, Father wrote a second letter in which he created a moral fable for us children about a man who traveled far and wide—even leaving his family—for the purpose of getting an education.

Luckily, Mother finally decided to write her family in Palestine about these events. They quickly solved the puzzle of Father's imprisonment. Her youngest sister and her husband had separated, and he was preparing their divorce. In order to shelter some of his funds, the husband, Uncle Iszo, a good friend of Father's mother, had, unbeknownst to anyone, sent funds to her account in Zurich. The account was registered in Father's name. This transfer had put our father into prison. Uncle Iszo promptly came to Hannover. He was put up in a hotel nearby.

Uncle Iszo, who had left Poland for Palestine in the 1920s, held a British passport, a circumstance that enabled him to arrive in Germany poised and certain that his testimony would carry proper weight. Our parents later described to us how his pronounced Semitic features and quite accented but impeccable German, one of five languages he spoke, had impressed the Court officers. He testified that it was he who had deposited the money in Grandmother's account. This seemed to have freed Father from prison.

But contrary to our understanding of the legalities, it was not the end of the case. Actually the accusations against Father went to three different levels of litigation, the final level being comparable to the highest and worst trial court, the Volksgericht, from which no appeals could be made. It took almost a year before Father was completely vindicated. The documents I saw pertaining to these trials speak with the utmost viciousness of my father; the prosecutor in charge accuses him of that special slyness to which Jews are known to be prone, and he made two appeals to have him retried. Interestingly, some of the trial judges who were assigned to his case may have been trained in Germany during the relatively democratic decade of the Weimar Republic (unlike many judges functioning after 1945), and that training may have been reflected in his being acquitted. He was not required to pay court costs. His final acquittal was dated September 1, 1938. During this period he could not work on his and his family's emigration since it would have been interpreted as an attempt by him to flee.

One evening in the middle of December, we heard the familiar sound of Father's keys in the door. We ran into the vestibule. After almost seven weeks in prison, pale but steady, Father stood before us.

For a moment we could not move. Then Father embraced Mother and Grete. Eva and I clung to his legs. When he had succeeded in freeing himself, he went to the telephone. He asked to speak to Joseph Berliner, the president of the Jewish community. "Herskovits here," he said with his usual emphasis on the first syllable as we watched him savor Herr Berliner's expressions of delight at the other end. Father and Joseph Berliner had maintained an excellent relationship over the years, and we regarded the old gentleman as a special friend of the family. Joseph Berliner had lost a son to World War I and a daughter to the influenza epidemic. Clara, a handicapped daughter, was his only surviving descendant, and she and her companion and cousin, Fräulein Wild, lived with him in his white villa. A few days later we went on our annual Chanukah visit to the Berliners, where as usual we children were treated with cakes and sweets and gifts of books. The visit was to be our last. Immensely relieved to have Father home, we celebrated Chanukah.

Because of what we read in the daily papers and the worries we often saw on the faces of our parents, we began to ask Father if we should not also try to leave Germany. Grete warned him that he would be the one "to lock the gate in Hamburg" after the other Jews had all left. I visualized a huge wrought iron gate, and the last boat leaving the harbor. I could not see if we were on it . . . But Father seems to have made some plans of his own before she warned him: A month after he returned from prison, having decided against sending her to school in Switzerland, he made his first inquiries to send Grete to England.

Father wrote to his half-brother in New York. Uncle Akos promised to send us the necessary affidavits. When these arrived, they were an invitation to visit the World's Fair in 1939. The intent of these papers was our permanent immigration, but Father explained that because he was born in a part of Hungary that now belonged to Romania, he could not get a permanent visa for the United States. The quota for Romania had been exhausted years earlier—shortly after

World War I. He could only qualify for a visitor's visa. His brother was aware of these complications. He advised Father to go to Canada after our visit in New York. We could then reenter America from there. Father knew that this was, at best, a semi-legal maneuver (it may be practiced to this day), and he would not hear of it. It was another instance of his integrity and unquestioning respect for the law—no matter whose.

2

The Nazi Noose Tightens

Nineteen thirty-eight was to be the last full year our family had together. Since Father's release from prison late in 1937, we children clung to him as never before. While he had safely returned to us, a steady stream of new anti-Jewish measures allowed for little letup in our anxiety. Often Father was detained by his work. When that happened, we felt his absence acutely and feared for his safety. Still, despite the many ominous political signs, our parents made a valiant effort to continue the pattern of our daily life.

Eva and I were looking forward to our tenth birthday on the eighth of March. Mother promised that, this year, the little cakes we would serve our friends would be store-bought rather than baked by her at home. None of the other mothers we knew baked their own fancy tortes, and while sighing at our foolishness, Mother understood how much we wanted to be "like our friends." There also was a cold supper, and Grete organized games and competitions and played the piano for a riotous game of musical chairs. And we were happy with our gifts and enjoyed the attention lavished on us.

Just a week later, Hitler marched into Austria. The picture on the front page of the *Hannoversche Tageblatt* told the story better than words: The streets of Vienna were lined with jubilant Austrians, who waved their flags and welcomed their Führer "home." The word *Anschluss* (coming together) was on everyone's lips. Hitler continued his defiance of the international community. The *Anschluss* was a blow to our parents and those thinking like them. They had expected that England and France would not stand idly by while Hitler enlarged his territory and his reach. But they did not abandon hope. They still thought the time would come when, with moral and economic pressure, the outside world would have to apply brakes to Hitler's aggressions, and as a result, the situation for the Jews in Germany would ease also.

A week or so before the festival of Purim, Father took out his Megillah (the scroll that records the story of Esther) and practiced his reading. We listened delightedly when, toward the end, according to the tradition, he clearly pronounced the names of the ten sons of Haman—the villain of the tale—in a single breath. They all met their deserved end on the gallows. Surely, I thought, that story is proof that justice prevails.

During the following weeks, our synagogue choir rehearsed the melodies we would sing on Passover, the next holiday of the Jewish calendar. Our teachers explained to us that Passover, aside from commemorating the Exodus from Egypt, also celebrates the start of spring, a time of renewal and hope. Father practiced one of his favorite prayers, *Tal*—a plea for dew—the moisture necessary for the growth of crops in the ancient Jewish land. At home, as usual for several weeks before Passover, everything was topsy-turvy. Our excitement at this upheaval was unaffected by Mother's worry that she might not be able to complete on time the myriad of tasks for a proper Passover.

Packages of large, round matzos arrived and were stored near the door in the dining room. I could not wait. Hours before the seder, even though it was strictly off-limits, I slipped into the dining room. I made a small tear in one of the packages and broke off a tiny piece of matzo. While a year had gone by, it tasted just like I remembered it, but also different, crisp and new. Then I began to worry that my parents would discover the small opening I had made in that package—or that punishment would come from on high. My parents failed to notice—but for a long time I was less sure about the Deity.

Finally by nightfall all was sparkling, and the unfamiliar Passover porcelain was in place. For the seder, Mother and Grete spread a snow-white damask cloth over the dining room table. At Father's place, the seder plate held the herbs and foods that served as reminders of our deliverance from oppression long ago. Eva and I needed no urging to wash and change into our new summer dresses. Mother had made us dresses of the raw silk that she had bought in Lucerne the previous summer, and she had embroidered small red and blue dots all around the neckline and sleeves. We were allowed to stay up late. And now my being the youngest—by forty-five minutes—was an advantage. At the first seder, it was my turn to ask the four questions: "*Ma Nishtanoh*," the first being: "Why is this night different from all other nights?" (Much of the readings in the Haggadah revolve around answering those four questions.) Eva got her turn at the second seder.

Six weeks after Passover, we celebrated Sh'vuot, a two-day holiday on which the giving of the Torah (the Law) on Mount Sinai is commemorated. The synagogue was beautifully decorated with white flowers. The custom to refrain from eating meat did not matter to us children at all because for dessert there was Mother's cheesecake to enjoy.

We spent our summer vacation in Geisa, a village near the university town of Tübingen. We followed our usual vacation customs and took long walks in the surrounding woods. The only Jewish residents were the Goldschmidts, an elderly woman blinded by diabetes, the widow of a scholar who had taught at the university, and her daughter. They lived in an old house filled with trophies and memorabilia. All the clocks in their house had stopped. To their delight, Father volunteered to fix them. (More than a decade earlier, his stepfather, the watchmaker, must have taught him the rudiments of his skill, when his mother and stepfather lived with our parents.) Towering above us on a ladder, Father spent hours until he had got most of those clocks running again.

Sometime during the summer of 1938, the Nazis ordered all Jewish men and women whose given name was considered "not clearly Jewish" to add the names "Sara" and "Israel" to their *Kennkarte* (an identity card). We were also photographed with our left ear exposed—the left ear having allegedly Jewish characteristics. I have Eva's and my photos, and we are both grinning! Even before Hitler's accession to power, Hans Globke, a Prussian government official, had recommended that Jews be forbidden to change their names to prevent them from hiding their Jewish ancestry. (This Hans Globke, incidentally, was quickly rehabilitated and served in Chancellor Adenauer's government after the war.)

Mother and the three of us had to add the name "Sara" while Father's first name, Samuel, was considered clearly Jewish. If our parents considered this order ridiculous, they muted their feelings lest they encourage us to make disparaging remarks about it outside our home. Inevitably, we made up for the lack of our freedom of expression in this and other respects by rambunctious and outspoken behavior at home. While we would not openly oppose our parents, Eva and I were now of an age to criticize each other's behavior quite mercilessly. It was our only real outlet.

Preparations for the High Holy Days started in earnest when we returned from vacation. Members of the congregation came to Father's office and purchased tickets for seats in the synagogue. Every seat holder received a color-coded ticket for himself and his family. Latecomers had to be content with seats in the old synagogue built in 1827, near remnants of the original city wall across the street, where services were held for the overflow. For many years, on Yom Kippur, a Christian woman and her two daughters had come to our house to supervise the children of the congregation who were too young to attend synagogue services. Two adjoining schoolrooms were turned into a large play area, and toys locked away all year were brought out of storage to entertain the children. The congregation provided lunch, and cots for the smaller children's afternoon nap. But now Father told us that the law forbade the Christian woman and her daughters to come to our house. A young woman from the congregation would replace her. Eva and I spent the morning participating in the choir. Around lunchtime Grete took us home. Our house was full of children, but I missed the two tall girls with their long blond braids who had played so patiently with us. I was glad when Father and Mother finally returned. As in previous years, Father assured us that the long service and fast had not tired him at all. He had "enough energy to start all over again." Not so John Mandelbrod, Grete's piano teacher, who was conductor of the synagogue choir. When some days later he came for her weekly lesson, bounding up the stairs two at a time, we heard him singing joyfully: "*Yom Kippur ist vorbei, Yom Kippur ist vorbei!*" (Yom Kippur is over, Yom Kippur is over!)

No sooner had the solemn High Holy Days ended than it was time for Succoth and Simchat Torah. Those two holidays I liked best of all. The succah of the Jewish community, a prefabricated wooden hut, was erected in the school yard. It was painted a light blue-gray, bordered with colorful garlands of fruit. Its roof, which according to custom had to be open to the sky to simulate the hut-like structure of ancient times, was divided into panels that were pulled upright with strong cords. The succah was large enough to have a coal-burning stove; its three tables were arranged in a horseshoe shape. The succah could seat thirty or more adults. We helped Father decorate the walls with multicolored paper chains that we had made, paper lanterns, and pictures of Rachel's tomb and other biblical scenes that were kept in a special box for this annual use. A truckload of evergreens and pine tree branches was delivered to the backyard and perfumed the air with the pine branches' pungent smell. Until Father found time to put the pine branches on the slatted roof of the succah, Eva and I had fun pushing each other on top of that prickly green. After synagogue services, the members came to make, or to listen to Father making, *Kiddush* (blessing over a cup of wine). In small colored glasses, brandy or liqueur was then served, and Grete and Mother offered crescent-shaped, chocolate-covered Balsen cookies. Dr. Freund, the *Landrabbiner* (rabbi of Lower Saxony), among many others, took his dinners in the succah. His wife brought him his food in an enameled, triple-decker food carrier, and their small white Spitz accompanied her. His piercing bark terrified Eva and me, but Mother, always concerned about good nutrition, looked at their soup and said worriedly to us that it looked to be too greasy. She did approve of Frau Dr. Freund serving her husband grapefruit—which they called *Pampelmuse.*

For Simchat Torah, a group of women of our congregation prepared bags of sweets, home-baked cakes, and small toys, such as wooden tops and mathematical games, for every child of the congregation. In one of the schoolrooms in our house, in assembly-line fashion, volunteers stood at long tables busily filling the bags, and we were allowed to help. The promise of these special gifts and sweets drew to the service even the children of families who did not usually attend it. The synagogue was beautifully decorated. All *perachot* (curtains that cover the doors to the ark) were draped over the railings of the three women's galleries. Many of these curtains had been handmade more than a century ago and had been donated to the community, sometimes in memory of a departed family member. Silk brocades of purple, yellow, reds, and blues, on which Hebrew psalms, sayings, and dedications were embroidered with gold and silver threads, lit up the usually somber sanctuary. During the service, carefully and with great reverence, all Torah scrolls were lifted out of the ark. Walking in procession and singing the traditional liturgy, Father, the two rabbis, and members of the congregation carried the Torah scrolls around the sanctuary.

The celebration of these festivals brightened our lives. I loved them for the peace and beauty they imparted to our surroundings. At home the atmosphere was transformed. This miracle was repeated every Sabbath: Not only our parents but every ordinary object took on a glow that changed its everyday appearance. On holidays I experienced these transformations even more intensely.

I was just beginning to understand that being Jewish brought both pain and joy, when, abruptly, violently, the cycle of holidays ended for me for all time. In an instant, our being Jews, until now "merely" a problem, became a calamity for us.

It began on October 27, one year after Father's arrest, when we heard that all Jews with Polish citizenship were being forced to return to Poland. It was the first time we heard the expression *Abschiebung.* (While I hesitate to call these events "deportations" because they were alleged to have had their origin in a Polish government threat to deprive these Jews of their Polish citizenship if they failed to return to Poland and request extensions, it is difficult to categorize them as anything else.) In Hannover they were being assembled and imprisoned in a large assembly hall without food or water. These Polish Jews, around seventeen thousand nationwide, were then forcibly put on trains to the Polish border. The German government for its part did not want to "risk" having these possibly stateless Jews in their midst and decided to forestall that "disaster" by expelling them preemptively. For a while the Jews were physically driven back and forth across the border by German and Polish border guards. The weather was bad, and they had neither shelter nor food. Eventually many were put into a camp-like prison inside the Polish border. All this happened fairly quietly, and if the world at large had an opinion about these inhumane actions, we did not hear about it.

My memory contains one small detail: Father asked our mother to prepare sandwiches for the Jews who had been taken from their homes without giving them any time to prepare even minimum necessities. He added that Mother should use cottage cheese only. I asked her why she had to make so many sandwiches and why Father would not allow her to use regular cheese. Mother explained that the very Orthodox Polish Jews did not eat hard cheeses, because these were prepared with rennet, an animal product. At that time no vegetarian equivalent was obtainable. Father must have taken those sandwiches to the Rüsthaus, located a few streets away from us, where Hannover's Polish Jews were held.

At that time Herschel Grynzpan, a young Polish Jew, who had grown up in Hannover, was living in Paris when he received a letter from his sister describing the situation under which she and their parents were forced to exist. He was so enraged that he purchased a gun and went to the German Embassy. There he shot and seriously wounded Ernst vom Rath, the first German diplomat he happened upon at the embassy. The diplomat died of his wounds. This murder was usually cited by Germans as the catalyst for the pogrom that was unleashed in Germany and Austria, the burning of synagogues and businesses, the violent death of at least one hundred Jews, and the incarceration in concentration camps of all the Jewish males they could find.

However, well before the shooting of vom Rath, during 1938, anti-Semitic laws, special regulations, and violent outbursts against Jewish property had steadily increased. In June, a synagogue in Munich had been destroyed by fire, and in August, another synagogue was destroyed in Fuerth, the old twin city of Nuremberg. How perpetrators of these staged crimes were "punished" would deserve another look at the legal procedures during the Hitler era.

The significance of this first deportation by the Germans in which a sizable group of men, women, and children of Polish Jewish origin were seized and expelled from the country where many had lived legally since the turn of the century—thirty or more years—has not been sufficiently investigated. It was no less than a harbinger, and perhaps even a rehearsal, of the persecutions to come. I do not know how it was assessed at the time. It was perpetrated upon a minority within a minority. Moreover, this group of Jews was not well integrated and accepted in the German Jewish community. As for the shooting of vom Rath, could it not be seen as an instance of that rare Jewish resistance or, more likely, revenge—with its predictable consequence of terrible vengeance?

Just three weeks later, very early on the morning of the tenth of November, Father received a telephone call. Wishing not to disturb Mother and us children, Father did not tell us of this call until much later. We were getting ready for school when we heard a tremendous thunderclap. "What happened? What was that?" we asked Father. His response was that two trolleys might have collided a block away on Goethestrasse. It made sense to us. We went downstairs to our classroom. Hardly had our class assembled when our teachers dismissed us "for the day." Upstairs we were surprised to find our parents intently discussing something. Father ought to have been in his office. Our parents told us that it would be best if we all went to spend a few days with friends, the Family Hahn. Father explained that these Jewish friends were Czech nationals. Their house should thus be off-limits to the Gestapo, a circumstance Father thought the "legalistic" Gestapo would take into account. Father did not explain why this circumstance was of importance to us. But his assumption may have been correct.

The apartment of Family Hahn—we had often met them at the Kaunitz *Schrebergarten*—was crowded with people. I went to the kitchen to say "hello" to Frau Fraenkel, the blind grandmother with whom I used to walk in the *Schrebergarten* of our friends. She had aged, and in the confusion, I could not be sure that she knew who was speaking to her. A year later the Hahns' Czech passport would become totally useless. Czechoslovakia had by then been occupied by the Germans, and both native Czech Jews and a considerable number of refugees from Germany and Austria were caught in the same net. Only four years later, on the second transport to leave Hannover, Mrs. Hahn was deported to the "East," to perish either in the Warsaw ghetto or in Treblinka. Where and how her husband lost his life, I have never found out. Nor do I know what happened to their only son. Frau Fraenkel was deported to Theresienstadt.

From the conversations of the adults around us, we children learned what Father seems to have known earlier: Many Jewish men had been "taken away." They were incarcerated in Buchenwald, one of the early concentration camps. A great many Jewish stores and apartments were destroyed, but not before they were ransacked and their contents looted. After several days of camping out at our friends' apartment, our parents decided to take us home. But despite what we had heard about the upheaval and destruction that had befallen the Jewish community, we could not imagine what we would find in our house.

As we walked up the three flights of stairs, we had to carefully pick our way on the stone steps to avoid stepping on glass and pieces of wood. And chaos confronted us when we opened our front door. In the spacious vestibule, three of the four doors to the two large yellowish oak linen closets were open. The closets had been emptied. Behind the still closed fourth door, a few apparently older or forgotten pieces of bed linens remained. Broken glass and broken dishes everywhere littered the floor, and silver utensils and candlesticks were missing from their customary place in the dining room cabinet. The furniture of Father's study—the room directly opposite the front door—had been methodically hacked to pieces. Hebrew books, their pages torn, were scattered on the floor. Many of these were *sidurim* (Hebrew prayer books for the Sabbath and the different holidays), and Father began to pick them up as he was stumbling over them. (According to Jewish law and custom, Hebrew prayer books and texts, which usually include the name of God, should be handled with reverence and are not supposed to lie on the floor.) In the vestibule, the cabin trunk that had held linens bought for Grete's planned emigration, was empty. Dumbfounded, afraid to move, Mother and the three of us just stood there.

Father tried to comfort us: "We should thank God that we are together and that we are unharmed. Luckily we decided to leave home and were not here when these people came." But while we continued to look at our ruined home, Father had other, much more terrible news: Our synagogue had been destroyed. That was the message of the telephone call he had received days ago. Someone wanted him to know that our synagogue was about to be dynamited. (Actually the synagogue had first been set on fire during the night.) Since the building was freestanding, there was less danger that the fire would spread to the surrounding streets. I recently received a photograph of the burning synagogue. Seventy-one years later this sight is as inexplicable and painful to me as it would have been had I seen it at the time. And this was one synagogue of close to one hundred that were vandalized, dynamited, and set ablaze all over the great German Reich.

From then on, services would be held in the old *Shul* across the street from the synagogue. Until then, this much older building had been used only for the services of the "overflow" during the High Holy Days, and for our Saturday afternoon youth services. During the week it became a gym for us students, and on weekend evenings an auditorium for the community's cultural activities. Father gave us to understand that the congregation would no longer need our choir. With that, he bent down and picked up the leg of what had been a black stained chair in the study. While he looked at what remained of its carved top, splintered beyond repair, he said: "Remember what I have so often told you. Mere material losses are unimportant in the total scheme of things."

Because Father was hidden with us at the Hahns', he escaped arrest. For the first time we children heard talk about prisons in our country—concentration camps—that were far worse than the place where Father had been imprisoned a year earlier. The men returned, but while they were warned not to speak of their experiences, some of the stories of how they were mistreated and even tortured made the rounds. Under orders of the Gestapo, they had to leave the country as soon as possible. Those who already had the necessary papers for emigration packed a few belongings, took the ten marks they were allotted, and with or without their families, fled the country they had not too long ago called their own. If Father had been imprisoned, he, too, would have had to find a way to emigrate—and his life might have turned out differently. I shall not speculate about the fate of the remainder of the family.

A few days after our return home from the Hahns', the Gestapo arrived in Father's office. They took Father to the nearby ruins of the synagogue in the Bergstrasse. He was to help them search for the safe in which the old ritual silver ornaments for the Torah were stored. Wading knee-deep in the rubble of what used to be his beloved synagogue, Father searched where his small dressing room had been. The safe and its precious contents had disappeared without a trace. The whole search was a charade, played for the benefit of some insurance company. Father returned home, covered in ashes and dust. Without changing his clothes, he sat silent and exhausted at the kitchen table. That was where we found him when we came upstairs after school. He seemed far away and did not hear our questions.

Our synagogue had stood in the center of a large open plaza, the first freestanding structure of its kind in Germany. This placement allowed a full appreciation of its architectural detail and impressive size. Its yellow-brown, glazed brick exterior, the material native to that region, clearly expressed the desire of Hannover's Jews to be members of their surrounding society. We took its presence in our life for granted. It was there and always would be—our synagogue was an integral part of our lives. Now, when we went to the old *Shul* for Friday night and Sabbath services, it was impossible not to pass those ruins. The sight was overwhelming. Those ruins were not just a bad dream: They were all that was left of our beautiful synagogue.[1] It looked like a monstrous skeleton. Above the entrance the huge rose window was a gaping round hole. The central dome had disappeared, the fire and later dynamite had collapsed it into the interior of what had been the sanctuary. Flanking the entrance, the two turrets whose stairs we had so often climbed hovered eerily in midair. Eventually the rubble was cleared away, and the Jewish community was made to pay for the cost of the cleanup.

Soon after those weeks, two oil paintings were brought to our dining room. One was a large self-portrait of Ernst Oppler, the son of Edwin, Hannover's famous Jewish architect, who had been employed by Hannover's royalty and who had designed the Lützowstrasse Gemeindehaus, where Eva and I were born and where we were still living. The intensity of Ernst's gaze, which only increased as we moved away from it, deeply impressed us. Only weeks earlier the Nazis had destroyed his father's greatest achievement. The grave eyes of the son seemed to express both rebuke and sorrow . . . I think that the second picture was a painting by Moritz Oppenheim. It depicted a Jewish family scene. I do not know who the owner of these pictures was, why they were stored in our dining room, or what became of them.

Abroad Jewish organizations began to make some effort to accelerate the emigration of those recently incarcerated. Of course, I do not know where our father would have gone. But late in 1938, our parents spoke about a possible rabbinical appointment in St. Gallen, Switzerland. Nothing came of it, perhaps because Mother was at that time making plans to enter the hospital for a long-delayed, though supposedly minor, operation.

After the destruction of our synagogue, our life was no longer the same. While in December 1938, the Jewish community—and our family—attempted to regroup and school was resumed in our house, our parents began to think of the possibility of sending Eva and me abroad. Plans to send Grete to England had been under way for almost a year. Some foreign countries willingly accepted small groups of Jewish children, but they would not do the same for their parents.

One evening at supper, Father broached the subject. Our parents had decided to send Eva and me on a children's transport to Holland. "Holland is nearer Germany than England, and besides, the climate is better." The bread on my plate took a long time to get down after Father finished talking. Eva jumped up from her chair. She pleaded with our parents not to be "sent away." It was the first time of many when she spoke up for both of us. Father told us not to be foolish ("*Seit doch keine Narren!*"). Life would be so much better for us in Holland.

"You will be able to go to school undisturbed, and with God's help, before long we will all be together again."

There was little joy that final Chanukah together as I listened to our parents enumerate the benefits of our stay in Holland. "You will have so much better nutrition; the political atmosphere will be calmer; you will not be taunted by other children." Mother was busy sewing clothes for our impending departure. Eva promptly refused to try them on. She did not want to cooperate in our separation. We had never been away from our parents, had never slept in a friend's house. My one independent foray into the outside world had been instituted not long before. On Thursdays when mother prepared fish for our midday meal, she sent me on an errand to a little shop several streets away. I had to cross a busy intersection on Goethestrasse near the Clevertor. Clutching a small white porcelain pot in one hand and some coins in the other, I had to ask for ten Pfennigs' worth of freshly prepared mustard. Now we were to be sent to Holland, a paradise of milk and butter, and peace and quiet. Who would take care of us, or what would await us there, was impossible to imagine.

Not until the archives in Hannover were opened some sixty years later did I get an inkling of what my father had felt by the end of that fateful year. In a letter to a financial official, probably someone he knew from an earlier time, he called 1938 an "indescribably difficult year." It had taken three trials from December 1937 until September 1, 1938, to legally clear him of all the trumped-up charges that had hounded him because of the bank account that, with official approval, he had held in Switzerland for his mother. The underlying difficulties Father seemed to refer to were those three trials that prevented him from even thinking about his and his family's possible emigration. And these personal difficulties did not touch on the destruction of our synagogue and what had happened to the Jewish communities in the rest of the country.

On January 3, 1939, our parents took Grete, Eva, and me to the photographer on Goethestrasse to document what would be our final day together. The next day we assembled with the other children at the railroad station. We joined a transport from Berlin. This was nothing like the vacation trips we used to take with our parents. The railroad station had lost its air of pleasurable anticipation. It was merely grimy and deserted that morning. Eva's protests had been to no avail. She and I were setting out alone.

3

Kindertransport to Holland

On the train, Eva complained that I was making her nervous. "Rutchen, sit down. You cannot see them anymore." She was right. The last few houses on the outskirts of Hannover had long since vanished. The train was speeding through a flat, monotonous landscape. I stood there, holding on to the leather strap of the window, my face pressed against the cold glass. I could not tear myself away from the window where, moments before, I had seen Father and Grete, their arms around our crying mother. Mother had to struggle to remain upright. "I know," I said to Eva. I sat down and landed on top of my carefully wrapped favorite doll. The package was crushed, the doll's sweet porcelain face a mess and her white wooden crib a jumble of sticks. In an instant I had destroyed my favorite possession . . . If only Eva had not told me to sit down, if only I had been more careful, if only I were still home . . .

Together with several hundred other German Jewish children from Berlin and other towns, the train was taking us to neighboring Holland. It was the first time in our life that we had been separated from our parents. Although they promised us that this would be a temporary parting, I could not imagine when or where we would see them again. Holland agreed to shelter us children from the ever more relentless persecutions by the Nazis, on condition that we leave our parents behind. Two months earlier our synagogue had been destroyed during *Kristallnacht*, and we had not recovered from the shock of that experience. And now we had to part from our parents.

I can still see their faces, especially my mother's. Her tears streamed down her face, but she made no effort to stop crying and to wipe them away.

Eva sat next to me. She was busy with a navy blue leather satchel that Father had bought us just a few days ago. Like me, she tried hard not to cry. The four other girls in our compartment had come from a Jewish orphanage in Berlin. For a moment, I wondered what it must feel like to be an orphan.

Eva and I used to love traveling on trains. But this trip was utterly different from the vacations on which we went with our parents, and the drab wintry landscape that rushed past the window of our compartment did not interest me.

It was night by the time we arrived in Amsterdam. We were greeted by members of a refugee committee. Perhaps they did not expect us that night. There were no beds or cots for us. We spent the first night away from home on a concrete floor covered with some blankets but without mattresses. Holland, it occurred to me, was not quite the paradise our parents had described.

The next day we were quarantined in Amsterdam-Zuid in barracks furnished with bunk beds. The food arrived in huge metal containers and tasted somewhat metallic. We lined up to get a scoop of thick, light yellow "chicken soup." It was almost inedible, and we were not yet hungry enough to have lost our fussiness. Outside it was chilly and wet, and the barracks were inadequately heated. It felt as if we were exposed to the elements. I thought of home, our cozy kitchen and warm *Kinderzimmer.* Until that time I had no idea that central heating could be something special and that many people lived without it.

Within days the first letter from our parents arrived. They sent us the photograph of our family taken the last day we were together. Eva's unhappiness, much more vocal than mine, was somewhat assuaged when she held the picture in her hands. It hurt me to see the grave expression in the eyes of Father and Grete. Our mother even sadder and resigned looked into the camera. Eva insisted that the picture be kept under her pillow, and she was relieved when I agreed to her demand. All I had to do to remember their faces was to close my eyes. Every night before I went to sleep, I saw them as clearly as if they were standing before me.

On January 10, we moved to Wijk aan Zee, a North Sea resort village, northwest of Amsterdam, where a Catholic organization maintained a children's convalescent home. Friendly nurses welcomed us. In Dutch, one of them tried to explain to us that we should undress to be washed by them. Repeatedly she pointed to large cakes of green soap (*Kernseife*), but we looked at her uncomprehendingly. Then, all of a sudden, I heard the similarity between her Dutch words and my German ones. Pleased with my discovery, I translated for the other children what the nurse was trying to tell us. She never forgot my help, and I became her "favorite"—something of an advantage in that very strict setting. She looked the other way when I took a book with me at nap time—or ate my ration of peanuts in bed. And in a small snapshot of our group, I sit next to her, with her arm protectively around my shoulders.

The German Jewish refugee children who had turned up in their home were very different from the children of the slums who were the usual wards of these Catholic nurses. With partial success we persuaded them that the older ones among us—we ranged in age from two to eighteen years—could wash themselves and had no need of regular afternoon naps. They agreed to let us wash ourselves, but we had to take our daily nap.

The food was much better than in Amsterdam-Zuid although meat was always ground up after it had been cooked. We took our meals in a large dining room at long, marble-topped tables. The milk, served in zinc beakers, tasted of the soap suds used to wash them. It was hard to get down, but we weren't allowed to leave it. The only way out was spilling the milk. At mealtime one could hear a musical "ping" as beakers hit the marble top—on bad days this swelled to a whole cacophony.

Daily, in rows of two, we were taken for walks on the windswept deserted beaches. The ocean and beach looked quite different from what I remembered of our summer vacations on the island of Norderney. Threatening, high greenish-black waves flooded the sand and sprayed us if we were slow to jump out of the way. Still, at times I enjoyed our walks and the starkness of those dunes with their spare tall grasses.

In February, a young Jewish teacher arrived and taught us Dutch and Dutch geography. Somewhat handicapped by a slight limp, she was kind and patient with us. For Purim, the older girls created a skit for which they used the music of a popular song: "Dreaming of the North Sea and the Home in Wijk aan Zee"; in rhymes they made fun of the home and its many rules.

Letters from our parents arrived with utmost regularity. We asked for and received a second family picture—the first one had been ruined by "excessive use." On our eleventh birthday in early March, a small parcel with chocolates arrived. The director of the home, an imposing elderly woman in a dark red robe-like dress, called us into her office. Our parents were on the telephone! I could not really understand what Mother said to me because she was crying while she tried to speak. Then it was Eva's turn, and Father talked with her. In a few moments it was all over.

During the second half of March, mail no longer arrived so punctually. We were worried. We only had to look at each other to burst into tears. Finally we decided to ask the director to let us call home. Despite our pleas, she refused. Deeply troubled, we participated in the home's unchanging routine. All tasks were performed together. Together we went to the bathrooms, washed, slept in the large dormitories, walked, and ate. Crying, Eva and I, holding hands or in close embrace, went along. There was no privacy, and the other children must have thought we were crybabies.

Finally at the end of March, a letter arrived. Father wrote us that Mother had been hospitalized. She had undergone minor corrective surgery for a gynecological disorder and was recuperating. We had known not only that she was in need of such surgery, but also that the problem was a consequence of our birth. Thus the news did not really surprise us. Father enclosed a short note from our mother, which puzzled us because it referred to our birthday as if she did not know that we had talked on the telephone and received the chocolates she had sent us:

> Dearest Little Ones: Now another year has passed and your birthday is here. [I wish you] good health and happiness until you are 120 years old! [A traditional wish] May gracious God permit our speedy reunion! But until such time we do not want to complain and argue with our fate. Rather we want to pray for good health, joy and contentment. I hope that the sweets from me will arrive in good time since I will be unable to call you—perhaps Papa will be able to reach you. Please accept my warmest wishes even if they can only be conveyed by letter.
>
> I hug and kiss you—unfortunately only in my thoughts.
>
> Your ever loving Mother

Early in April our refugee group left Wijk aan Zee for the very old Burgerweeshuis (orphanage) located on Kalverstraat in the heart of Amsterdam.

The Dutch orphans in the Burgerweeshuis were living in a separate wing. We could see them exercise or play games in the inner courtyard of the building. Their dresses had sleeves of different colors, one red and one black, and the bodice was gray or striped. This clown-like uniform was meant to deter their escape or assure their swift return should they manage to run away.

Our life, unrestricted compared to what we saw of theirs, was beginning to take shape. The same central refugee kitchen as during our first brief stay in

Amsterdam fed us. The food had not improved, although there was a weekly treat of a small piece of pastry and a bag of peanuts. Those peanuts were actually intended for the monkeys on our regular visits to the zoo. Quantities of white rice with a sprinkling of brown sugar were part of the daily fare. On Sundays dried apricots replaced the sugar. It was then I remembered our mother's dire warnings—when she was exasperated with our poor eating—that the time might come when we would be glad to have the spinach or carrots she was begging us to eat.

The woman in charge of the home began regular hair inspections to see if we had acquired lice. Evidently despite Holland's vaunted cleanliness, head lice were a common occurrence among children. One by one we had to submit our heads to the woman's close scrutiny. If, during this procedure, she paused for only a second as she pulled the comb through my hair, I would wonder in dread if she had found a louse. The whole procedure deeply offended me, and I hated to submit to it.

For the first time in my life, I hated to get up in the morning. I would wake with a start, and immediately my worries threatened to overwhelm me, especially my gnawing worry about our mother. It made the cold, unfriendly dormitory and the damp washroom that awaited us even less inviting. At home Father had insisted that we wash with cold water in the mornings to "toughen" us, but it had evidently not been successful.

We had been worrying about Mother for about a month; it seemed like an age. Two more short notes from her were included in Father's letters to us: One stressed that she was in a great hurry, but "Papa and Grete will write you everything. Just stay healthy—that is the main thing. In my thoughts I kiss you a thousand times. Mother."

At the end of April, Father had exciting news: Grete would stop off in Amsterdam on her way to England. We were so happy at the prospect of seeing her—it was now four long months since we had left Hannover—we could hardly wait for her to arrive. One of my newfound friends in the home cautioned me: "If I were you, I would not be all that happy." It shocked me to hear her hint at what we ourselves feared: Grete would bring us bad news from home.

Meanwhile we had been enrolled in a home economics course in a vocational school. We were to learn to iron, sew on a hand-cranked sewing machine, and do a little cooking. One day as we were leaving the school building, we saw Grete. She was at the opposite end of the street, walking swiftly toward us. Grete had just turned seventeen. She was a tall girl and looked serious and adult in her traveling clothes. We hugged her and clung to her and did not want to let go.

Mrs. Wijsmuller, a senior official of the Refugee Committee who with her husband's occasional assistance supervised our group home, had arranged to give us a few hours of complete privacy for our reunion with Grete. We went to her home, located in a beautiful old house on Nassaugracht, one of the streets bordering on a canal. Her housekeeper, whom we also knew from her visits to the Burgerweeshuis, showed us into a dark, though highly polished, dining room. Lunch, set on a table by the window overlooking the water, consisted of white bread with chocolate spread, a favorite treat in Holland. As soon as we were alone, we began to question Grete about our mother. Haltingly she told us what had actually happened at home in Hannover. Our mother had died. On our birthday, right after she spoke to us on the telephone, she entered the hospital, for what was considered a minor surgical procedure. A week later, early in the morning of March sixteenth, just as Dr. Bergmann, our family physician, entered her hospital room to visit her, she died, probably of pneumonia. The notes Father sent us from her were written in preparation for her stay in the hospital. By the time Father finally told us that she had undergone an operation, she was no longer alive.

I looked at the table that had been set so elegantly for us and out the window at the sunny canal on which sightseeing boats were passing, and thought: So that is what it is like to be an orphan. I, always called the crybaby of the family, did not cry when I heard that I had lost my mother. Eva, too, was totally silent. We were too stunned when Grete confirmed our worst fears. As usual, Father had tried to protect us as long as possible. He sent Grete to tell us the terrible news that he had been keeping from us. I could not help remembering that Father, whose tact in these matters was well known in our congregation in Hannover, had often been asked to break sudden bad news to the wife or husband of a member. When the friend of our parents, Dr. Lesser Knoller, the director of the Jewish Teachers Seminary, was fatally injured while crossing a busy street, it was Father who had to tell his widow. Grete stayed with us for several more days, but I do not recall a single thing about the remainder of her visit in Amsterdam.

Grete arrived in Middlesbrough at the beginning of May. She had a work permit from a Jewish family to teach the piano to their small daughter. Father had been helped by a member of our congregation who was acquainted with the British family, and she recommended Grete to them. No sooner had she arrived than the family dismissed their household help. They decided that Grete might as well perform the domestic chores also. Grete was very disturbed by these developments and wrote us repeatedly complaining about her plight. Like other girls in her circumstances, she had the choice of working either as a domestic or in a factory. The only other possibility was to learn nursing. Within a short time she had got in touch with Nathan Laski in Manchester—father of the more famous Harold and a friend of Churchill's ever since the latter switched to the Liberal Party in 1904 and represented North-West Manchester in Parliament.[1] Nathan Laski was president of the Victoria Memorial Hospital ("the Jewish," as they called it) in Manchester. Grete got Mr. Laski's agreement to begin work immediately as an aide in the hospital. Her formal course of nursing studies could not begin until she was eighteen years old in April 1940. Grete later wrote us that Mr. Laski had asked her what she had learned at home. Her answer that she learned to play the piano did not put him off. He pointed to his piano and asked her to play. He seems to have been satisfied with her performance, because he handed her a five-pound note—at the time a small fortune—for a movement of a Mozart sonata. My guess is that she played the C Major Sonata, K. 545, which she usually chose when she was asked to "play something." (It is beautiful and short and perhaps one of the most studied by young students.) The Laski family collected her from the railroad station when she moved to Manchester, and individual members were both kind and attentive, so that when she described her experiences to Father and us, we were briefly tempted to hope that they might be helpful in his emigration as well.

In Amsterdam, Eva and I learned that Father had written to the woman who ran our home to ask that she keep an eye on us. She must have told some of the older girls of the death of our mother—which resulted in the cryptic, even spiteful remark the girls made to me. The aides in the home were quite kind, but I do not think that they treated us different from the other children. There were two very small boys, barely two years old, and I was assigned to prepare and give them their supper. Almost nightly this consisted of "pap," bread cubes that had been soaked in warm milk. They seemed to like it. I also volunteered to sweep the girls' half of the large dining hall. As a reward, I was allowed to stay up half an hour longer. An aide of the home, a dark-haired, young Dutch Jewish woman, befriended me. She taught me to fix the runs in her silk stockings, using a special crochet hook. It required good eyesight and a lot of patience. I set to work, and when I had completed three pairs, she took me to Maison de Bonneterie, a fancy department store, for a treat of ice cream.

When one boy died and several children fell gravely ill with diphtheria, our home economics course was stopped. We wondered who would catch the disease next, but most of all, we feared the discomfort and pain when the doctor lined us up to take weekly throat cultures from us.

Now we had time on our hands. Eva and I eagerly immersed ourselves in the activities that were arranged to amuse us refugee children. Teachers came to the home to teach us Dutch songs. We were even taken to a horse race. Before the diagnosis of diphtheria was made, we went swimming every week in Amsterdam's huge public indoor pool. I wrote Father: "Is it all right with you if I jump from the three meter board?" By the time his negative response arrived, I had jumped. In most things, Eva had far more courage than I, but because she was rather nearsighted, she did not want to jump from that height. But then she consented to at least go up with me. She ventured to the edge of the board, and I gave her a light tap. Down she went. When she reemerged wet and spluttering, she was furious.

There were other ways in which I exasperated her. I did not like letter writing nearly as much as she, and she would stand over me, commanding: "Write!" Grete preserved our letters, and while Eva's handwriting looks firm and determined, my additions to her letters show a more tentative, hesitant handwriting. Occasionally I expressed sadness at the loss of our mother. I complained to Grete that there was no one I could talk to and that I could not cry. Eva also mentioned Mother on her birthday on May 19, and she wrote of her sadness when the other children celebrated Mother's Day.

The Refugee Committee was led by Siegfried and Lola Kramarsky. A well-to-do art collector and banker, he had emigrated from Germany with his wife and children. (When in 1940 there was a danger that the family might not succeed in leaving Holland in time, Chaim Weizmann is said to have helped. Mrs. Lola Kramarsky, accompanied by her daughter Sonia, regularly came to inspect the home. Sonia, not yet twenty, was an ardent Zionist. A good-looking, sturdy girl, she wore her long dark braids coiled around her head. The Kramarskys knew that we had lost our mother. When Mrs. Kramarsky wanted to know how Grete was doing in England, I told her of her unhappiness. Mrs. Kramarsky reacted rather sharply: "Tell her not to complain too much, she could be sent back to Germany!" Her daughter took a genuine interest in our activities and helped to organize some of our performances and festivities.

The news from Hannover was startling: Our father planned to remarry. His future wife, Marie (Mania) Münzer, had been widowed in early February. Her only child, Lotte, was a little more than two years older than we. We had not met Lotte although we thought that we might have seen her once or twice, perhaps in school. Sometime in July we heard that their marriage had taken place on June 16. It was the last official act of our *Landrabbiner*, Dr. Freund, who, Father wrote, was by then very frail. He died a couple of weeks later. Grete must have asked Father about Lotte, and sometime in July he responded: "First of all I want to answer your question regarding my wife's child. She is almost fourteen, and was born on the 11th of December 1925 in Hannover. She is a German citizen. She is called Charlotte Sara. She is a good student and has good natural ability. She is very well developed for her age and is consequently quite sturdy. I think you saw her before you left so you know that she is also very pretty."

Father, we later learned, had other, urgent concerns. He had a permit to go to England, but his new wife did not. Many members of the Jewish community were leaving Germany, and others anxiously tried to get the necessary papers to get out. Mania, as she asked us to call her, was terrified that Father might leave without her, as happened in some families.

Years later I surmised that Father's early remarriage after our mother's death was a response to the uncertainties of the summer of 1939. It was one way to reassure his wife-to-be that he would do everything in his power to get emigration papers for her as well. At the time of his remarriage, we were incapable of understanding his situation. Eva and I, and this must have been true for Grete also, were shocked and hurt by what seemed his undue haste.

Meanwhile, Father repeatedly prodded Grete to attempt by various routes to get a permit for his wife. He stressed both his and her ability to perform any kind of work.

> August 6, 1939
> Dearest Gretelchen:
>
> . . . Enclosed are four photos [of my wife] and a health certificate. If you need them I can send you excellent references. From my own knowledge I can attest to the fact that there is no more decent Jewish woman in Hannover than she.
>
> Since I do not have a work permit for abroad [England is meant] I can work with my wife. You can assure people that in all of England they would find no more suitable housekeepers than us.
>
> You can also tell them that I could entertain a whole audience with

> song recitals. I really do not have to tell you what you can or should say without exaggeration. . . . Warmest kisses, your loving Vater.

Already in July he had written: "I have not yet given up hope that one day we will be together again with you, Eva and Ruth. How we will achieve it I cannot, at the moment, say. It could be that you children will succeed in arranging it." In another letter, he again assures Grete that he would be willing to do any kind of work, manual or not. "We are both very skilled, and more than willing to do what is necessary. We would be an asset to any staff." We found out that he also wrote to Hannoveranians in Amsterdam, who, he knew, had relatives in England to help Eva and me get to England. But he warned Grete not to raise our hopes. When he learned that our school friend, Ellen Neumann, had to attend Catholic church services in Scotland, he worried about such possibilities for us. And while he reported on his activities in the office and wrote Grete about singing techniques and singers, his letters sounded full of intense longing to be reunited with us.

More than fifty years later, his pleas are as heartrending as if they had just been uttered. Eva and I also spoke with each other of our hope that Margaret would help Father and Mania to get to England. And Eva wrote to Margaret in her new, forceful style:

> Amsterdam, 8. 8. 39
>
> Dear Greti!
>
> You will be surprised to have mail from us so soon again, but the reason for it is extremely important. Since more and more people are emigrating, it is very important that Papa also emigrate. I ask you therefore to get in touch with Mr. Laski and the Woburn House [site of the Refugee Committee in London] so as to leave no stone unturned to enable Papa and Frau M. (of course also!) to emigrate to England! You are in the country and can see to it that P. gets out. So please apply yourself to it in earnest. You know that we rely on you, you have to help!! We have had no mail from you. We will be writing a letter tomorrow. I am hoping to hear in your next letter that you are really doing something for Papi. Please confirm this to us as soon as you get this letter. Our entire hope rests with you!
>
> Many many 1000 kisses sends you your Eva who relies on you.

My contribution to this postcard:

> Dear Grete:
>
> Eva has already told you everything. Please make every effort and do your very best. Perhaps Mr. Laski could help you if you tried to turn to him. Who knows? I am very worried that again we have had no mail from you for eight days. Are you perhaps ill? Please write soon. 1000 kisses from your Ruth. On Friday we had a card from Papi.

Grete seemed powerless. She was not a very practical person, and being very much the oldest offspring, she was also quite self-absorbed. (Years later, perhaps in a moment of confession or, indeed, self-doubt, she wondered if she would have worked harder on her father's emigration if our mother had still been alive. . . .) The Hannoveranians she spoke to refused to see the urgency and made no effort to help. Fortunate to have reached England, they themselves must have been overwhelmed by their financial insecurity and unfamiliar surroundings. But having only recently escaped from Germany, they should have known that their new difficulties could not compare with the accelerating threats faced by their compatriots still in Germany. Although it required a mere fifty-pound deposit in a bank, no offer of practical assistance was made. Help from British Jewish organizations and the British government was too little and came too late.

Father's work seems to have become increasingly complex and time-consuming. As late as 1940, an additional bookkeeper had to be hired for the office. This was extraordinary since there were at most two thousand Jews left in the congregation. It was probably due to the increasing demands of the Nazis for financial reporting to extract the last drop of Jewish resources.

War broke out on September third. We were still in Amsterdam, and plans were being made to send us refugee children to private families. Vaguely I sensed that this war would complicate our lives further and demand many sacrifices of us. I spoke of my fears to Trixie, who, at eighteen, was the oldest girl in the home. In response she slapped my face. I turned away in shock and disbelief. My eyes filled with tears. Her slap burned my cheek. If only I had not said anything! I had probably touched on her own fears for the future, and this was the only answer she had.

The only immediate consequence of the war was that Father now addressed all three of us in the letters he wrote us, and Grete used the same route in reverse.

Letters to our relatives in Palestine went by way of Zurich, where the Karos, old friends of ours who were Swiss citizens, had settled earlier.

By September sixth, Eva was copying Father's first letter to Grete, because she did not want to part with the original. Later he would send a carbon copy to spare us the work of copying letters that were often one or two typewritten pages long. He urged us, but especially Grete, to obey all air-raid sirens and not to take for granted that she was safe because she lived in a hospital: "Planes fly off course and even military hospitals were occasionally hit during 1914–1918. Act as if you were housed in a munitions factory rather than a hospital. Do not play the hero [he demanded], you help no one and only injure yourself." (A year later the nurses' residence in Manchester was demolished by a bomb. Fortunately Grete was visiting friends at the time.)

4
Families Bloemkoper and Meijer

In early November 1939, the director of the home told us that two Jewish families in Leiden had agreed to have Eva and me live with them. While we were going to be separated, the two families both lived on Thorbeckestraat. I did not mind leaving Amsterdam, but the thought of being separated from Eva made me quite apprehensive. The opportunity for us to live in private homes was envied by many of the girls who stayed behind. Less than a year later their own lives would change dramatically. Eva's hosts and mine turned out to be quite different, in circumstances and outlook and in their eventual fate.

I felt that Family Bloemkoper was pleased to see me. Three little boys looked me over curiously as their mother introduced us to each other: "This is Ruth, and this is Jacob, our oldest; he is five. This is four-year-old Eli, and there, in the playpen, is our youngest, Abrammetje. He has just turned one." Missing in this lineup was their only girl, three-year-old Roosje, who was visiting her grandparents in Amsterdam. All were dark-haired and brown-eyed but did not otherwise look or act alike. I was excited to be with them, but not having had younger siblings or brothers, I had no idea what to expect. In Amsterdam I had enjoyed taking care of the two smallest boys, and I was sure that I would get to like these little boys as well. Their father, Victor Bloemkoper, was thirty, and their mother, Jeanette Bloemkoper de Hartog, twenty-nine. They appeared older to me.

When Father heard about our impending move to Leiden, he sent us instructions for our new surroundings: "Even if these families have help with their household chores, you must always be helpful. And if they have children, you must be sure to get on well with them." Whether as a result of his admonitions or not, I resolved to be on my very best behavior. And fear of doing something wrong made me act very diffidently. In Amsterdam, because I missed my mother, I had sought out the friendship of the aides, but it took me a while to feel at ease with Mevrouw Bloemkoper. They immediately asked me to call them "Aunt" and "Uncle." Try as I might, I could not do it and avoided calling them anything. Finally they promised me a bar of chocolate if I succeeded in calling them "Aunt" and "Uncle"—without backsliding—for a whole week. It was hard work, but I earned my chocolate.

The Bloemkopers lived in a small, modern two-storied row house, and I got their guest room in the attic. It had flowered wallpaper and simple white furniture, and I liked that room a lot. But it made me uncomfortable to have to share my bed with one or the other of Mvr. Bloemkoper's younger sisters when they came for visits. They were the daughters of her father, Mijnheer de Hartog, and his second wife, the aunt who became her loving stepmother and brought her up when Jeanette's mother died giving birth to her. She was a sister of Jeanette's mother. The De Hartog and Bloemkoper families all accepted my presence and seemed to feel quite at ease with me. A month after I arrived in Leiden, I got to spend a week on vacation with the De Hartog family in Amsterdam and felt sorry when it was over. Mijnheer de Hartog was a retired post office official, who gave the impression of not needing to worry unduly, and he enjoyed having the grandchildren visit with him. When I think just how many similarly blameless lives in around a dozen European countries were destroyed by the evil that overran Europe and Russia, it is not fathomable to this day.

The house in Leiden had small front and back gardens, and a few purple and white asters and cosmos with their wispy leaves were still in bloom when I arrived. The living room and the rarely used front parlor were comfortably furnished. Compared to the large, old-fashioned house with its unwieldy old oak furniture at home in Hannover, and the large halls of the Burgerweeshuis, everything seemed miniaturized.

Mijn. Bloemkoper was the cantor, teacher, and *shochet* (ritual slaughterer) of the small Jewish community. The family was strictly Orthodox. Every Sabbath I attended the services led by Mijn. Bloemkoper. The small synagogue, while quite inconspicuous on the outside, had an interior of dark polished wood. The women's gallery was almost completely closed off, and little could be seen of the service in the sanctuary. But regardless of how much I might have liked the synagogue, the service meant little to me, because I could not warm to the different voice and unfamiliar melodies. The Dutch pronounced Hebrew slightly differently. (The *ayin*, a silent letter in our pronunciation, had a nasal *ng* sound in theirs, following their Sephardic customs.) I quickly became aware of real differences between the observances of religious Jews at home and those in Holland. It was inevitable that I would compare the religious customs of my parents with those of the Bloemkopers. And my parents always "fell short." This feeling was confirmed for me when the Bloemkopers assured me that their way was the correct one. I did not want to feel critical of my parents, and these comparisons were painful and worried me.

Eva had come to a family of cattle dealers. While Family Meijer lived in a similar house, they were more affluent than "my" family. They also had four children—but their oldest daughter, Gerda, was seventeen like our sister Grete, Harry was fifteen, and Ben one year older to the day than Eva and I. Betty, the youngest, was a beautiful, blond three-year-old on whom the whole family doted.

A day or two after our arrival in Leiden, Mijn. Bloemkoper took both Eva and me to the local elementary school. It was pointed out to us with some pride that our school was located across the street from the Nobel prize winner Kamerlingh Onnes's laboratory, named for the Dutch physicist of superconductivity. The principal enrolled us in the fifth grade—although we had completed it at home—to give us a chance to learn Dutch grammar. The elderly, very friendly teacher seated us in the front row, and he worked hard to make us feel at ease. During dictation exercises, he pronounced every syllable with great precision and even greater patience to help us hear the nuances of the quite difficult Dutch spelling. He told us that, a long time ago, he had visited Hannover. When he showed us pictures of its famous Rathaus (city hall) and other sights with which we were familiar, he made me terribly homesick. But he meant well, and we learned quickly. Before long, we began to neglect our German. In his letters, Father now listed the words we had misspelled when we wrote to him. With some forbearance, he added that he thought we were careless rather than ignorant. Actually, since we had no chance to read or study German, our spelling did become quite atrocious. But when Eva won a prize of a gulden and a half in a story contest, Father delightedly reported the news to his friends, the Karos, in Zurich: He was not at all surprised, he wrote, because writing, rather than schoolwork, had always been her strength. Her story of the friendship between a cat and a dog was pure invention, and all the more impressive since we had never owned a dog while our experience with a newborn kitten was confined to a few weeks in the summer of 1938 when we were on vacation in Geisa.

The subjects I enjoyed most were Dutch history and art. For the first time I learned, in a systematic manner, about the past of another people. Pivotal events were listed chronologically in a separate booklet, and we were tested to see if we had memorized the dates. In art class we sight-copied small reproductions of Dutch master drawings and etchings of the seventeenth and eighteenth centuries. When I was busy with my drawing, I became totally oblivious of my surroundings and forgot my worries.

The Bloemkopers lived on a strict budget, and sometimes I worried that I might be eating too much. Actually my stay in their home may also have been of some help to them. I became a ready-made babysitter. Their own parents were living in The Hague and in Amsterdam. The Dutch girl who helped in their household went home in the evening. At first this new responsibility scared me quite a bit, but while I never stopped being anxious about being alone with four small, lively children, I got used to this new kind of responsibility. Eli and Abrammetje were my favorites. Eli was an extremely good-natured, thoughtful boy who never stopped asking questions about the relative sizes of the sun and the moon. Since I did not know, he quickly thought of something else to ask. Little Abrammetje and I made friends immediately. Roosje was not deterred by being outnumbered. A comical little girl with glasses, she made good use of her sense of humor to defend herself against her three brothers. The oldest, Jacob, was rather sensitive and at times cranky, and he often complained of pain and cried when his parents went out in the evening. The "medicine" I gave him—my concoction of vinegar and some spices—was evidently vile enough to convince him that it would help.

I got used to my life in Leiden. It was years later that I questioned the cost of my adjustment, which had helped to propel me into a premature "adulthood." Physically I hardly developed at all during the two years I spent with the Bloemkopers, and they seemed aware of my slow growth. In jest, Mijn. Bloemkoper would check my index finger to see whether I was getting any fatter. Eva, who was now quite a bit taller than I, spent an occasional weekend with me, but she complained about being unhappy living with the Meijers. She felt sure that she was not treated as an equal of the Meijers' own children. She expressed herself openly, leaving little doubt about how she felt. We did not confide in our father because we did not want to worry him. However, since Father and these two families corresponded, he was probably better informed than we knew. Occasionally Mvr. Bloemkoper added a few lines to the letters we wrote to Grete. Grete preserved our letters for more than fifty years, and as I reread them, I realize that this young mother of four small children must have known how we longed to be reunited with both Grete and Father. Nevertheless, she told Grete not to worry too much about Eva, who, she wrote, "liked" to complain about her life. Even though Eva told us what she felt, this separation left a lasting hurt.

The tenth of May 1940 was a beautiful spring day. Three days earlier we had celebrated Mvr. Bloemkoper's thirtieth birthday, and a colorful bouquet of her favorite anemones still stood on the living room table. Very early in the morning, to my surprise, Mvr. Bloemkoper came upstairs to wake me. It was so sunny that I had trouble opening my eyes. She told me to hurry and take my clothes. "You can dress downstairs," she said very agitatedly. Sleepily I thought: Father must have come to fetch us home. That wish was never far from my thoughts. But it was Hitler who had invaded Holland. The Bloemkopers' first thought was of me since I was sleeping in their little attic room. There was real fear of a possible bombardment.

The next few days were filled with anxiety and rumors, most of which turned out to be false. The radio and newspapers could offer little reassurance. We continued to fear German bombs, and the recurrent sound of *flak* (anti-aircraft fire) did not make us feel any more secure. Hitler, we had been told, would be stopped by the elaborate defense system of the Dutch. It was planned that, at a certain signal, the locks of a whole network of canals and rivers would open and flood the countryside to stop the advance of the invaders. Looking out of the window, we saw small black shapes, which turned into parachutists floating to earth. They were said to be German soldiers disguised as nuns and Dutch workmen. Landing behind the Dutch defense lines, they pulled their weapons on the unsuspecting population and first sowed confusion and then death.

Only a few days later, Holland capitulated. There had been no defensive flood. On the contrary: The system had been sabotaged by an extensive fifth column operating behind Dutch lines. Queen Wilhelmina spoke to her people on the radio. Then she and her family fled to England.

On the day of capitulation, the small Jewish community of Leiden made an attempt to flee to England. We all assembled in the Jewish orphanage—where Eva had recently moved from the Meijers'—and spent a whole night camping out in the large lobby while we waited for a signal that there was a boat for us in Ijmuiden—a harbor slightly northwest of Amsterdam. But there was no boat, and no crossing to safety for us. Early the next morning the Bloemkopers with their four young children and me, and the other families who had waited with us, walked home through the deserted streets. The little row houses with their neat flowering front yards looked totally peaceful, totally undisturbed. They seemed to be tokens of reassurance that things would not be so bad. The Bloemkopers were immensely relieved to be returning home to their familiar surroundings and possessions—although only hours earlier they had hoped to reach England, fully prepared to leave everything behind. I did not tell them that I was disappointed that we had to stay.

Meanwhile in Amsterdam, Mvr. Wijsmuller, worried about the German and Austrian Jewish refugee children in her care in the Burgerweeshuis, persuaded the captain of a Dutch freighter in Ijmuiden to take a group of Jews on board. He agreed and helped around two hundred Jewish men and women, among them eighty Jewish refugee children from the Burgerweeshuis, to flee to England.[1]

Until Hitler's attack on Holland, letters from Father to Grete continued to come to us or went by way of Zurich. On February 25, 1940, Father had written her:

> Dearest Gretelchen:
>
> The Little Ones have told me that you continue to write them regularly. I think that is very nice of you, especially since I know how many demands are being made on your time. In one week they received three letters from you, which Ruth reported with three exclamation points, proof that it was a big thrill for them. I am thinking that with your 18th birthday on April 10th, your training period is approaching. I assume that this has not changed. I am counting on your receiving some credit at the end of your training for your work since October 1939.—
>
> Please write to Iszo.[2] If Iszo could arrange my and my wife's emigration to any country whatsoever. The child [Lotte] is soon to leave for the U.S. so no intermediate stop-over is needed for her. Iszo should get in touch with Uncle Akos if he needs to. I would like to work on our emigration so that I can again have you children with me. Wherever it might be, I shall strive to have that wish fulfilled. We are all well, thank God, and our days are taken up with a great deal of work. Some times they are too short. I practice voice technique, have heard Jan Kipura for the first time. His voice sounds rather worn in the higher register, at least, that is how the record sounds. In the middle range where he is singing more softly, he can be bewitching.
>
> I send you fondest greetings—your ever loving Father.

Eva and I caught the urgency of his appeal, and both of us pleaded with Grete to write to Uncle Iszo "immediately and without fail" and to "keep up her correspondence with him" to remind him of Father.[3] Eva's eloquent letter to Margaret shows her at her best. She advises Grete, by six years her senior, to be polite but insistent! Father evidently expected that Lotte would get her visa for the United States since she had a low quota number. By fall he reported that our friends, the Kaunitz family, had succeeded in leaving for the United States in the summer of 1940.

Winters in Leiden did not seem as hard as in Amsterdam although my attic room was quite cold, and only the living room had a coal-burning stove. Eva and I learned to skate, and while we could get all the way to school on our simple wooden skates, Eva enjoyed that activity much more than I.

Summer vacations in Leiden were spent at home except for day trips to amusement parks. One of my trips to a playground ended unexpectedly. While waiting my turn, a boy on a heavy, boat-shaped metal swing hit me full force on my forehead. When I came to, I was in the emergency room of a local hospital. At the Bloemkopers, I was installed on the second floor in the children's room. Lying still for four weeks to cure the concussion I had sustained was rather boring because I was not allowed to read. A couple of weeks after I was allowed to get up, Eva crossed a busy street in front of a bus, and unable to see an oncoming car, got hit and catapulted on top of its hood. She was badly shaken up and bruised but miraculously escaped other serious injury. Now it was my turn to visit her, and she, too, soon recovered. When Father heard about these accidents, he became extremely alarmed and wrote to both families imploring them to take good care of us.

The Nazi occupation in Holland incrementally curtailed our ability to move about and live normally. However, Father could now send us money for clothes and, separately, reimburse the Bloemkopers for some of the expenses they had incurred on my behalf. Pleased with this development, the Bloemkopers put these funds into a special account but rarely or never made use of them. In late spring 1941, Eva and I graduated from the sixth and final year of elementary school. For several weeks during the summer the principal of our school coached his daughter and me to take the entrance examination for the HBS (high school). I was happy when the news arrived that I had passed. Mvr. Bloemkoper served vanilla pudding—usually a Sabbath treat! But my happiness did not last. Hitler's racial laws had caught up with us. Jews were no longer permitted to enroll at the high school. Eva planned to go to a Froebel school to begin training as a kindergarten teacher, but this, too, was no longer possible. The Bloemkopers then decided that I should learn sewing and take courses in mathematics and English. Alternate plans for Eva were to be made by the orphanage.

During the first days of November 1941, Eva and I received a terse letter from Father, instructing us: "You are to pack and return to Hannover immediately."

We were given the name of an official whom we had to see for our travel papers. I was too excited and preoccupied with this new development to feel very sad at having to part from Family Bloemkoper. The thought that I was soon going to be with Father again took precedence over everything else. Still, it hurt to say good-bye to Abrammetje. He was now three years old, and I had helped watch over him for much of his short life. When would I see him again? When he cried, his mother comforted him: "Ruth will come back when the war is over," which the Dutch express as "when the war passes [by]."

5

We Are Back in Hannover

On November 7, 1941, Eva and I arrived in Hannover's central railroad station from which we had left almost three years earlier. Father was nowhere to be seen. A tall, straight-backed woman was walking alongside the train. She caught sight of us and waved. It was Mania, our stepmother. She appeared relieved to have found us. The first thing I saw was the yellow patch on her coat. The word *Jude* was imprinted in black in the center of the yellow Magen David (Star of David). She was anxious to get us home. While we lived not far from the station, she was worried to have to walk through a busy section of town with the two of us who, while obviously Jewish, wore no star. She explained that Father had to be in town on urgent business. We would see him later. Eva and I were terribly disappointed. Carrying our suitcases, we quietly walked home.

When we entered our house, we found the familiar surroundings greatly changed. To my surprise, there were people everywhere. Although the year before, Father had mentioned in one of his letters that several families, including Lore Pels, a school friend of ours, had moved into some of the schoolrooms, we did not really grasp what this meant and were unprepared for what we found. Along the walls of both flights of stairs, all kinds of chests of drawers and cabinets were propped up, leaving a much narrower staircase.

In our own apartment one wing was occupied by other people. Our family still had the two bedrooms, a small living room, and the kitchen. How exceptional this wealth of space was, I would soon learn. The grand piano—under which I remembered crouching to listen to Grete play—was no longer there. Mania took us into the kitchen and asked if we were hungry. We did not feel like eating.

Finally the kitchen door opened and Father stuck in his head. He explained that he had been detained by the *Behörde* (authorities); we had not forgotten that it was one of his euphemisms for the Gestapo. He was very tired. I was shocked when I saw him. The changes in the house had not prepared me for how changed he appeared to me. He was smaller, his hair much whiter than I remembered. Father held us close to him and kissed us. Still I felt safe in his embrace and happy to be with him again.

Our stepmother spoke to us in a controlled, cool manner. I thought that her slightly accented speech had a harsh sound, but unlike our mother's, her German was grammatically perfect. Her daughter appeared to be a young adult next to us. Lotte, who was not yet sixteen, had dark brown hair and dark, almond-shaped eyes, and she was almost a head taller than her tall mother. Smiling shyly, she shook hands with us. I thought I could like Lotte, but I could not tell how Lotte felt about meeting Eva and me.

From Father's conversation with Mania, we gathered that there was no longer even a slight chance for our family to be able to go to Cuba. His hope to be able to emigrate to Cuba had been the reason for his request that we be allowed to return to Hannover. Had we arrived home too late, and if so, had our lateness prevented their timely departure? We did not ask and Father did not say. (From Zurich our friends, the Karos, wrote a postcard to Grete in Manchester in which they told her that Eva and I had returned to Hannover, and they expected we would be arriving in Cuba any day now.) Less than a month earlier, a small group of members of our community had managed to leave for Cuba. They may have been the last to reach safety. A year earlier Father and Mania fully expected that Lotte would emigrate to the United States. Her emigration was no longer even mentioned. Actually, two weeks before our return, by a secret decree of October 23, 1941, the Reichssicherheitshauptamt (RSHA), the central SS office in Berlin under Himmler, prohibited, "without exception," all Jewish emigration from Germany and its occupied territories.[1] Nevertheless, the permission Father received to bring us home, regardless of whether he knew of that decree or not, was to be decisive for Eva and me.

Since Father had no common language other than German with Polish-born Mania, Eva and I understood far more of their conversations and concerns than we had of those of our parents before we went to Holland. Father seemed harassed and impatient. Eva and I had not spoken German with each other for at least a year, and now, too, we often lapsed into Dutch. Irritated, Father said that he disliked the recurring, guttural *ch* sound, and he asked us to speak German. He encouraged us not to forget Dutch—we just shouldn't practice it in his presence. Neither of us reminded him of his habit of speaking Hungarian with our late mother.

Two months before our return, Lützowstrasse 3, the Jewish community house, had been transformed into one of the sixteen Jew houses (*Judenhäuser*) for the remnants of the Jewish community.[2] For almost twenty years, our family had made its home on the third floor. In the dining room, on a couch our mother had occasionally pointed out to us, both sets of twins were born. Now, like the other Jew houses, our house served as a collection point or way station, hardly more than a holding pen, for about one hundred persons, young and old, both families and single individuals. They had been evicted from their own houses and apartments. We were appalled to see under what conditions so many people were existing—and in an instant the image of our home that I had held on to while I was in Holland was destroyed.

The two classrooms on the ground floor housed several families. The same was true for the second-floor classrooms and the library. In our apartment, which had always encompassed the entire third floor, eighteen men and women were "living" in the dining room. A small number tried to fit into the much smaller *Herrenzimmer* (father's study) next to it. Two small rooms, the maid's quarters of years ago, were also occupied. People were even sleeping in our attic. They seemed to prefer its privacy but instead had to breathe the dust and dirt of age-old storage. Those living in our apartment cooked on small cookers in the vestibule and, once in a while, at the invitation of Mania, in our kitchen. They shared the one toilet and bathroom with us. The people living in the schoolrooms and offices had to use toilets located in the school yard, the only ones available. I do not know whether they were able to bathe unless they used the *mikvah* (ritual bath) in the basement. The few toilet facilities of which the house could boast must have been considered adequate for its original purpose when it was built by Edwin Oppler in 1875. The *mikvah* itself was a much later addition to the house. Conditions in the other *Judenhäuser* were as bad and, in some cases, worse.

Our children's room was also changed. But its wallpaper was the same and reminded me of how often I had stared at its winding, flowery pattern. Once I had "seen" a threatening figure hidden in its trellises, it became difficult to see the pattern in any other way. Our small desks at which we had done our homework and where I used to hide Grete's books were gone. Once when I had gotten up very early and sat reading at my desk, I found a piece of a cookie on my desk. Not until I had gobbled it up did I realize that it was Yom Kippur, the holiest fast day of the year! For a while I was so overcome by guilt, I could not think. After a while I hoped that God would not remember or that He did not bear grudges . . . Lotte used Grete's old bed. But one of our beds had been given away. Eva and I had to share the one remaining bed. At first we quarreled quite a bit over space, but then we learned how to be a little more accommodating, a skill that would be a requirement during the next few years.

Despite these troubling changes in our living arrangements and the evident misery I saw of those sharing our quarters, I was intensely relieved to be reunited with Father. The comfort I derived from being near him cushioned the impact of the upheaval that surrounded us. But the restlessness and tension in our house and the uncertainty and worry I often felt soon absorbed all my attention. It blotted out the years I had spent in Holland and the friends I had left behind until sometime during December, around a month after I had left Leiden. In short succession, I received two letters from Mvr. Bloemkoper.

Mvr. Bloemkoper wrote that three-year-old Abrammetje often stood at the bay window of the front parlor and watched the street. Patiently he was waiting for the war to pass [by] because "then Ruth will come back." And his mother fervently shared his wish. Her hastily written second letter sounded extremely anxious. The family was no longer together: Mijn. Bloemkoper had been taken to Westerbork. She also expected to be leaving for Westerbork shortly with her four small children. I had no idea where Westerbork was or what it meant. Worried, I asked Father. He could give me no explanation. (It was the Dutch camp and collection point where Dutch Jewry was concentrated and selected before being deported to concentration camps for "work" or immediate annihilation.) I do not think I was able to grasp just how ominous her letter was. It was the last time I was to have direct news from them. I feel certain that these young children suffered terribly before they were murdered. That is to say nothing about their parents. Thinking of what happened to this family hurts me like no other loss I have suffered. That pain will not go away, nor will it allow me to spout fine sentiments about "forgiveness."

Mania took me up on my offer of help with her chores. I was to dust and straighten out our bedrooms. She told me to take a dust cloth from a small room next to the kitchen that used to be our pantry. Among the odds and ends and cloths lying in a corner for housecleaning, I found my mother's navy blouse with the tiny flowers. She wore it when our father took us for the family photograph on the last day we were together on January 3, 1939, the day before we went to Holland. I ran my fingers along the edge of the soft navy blue binding around its neck and took another cloth for my work.

Like my own mother, Mania must have liked reading in bed, because *Vom Winde Verweht* (*Gone with the Wind*) was open on her night table. So I dawdled, reading and dusting by turns. The story quickly transported me to the American South of the Civil War era, a time and place so alien and distant, it might have been happening on a different planet. When I finally returned to myself and my work, I thought of my mother and her blouse, and I could not shake off my sadness.

I was as inquisitive as ever, and one day when Mania sent me to clean up their bedroom, I found old letters my father had received and copies of those he had sent. I was both puzzled and hurt to read a letter from some German authorities telling Father that our sister Klara had died of *Ruhr* (dysentery) early in 1941. I only knew that *Ruhr* was a disease one contracts in unsanitary conditions. Klara was said to have died in "Cholm, near Lublin" in Poland.[3] This was puzzling news. In 1934, Klara was taken to a Catholic home for the mentally disabled in Bavaria when the Christian family in Norderney was no longer able to (or allowed?) to take care of her. I had heard my parents talk about the need for Father to deposit a substantial sum of money in escrow (in German: *Kaution*, a word my parents had to explain to me) to ensure her upkeep in the event he were to emigrate.[4]

Another letter informed Father that his mother, our Oma Cillie, had died on a visit to Tel Aviv. As she had wished, Uncle Iszo had taken her remains to Jerusalem for burial on Mount Olive. It hurt me to read these letters, but I could not speak to anyone about them since my discoveries were the result of my snooping. I had to keep my pain to myself. I also found some love letters and poems Father had written to Mania in the summer of 1939. For the first time it dawned on me that he was a person with a life of his own. When I thought of him, how he looked now, gray-faced and exhausted, I was glad that he had experienced some personal happiness before his world had begun to crumble as it was doing right now, in front of my eyes.

Like those chests and wardrobes propped up and wobbling on our staircase, an atmosphere of uncertainty and fear, of provisional arrangements and anxious anticipation, was all around us. Mania told me about some of the changes that had occurred during our stay in Holland: Sometime between September 1939 and November 1941, Father's salary had stopped. I was not surprised to hear that he had no resources since he had literally given to those in need every penny he, and we, did not need. We now were living on a portion of Lotte's inheritance from her father. When my father and Mania married in 1939 and she saw how modest and old-fashioned our furnishings were, she persuaded him to buy two easy chairs and a small table to refurbish the living room. She also brought her Persian rugs and Hutschenreuter dinnerware with her. It was obvious that these tokens of her former life could no longer assuage her anxiety. Despite her deep reserve, I sensed that at times she was both angry and despairing.

I did not find it difficult to get along with Mania if I agreed with what she said and spoke with her of what was on her mind. I did my very best to please her and to win her approval. Mania was not demonstrative and showed little warmth, so my sole gain was the peace among the five of us, which I was hoping to maintain. I disliked the disagreements that sometimes flared up for what I thought were trivial reasons. Eva, with a different and prouder nature, wanted to have little to do with Mania, and remained barely within the bounds of politeness with her.

Eva and I were beginning to grow apart. I could no longer assume that I knew instantly and automatically what she was thinking. Even though we had always competed for our father's affection when we were younger, it now puzzled me to see Eva compete with Lotte. Lotte and Father got on quite well with each other, and it seemed to me that he understood her better than her own mother. But most of the time, Father was too distracted to notice any of us.

A few weeks after our return from Holland, an acquaintance of Father's, a Jewish man married to a Christian woman, visited us. Herr S. was interested in good health and nature "cures." He strongly urged me to throw away those "miserable crutches"—by which he meant my glasses. He told me to do eye exercises and to focus as much as I could on the color green. My vanity was aroused, and before long I stopped wearing my glasses. Father was suspicious of these theories and perhaps of the man's motives. He warned me not to discard my glasses. I disobeyed him. It was my first attempt at independence, and the time would come when I would rue it. After his initial opposition, Father did not even seem to notice that my glasses were no longer on my nose. Eventually the glasses were lost. I had worn glasses since the age of nine and not until I was eighteen did I get another pair.

Father was not himself. He seemed troubled and preoccupied. We were so used to hearing him vocalize or hum; now he was silent most of the time. His face had lost all color, and strangely, he walked with a limp. All he would tell us was that he had more work than usual. "Go, go. Be good children and help Mania with her chores."

It may have been late November when the reason for his strange demeanor became clearer to us. He had been told by the Gestapo that one thousand Jews were to be "resettled" in the "East." Despite the use of these euphemisms, it seems to have been known that the destination for this deportation was Riga. (From most German cities the first Jewish deportations numbered approximately one thousand each, and many went to Riga, Minsk, and Lodz. Several of the transports had hardly arrived with their "cargo" of one thousand Jews when they were taken to a cemetery and killed on the spot. This was allegedly stopped by orders of Himmler because it caused too much "alarm" among the Jewish communities that were still in Germany, anticipating their own "resettlement." The Nazis preferred doing their killing of innocent people quietly. Members of our community must have learned about these events, since the transports began in October, and the first Hannover transport was also scheduled for an earlier date originally. All those on the transport list were required, sometime before their departure, to complete a detailed questionnaire about their financial resources and possessions. Father spent even longer hours in his office. I heard a great deal of talk about lists. These lists enumerated the names of all the men, women, and children who were "chosen" to be deported. For decades I assumed that it was Father who was required to make up the lists of names for this, and subsequent, transports. In 1989, I learned it might have been the Gestapo who assembled the lists and handed them to Father. This is no longer a certainty either.[5]

Father prepared a circular with instructions, which he mimeographed and gave to the members of our congregation who were to be deported to Riga. He asked members of the community to act in a communal spirit toward each other despite the hardships they might encounter. Among other topics, I read his advice regarding problems of hygiene under less than optimal conditions. I remember those instructions because his advice that one's urine could be used as a disinfectant was so disturbing and puzzling to me. While I have seen several circulars prepared for different transports and written in my father's unmistakable style, I have not seen that first one with its advice on behavior and hygiene since December 1941.

Five brand-new rucksacks of drab olive canvas with leather reinforcements and leather straps, especially made for each of us, appeared in our living room. Father seems to have requested that we be allowed to join this transport on which a majority of the remnant of our Jewish community in Hannover was to leave. (Those rucksacks are the only proof I have for my assumption that Father either requested or expected to be on that Riga transport.) The Gestapo must have denied his request. This denial could hardly have failed to be a signal for Father that they fully intended to continue making use of him.

On December 11, Lotte's sixteenth birthday, she, Eva, and I helped carry rucksacks and suitcases downstairs. The day everyone had been dreading had arrived. In our house, several people committed suicide. In broad daylight the Gestapo took one thousand individuals from the different *Judenhäuser* on streetcars, used simultaneously by the staring but uncaring German population, to the horticultural school, Ahlem. Lotte went along to Ahlem to help. They were deported on the fifteenth. They went in real, if very old, trains. Open coal and transport wagons came later. During those four days, having been bodily searched for any possible valuables they might have hidden on their persons, anxiously waiting in uncomfortable, crowded conditions, without even cots to lie on, they got a foretaste of what was in store for them.

Our house was silent and empty after the people were taken away. The next day Eva and I were sent to clean the rooms in our house and in some of the other houses that had served as *Judenhäuser* and now stood empty. Father helped us. I felt acutely uncomfortable in those disheveled, deserted rooms, and Father tried in vain to put us at ease. I was too troubled by what I saw. An odd assortment of stuff was scattered all about: an old doll, a colorful silk blouse, a leather case for sewing thread. Amid the chaos, these things, left behind by the men and women who until a few days ago occupied these rooms, were proof of how their owners had clung to their customary civilized ways and last possessions. Now they had been forced to relinquish even these vestiges of their former lives. I was startled out of my reverie when several Gestapo men suddenly strode through the room. They checked if anything of value had been overlooked. One of them made straight for some bottles left on a dresser and, after a quick look at their labels, thirstily drank any hair tonic that contained alcohol.

Lotte and the two of us were sent to work in what remained of the Jewish hospital. It now served as an old age home. Lotte and Eva made beds and swept the rooms, and I helped the cook and washed huge pots in the kitchen. The home was desperately short of staff. One evening we reported to Father that the usual afternoon coffee was no longer being served to the residents and that they missed it terribly. Father asked Mania to bake some *Hefekuchen*, and we took that freshly baked, slightly sweet cake-like bread and ersatz coffee to the home. The old people were delighted when they were served this unexpected treat by the five of us. Father intended to show those responsible for their care that, with a little extra effort, it was still possible to provide nourishment and diversion for these old people who were so much in need of both. While his gesture was totally in character for him, it was hardly calculated to make him popular with the person in charge.

Early in January 1942, the German government decreed that all Jews who owned fur coats, mountain boots, and similar items were to "donate" them for the winter campaign then under way against the USSR. The anteroom to the *mikvah* in the basement was used to store the coats and other goods that were brought to us for delivery to the Nazi authorities. Our stepmother's elegant black Persian lamb coat hung next to the long sable-trimmed broadtail coat that had belonged to Clara Berliner's late mother and was delivered by Clara. Father relinquished the heavy boots he had worn in happier times on his hikes in the mountains. Mania was extremely upset to lose her most precious possession: Her Persian lamb coat represented the proceeds of the sale of her real estate, consisting, she said, of two (or three?) houses she had been forced to sell in 1939. Because her first husband had long been ailing—if I remember rightly as a result of injuries sustained during World War I—Mania had managed his business. She had been very astute and succeeded in increasing their holdings. She told me that the coat had been especially made for her, because she thought that once she was abroad, it could be turned into cash to feed the family. We were sitting in the kitchen the evening before the collection began, and Mania was fretting about having to give up her fur coat. In her anguish she said to Father: "If I cannot take my fur coat, I won't emigrate!" Father's retort was instant and shockingly honest: "If I could, I would leave today—in my underpants!" (*Wenn ich es könnte, ging ich heute, in meinen Unterhosen!*)

Sometime in January we had to move from Lützowstrasse 3 to Ohestrasse 8. That complex actually included two buildings that were owned by the Jewish community and had previously served as the day care center and Welfare Office. We took only our household items—and no furniture. I never saw our home again. It is not known how or even if the house was utilized after we had to leave. It was said to have been destroyed in the fall of 1943, in the first of a series of massive bombing raids that were to hit Hannover as well as Hamburg and other cities. There were several elderly Jewish women living in the Ohestrasse 9 building. Our relocation was evidence, if any was needed, that the Gestapo meant to concentrate the remnant of Hannover's Jewry in ever fewer locations so as to make controlling us absolutely foolproof.

Late in February, we again saw those telltale signs in our father's demeanor. Although as usual he did not confide in us, the change in expression in his face was striking. It told us what he would not divulge. It was as if this once so robust man was shrinking. There was the same limp of whose origin we were completely ignorant. Clearly another transport was being prepared. We heard that the destination was Warsaw, later it was said to have been Trawniki, then it reverted back to Warsaw. Frau Minnie Hahn's name was on the list. I do not know if her husband died earlier. But I do know now that her old mother, Frau Fraenkel, my blind friend whom years ago I had taken around our friends' garden, was not fortunate enough to have died so that she did not have to go on that final journey. She had been put into a home in Langenhagen and, at almost ninety years of age, was deported to Theresienstadt. Whether their only son managed to emigrate, I do not know.

On Purim in the Ohestrasse house, Father organized a get-together for the few remaining Jews with whom we lived together. Mania served her cakes. She had managed to make *Hamantaschen* (a traditional pastry filled with poppy seeds or prunes) despite a shortage of many of the proper ingredients. I do not think that Father read the Megillah. Jews may no longer have been permitted to hold religious services. He regaled the old people with songs and arias of Lorzing operas, such as "Auch ich war ein Jüngling mit lockigem Haar, an Mut wie an Hoffnungen reich." (I, too, was once a young man with curly hair, rich in courage and hope.) The old ladies nodded, smiled, and applauded. For Passover, miraculously, Mania obtained some flour, and instructed and supervised by her, we girls baked our own matzos.

I had another chance to see with what pronounced, almost exaggerated, courtesy Father treated elderly women. One of them, a tall thin woman, often came to speak to him. She lived in a tiny room under the roof all by herself and suffered from arthritis. She was a Hungarian citizen. He invited her to share our seder. Mania and we three girls would have preferred to be by ourselves. Long after she had left the room, a pungent smell of the wintergreen ointment she used for her rheumatic pains lingered in the air. We girls held our noses, but Father scolded us severely. For the first time since we came back from Holland, I saw flashes of the old anger.

During this time Mania was receiving letters from her sister and brother in Poland. Her brother, a lawyer, had lived in Kraków with his wife and only son. When the Germans invaded Poland, he and his family were on vacation. Unable to return home, they were stranded in Przemysl without any means of support. Invariably his news was heartbreaking. One day Mania showed me a photograph he had managed to send her. She told me that he had been a very successful and prosperous man, but his picture showed a bearded face, emaciated and marked by suffering. Mania, usually so composed, was very upset. Although she said that he had sent her the picture to rouse her to action, she realized that he was in a pitiful state. She began making up parcels for him with sheets and pillowcases and some nonperishable food stuffs. To mail them, she used fictitious return addresses. She warned me not to tell Father because he would surely worry about the possibility that her subterfuge would be discovered. Her brother thanked her profusely when he acknowledged receiving some of these packages. He wrote that he was waiting with such obvious anxiety for the mailman that he must have aroused the man's suspicion. He was convinced that the mailman eventually stole several of these packages. A sister of Mania's and her family were in the ghetto of Lvov. I think she lost touch with both families before the end of 1942.

Ahlem

At the end of June 1942, we had to move again. This time we were sent to Ahlem, the Jewish Horticultural School just outside city limits. The school was founded in 1893 by Alexander Moritz Simon, a banker and Jewish philanthropist, to teach (mostly poor) Jewish youths the skills of agriculture and horticulture. The end of the nineteenth century saw a fair amount of anti-Semitism, and teaching Jewish youths agricultural and horticultural skills instead of strictly academic subjects was intended to demonstrate their love of the German land. Aside from German Jewish youths, during the early years of the twentieth century, young orphan boys came to study in Ahlem from as far away as the Ukraine, the Crimea, and other parts of Russia to flee pogroms and the war. Several of them, after completing their studies, emigrated to Palestine and created an impressive legacy of garden designs for Chaim Weizmann, a branch of the Rothchild family's cemetery, and other prominent individuals, and several memorial sites and towns, such as in Tel Aviv, Haifa, and Safed.[6] For a while, manual trades were also taught in Ahlem, such as bookbinding and shoemaking. In the 1930s, the school largely served as a *Hachscharah* (training) for Palestine. At the time we had to move to Ahlem, all formal education for Jews had been outlawed, and most of the young students had emigrated or returned to their families and been deported with them. Meanwhile, Ahlem was turning into a collection point for the Jews of Hannover before they were deported.

Eva continued for a while to go to Hannover to work in the same hospital that was now used as an old age home. I did not ask her how she felt about being in the building where our mother had died a little more than three years ago. We had neither the time nor the ability to speak about our feelings during this strange period of our life. We were expecting that the worst was still to come for us though we were unable to say what that might be. I hardly saw Eva since her walk to and from town was quite long and Jews were forbidden to use public transportation. Meanwhile Lotte and I were sent to work on the land and in the greenhouses.

When we arrived in Ahlem, we found that aside from Dr. Max Schleisner, the last president of the Jewish community; his wife; and Eva, their oldest daughter, the Jewish population of the school was reduced to the former director, Levy Rosenblatt; his wife; his daughter; his son; two handicapped young men; and a married couple, Fritz and Erika Blankenburg. In addition, there were two young gardeners, Helmut Bloch and Oskar Windmüller, both of whom had been horticultural students. Mrs. Bloch, Helmut's mother, and the parents of Oskar Windmüller also lived in one of the buildings. While I have no recollection of seeing them, I have since learned that around one hundred other Jews were said to have lived in Ahlem at that time. Ahlem had several buildings that were still in reasonable condition, and the place was large enough not to appear overcrowded. Our family lived in a shed-like structure that was divided into very small living spaces: a kitchen, a front room, and two bedrooms and a bathroom. We have not found any structure in today's Ahlem that would resemble my description.

Fritz Blankenburg had been a judge (*Amtsgerichtsrat*), and he and his wife, Erika, became gardeners when he was no longer allowed to work in his profession. Even so, his lawyerly thinking stayed with him, and his gardening was done methodically and according to the rules as befitted a lawyer. Theirs was a "mixed marriage," but Mrs. Blankenburg was a convert to Judaism, and although she was pressured by the Gestapo, she refused to return to her original faith. They always spoke with happiness and relief of their good fortune—and good sense—to have sent their two intelligent and accomplished young daughters to England in 1939. They taught me a good bit about gardening, and I became their willing apprentice. Fritz Blankenburg, a lanky man with boyish features accentuated by slightly protruding front teeth, liked to expound on theories of law while we were working in the greenhouse or packing hotbeds to "force" rhubarb. (The hotbed created the environment to grow flowers or vegetables out of season.) If he guessed it, he was undeterred by my total incomprehension. All he required of me was silence. Meanwhile I thought of how much school time I had already missed, and for the first time, though hardly for the last, I had a gnawing sense of regret that I would never be able to learn the things that interested me. And I felt a twinge of envy for those two lucky girls in England whom I had never met. (Decades later I did meet one of their daughters, who had become a lawyer and a judge.)

I worked hard in the greenhouses, where we raised tomatoes, cucumbers, tulips, and amaryllis among other vegetables and flowers, and I carried heavy watering cans and pushed wheelbarrows heaped high with compost or soil or rocks. While I worked alongside her, Frau Blankenburg taught me the different methods for propagating begonias and hydrangeas. She was calm and fair, and every task became a lesson on the needs of the plants we grew. My first task became the watering of the many tomato and cucumber plants in the greenhouse. "The cucumber plants are very delicate," she told me, "and must receive neither too much nor too little water." Gradually I learned what was meant by such strictures. Outdoors I helped plant large fields with a variety of cabbages and other vegetables. We harvested buckets of red currants, and although almost all had to be turned in, Mania made jelly with what little we were allowed to keep. Cherries were grown espalier fashion and were especially beautiful and tasty. In the fall I was surprised to learn how many varieties of pears there are. Much of our harvest was the result of the devoted labor of students and their teachers over a period of many years. If we were supervised by a German official, as I was told recently, I do not recall ever seeing him or hearing that he interfered in our work. In this way, from the summer of 1942 to late spring 1943, over a period of eleven months, I experienced one complete cycle of the seasons, sowing, weeding, and watering, and even harvesting. It was my first experience of hard work, and I enjoyed doing it and being responsible for my tasks. Every evening I collapsed on my bed, physically exhausted but mentally alert and eager for my books.

The three of us kept—but did not eat—rabbits. One morning we were horrified to discover that Lotte's purebred white, blue-eyed rabbit had smothered its only offspring. Lotte and I wondered whether such things happened accidentally. Eva and I had an ordinary brown and white rabbit that appeared to be happily nursing her large litter.

The group of Jews who lived in Ahlem seemed no longer to constitute a Jewish community. No services were held, and the Jewish holidays passed without observance. But I also remember no instances of anyone getting together, any conversations among us, who were the remnants of what once had been a vibrant community. The air-raid shelter was in another building, to which we had to run when we heard the sirens. It was our only meeting place. It is impossible to say whether the Jewish adults feared and mistrusted each other or whether it was the anxiety and uncertainties that enveloped us all: Who would be the Nazis' next victim for deportation?

I heard Father sing two songs: one Yiddish, called "Teut is a kim óif der velt, ain toiter kan nit werden oifgestellt" (Death has come to the world and a dead [person] cannot be resurrected). The song ends with the words: "Whether one seeks pleasure or bread—death is at the end of the road."[7] The other was a German song, "Kein Haus, keine Heimat, kein Weib und kein Kind, so wirb'l ich, ein Strohhalm, durch Wetter und Wind" (Without house or homeland, without wife or child, like a blade of straw I drift through weather and wind).[8] Unlike the Yiddish songs we used to hear Father sing in which comic and tragic elements mingled, these songs had an unrelieved, terrible sadness. It was not difficult to imagine what Father was expressing.

Father called me a compromiser because I had less trouble getting along with Mania than Eva. I did not take it very seriously—perhaps I did not fully understand the term, but I thought that he was making excuses for Eva. She liked to assert her independence and fought anyone's attempt to direct her. On another occasion I proudly showed Father the new muscles in my upper arms. He understood this as my unhappiness over developing so much more slowly than Eva. He consoled me by telling me to be patient: He recalled that he had not begun to grow and mature until he was eighteen. For the first time, he also spoke to me about our late mother, and he made me very happy, but speechless, when he asked me: "Do you know that your mother was a very musical and highly intelligent woman?"

Outside the building in which we lived, there stood a large wooden overseas shipping crate, called a lift. Its owner, Siegfried Bacharach, a bookseller, and the longtime editor of the *Jüdische Nachrichtenblatt*, the local Jewish community newspaper, had given Father the key when he and his wife managed to leave for Cuba in the fall of 1941, among the last to do so. He was a veteran of World War I and had lost a leg, which may have earned him the Iron Cross. This may have entitled him to that late chance to emigrate. Occasionally Father opened the lift for us, and when we walked into the rectangular, shed-like structure, we were surrounded by books. Father gave me stories by Stefan Zweig, novels by Jakob Wassermann, Warren Deeping, and John Galsworthy. I read Sammy

Gronemann's *Tohuwabohu* (the expression for Chaos in Genesis), in which he describes the life of turn-of-the-century Berlin Jewry and the impact of the arrival and settling of Eastern Jews in their midst. Its humorous tone appealed to me until I realized that its descriptions were based on reality, the conflicts between German and Eastern Jews about which I had heard for a long time. Sammy Gronemann was the son of Landrabbiner Selig Gronemann (1883–1918) of Lower Saxony. The Rabbinate of Lower Saxony had been established in 1687. But only the *Schutzjuden* (Jews under special protection because of their financial usefulness to the State) had any voice in how the Rabbinate was to be governed.

Once as we were looking for suitable books, Father said: "Here, you Romantic, is Heine for you." In the *Buch der Lieder* (Book of Songs), I found the words to songs I had heard Father sing when we were little: "Der Asra" (a mysterious young slave who belongs to a tribe that dies when it loves); "Morgens steh' ich auf und frage / Kommt Feinsliebchen heut" (In the morning I rise and ask / will my sweetheart come today?); and "Die Zwei Grenadiere" (The Two Grenadiers). Father pointed out his own favorites, such as the scathingly satirical "Donna Clara," and "The Disputation," in which neither of the disputing religions does very well, and talked of Heine's prose writings: Heine wrote about his travels after he visited the Island of Norderney and the Harz Mountains, cultural events in Paris, and other subjects in a prose style that equaled and at times surpassed his poetry. But because he had been a Jew, who converted when it was the only way to be accepted and gain access to the larger society, a century later the Nazis would not acknowledge his greatness. German songbooks of the 1930s attributed the authorship of the popular "Lorelei" among other songs to "Anonymous." Some schoolchildren assumed that "Anonymous" was indeed the name of a poet. These occasional forays into the lift with Father, and the few conversations we managed to have, helped me to define myself aside from being Eva's twin. In the process I also began to observe my environment a little less and to pay more and more attention to myself and my feelings.

When the next transport was assembled in Ahlem in July 1942, only a month after we were moved there, we only had to look closely at Father to know what was going to happen: The news was there in his haunted, sad eyes and posture. This was the first transport from Hannover to Theresienstadt. It arrived in that ghetto at a time when it was terribly overcrowded, and many of these very old men and women were almost immediately sent to their death in Minsk. The people we knew in Ahlem were deported to Theresienstadt in March 1943. That group included the remaining elderly; (disabled) veterans of World War I; the director of Ahlem, Levy Rosenblatt, and his family; Clara, the daughter of Joseph Berliner; and Dr. Max Schleisner and his wife and daughter, Eva. Jews who lived in the few remaining *Judenhäuser* in the city were brought to Ahlem. This was the routine for each transport. However, this was the first time Eva and I saw firsthand the extent of the commotion, unhappiness, and discomfort of a large group of people, confined in crammed, and wholly inadequate, quarters and expecting even greater miseries and hardships to come. The makeshift conditions lasted "only" a few days, but they were enough to cause intense fear and anxiety, in anticipation of the journey "east."

An old woman, Frau Rothenberg, long known to us as a peddler, was included in the earlier of the two transports. Every Friday afternoon she had come to see our mother as far back as I could remember. Every Friday afternoon, Frau Rothenberg had sat at our kitchen table, eaten a sandwich, drunk a cup of coffee, and sold Mother some shoelaces and shoe polish. Then, with some relish, she would report her dealings with other members of the community. Her "wishes" for them depended on how she judged their generosity, or lack of it, toward her: "May Frau A. gain a pound a week, and Herr B. lose a pound." (Frau A. was quite well endowed; Herr B. was, on the other hand, rather thin, and rightly or wrongly, neither measured up to her standards of philanthropy.) Weekly, Mother gave her a challah, and Frau Rothenberg would thank her by asking for some butter to go with it: the size of a walnut ("*a Nuss gross*," as she put it). After she had tucked the bread and butter safely into her basket among the shoelaces and sundries, she'd pronounce a blessing on Mother. Then she'd leave and we'd hear the clop, clop of her high-laced boots as she made her way downstairs to Father's office. She knew he would have her weekly money for her. Her husband was considerably younger than she, but he relied entirely upon her peddling or so we understood. Now she was here in Ahlem, as always wrapped in her black knitted shawl, wearing voluminous layered woolen skirts, her wispy white hair held in a tiny knot on top of her head. Her voice was still as shrill, and we heard how peremptorily and in no uncertain terms—"Rudolf, lift up my skirts"—she called on her husband to help her with her toilet needs. She was very frail and was around eighty-seven years old—her husband was only seventy-nine. Although just a few years had passed, those Fridays at home in Lützowstrasse and Frau Rothenberg's weekly visits to our mother belonged to another world. There was almost no one left to connect us to that time.

The two handicapped young men, who were friends living in Ahlem, were among this group of men and women who were to be deported. One was a blind merchant marine. Malaria treatment for syphilis was said to have caused his blindness. When we knew him, he was quite well and of sturdy build. The other man was confined to a wheelchair. The two men depended on each other to get around. It was the blind man who would gather his paralyzed friend in his arms and put him in the wheelchair. Early on the morning of the transport, or perhaps the day before, the young man in the wheelchair disappeared. Father knew that he could not have left Ahlem without the help of his blind friend. The blind man denied any knowledge of his friend's whereabouts. Father explained to him that unless his friend was found, someone else would have to take his place in the transport. The blind man reiterated that he did not know what had happened to his friend. Aside from one other person, Dr. Hans Meyer, a physician, who was rumored to have fled to Switzerland, but was probably hidden in a mine shaft in Ahlem, the only Jews of Hannover who put up any kind of resistance to being deported began and ended with the action of these two young Jews, one blind, the other lame.

The upshot was that Father walked for hours all over Hannover. He found the young man in his wheelchair in the *Tiergarten*, a park at the other end of town, and returned with him to Ahlem. If nothing else, this episode confirmed for me that the Gestapo made Father responsible for the delivery of the deportees.[9]

Lotte developed a friendship with Helmut Bloch, one of the two remaining young Jewish gardeners. She had met him first on December 11, her sixteenth and his nineteenth birthday, when she went to Ahlem with the group of Jews from our house who were about to be deported to Riga. That was when she and Helmut discovered that they shared a birthday. Helmut was blond, wiry, and much shorter than Lotte. I believe that he was acutely conscious of that difference in their height and exerted pressure on her to "prove" her love for him despite of it. Father occasionally told Mania that he was worried about this friendship. He said Lotte was spending too much time alone with Helmut. His concern seemed lost on Mania, who pleaded for her daughter, and Father was too preoccupied and busy to insist on a change.

I, too, liked Helmut a lot. But I don't know if I really admitted that to myself. Without knowing that saying, I held to the principle: "What business is it of yours if I love you?" But it was impossible not to blush when Helmut turned up in the greenhouse. I do not remember that he ever so much as looked at me. He certainly seemed to know everything about the business of gardening, and I could not help feeling critical of his evident attitude of being the "real gardener" in distinction to the Blankenburgs, who had only recently undertaken to learn to be gardeners.

Among all the other worries Father had to cope with was the Gestapo's disconcerting habit of suddenly showing up at Ahlem. They came to demand quantities of its produce and fruit. Not content with an ample supply of produce, they asked that Father cut big bunches of the double-blossomed purple and white lilacs for them. Perhaps they loved flowers like the rest of us.

Each season brought its duties. In autumn we had to plant the tulip, daffodil, and hyacinth bulbs for next spring. The winter of 1942–43 was very cold, or so it seemed to me. I spent long hours outside with Fritz Blankenburg digging up frozen patches of ground that had never been cultivated before. We had been ordered to utilize all arable acreage for the production of food. It was strenuous work, requiring the excavation of a one-meter deep channel, to ensure that the soil that ended up topmost was the layer that had been the lowest originally.

Allied planes frequently flew over Ahlem on their way to nearby Continental, the big (synthetic?) tire and rubber factory. The one-storied house in which we lived had no cellar or air-raid shelter, and so, to the accompaniment of sporadic *flak*, we ran some distance across the yard to the shelter. Lotte rarely came to the shelter with us, and it was then Mania worried about her absence. While I was not afraid of a possible bombardment, we were extremely anxious if Father wasn't home yet. Once, on his way back from town, he was caught in an air raid. He told us how he had run from shelter to shelter. The police would chase him into a shelter because Jews were forbidden to be on the street, but when the shelter's occupants saw the yellow Jewish star on his coat, they chased him out. According to the regulations, Jews and Aryans were forbidden to occupy the same shelter. This routine was repeated several times until he finally arrived, totally exhausted, in Ahlem.

Because we worked on the land, we did not lack either vegetables or fruit, and Mania even managed to preserve some of this produce for winter. She was an exceptionally capable cook and baker who made imaginative use of what little foodstuffs she had. I can still see her firm motions as she scrapes clean the bowl in which she has mixed some dough. This, she always reminded me, not only utilizes the precious ingredients but helps to make a better product. However, we had no eggs, milk, or butter. When we were still at home in the Lützowstrasse building, a Frau Nyszli had come to see Father in the office to ask for some advice. She was the non-Jewish wife of a Hungarian Jew who, at that time, was still living in Hungary. She had a young son named Geza. This woman now visited us occasionally in Ahlem. She brought us some news of the outside world and, perhaps more important, one or two eggs or a small piece of butter or margarine. Clearly she put herself and her child at some risk by helping us. In return, Father and Mania would give her a piece of porcelain, some coins, or linens or whatever else she accepted in return. When we were about to be deported, we left our very few remaining small valuables with her.

In the spring of 1943, Father asked me to come with him to the offices of the Gestapo in the Schlägerstrasse. I was to plant tomatoes on their balcony in boxes usually used for geraniums and other flowers. We packed tomato plants, some radish seeds, soil, and small tools. When we arrived, I was shown the balcony and began my work. Father came outside to help me water the new plantings. Just as I was finished and we were about to return to the office, we heard awful screaming; the screams seemed to come from another floor of the building. As we were leaving, I was amazed to see that, next to me, Father was walking *backward* out of the room, facing the Gestapo official who sat at his desk, until we closed the door behind us. Back on the street we had a long walk ahead of us. I breathed a sigh of relief. I did not dare ask Father about his strange mode of exit. But I did ask him if he knew whose screams we had heard. Father answered with uncommon openness: He thought that Polish slave laborers were being beaten on the floor above. (In our final two years in Hannover, Bremer and Nonne were mentioned most often as the two Gestapo men involved in day-to-day dealings with the Jewish community, and they were notorious for their brutality. While Heinrichsmeier, whose involvement spanned a longer period, had a better reputation, this may be based largely on a comparison with those two.)

In March 1943, another small transport of Jews left Ahlem. We were unaware that its destination was Auschwitz—but even if we had known, the name would have meant little or nothing to us. The only people we knew among those to be deported were Lotte's friend Helmut Bloch and his mother, and Oskar Windmüller and his parents. Plainly Lotte was extremely agitated, but she would not confide in any of us or even speak to anyone. She could not sit still, and in total silence she took to pacing the narrow hall from one end of the apartment to the other. For days (or weeks?) after the transport, Lotte remained like a wordless stranger in the family, unwilling or unable to acknowledge our concern or even our presence.

The development Father had predicted for me finally began. While I stayed very skinny, I was very happy when at fifteen I menstruated for the first time. I had caught up with Eva! My stepmother now considered me mature enough to be able to make up a bed correctly—having told me for a year that it was a sign of my immaturity that I was doing it wrong. Even though Lotte's boyfriend had been deported, I continued to carry my warm feelings for him, and I steeped myself in Heine's ironic poems. For months I made a valiant effort to win Lotte's affection, because seeing Lotte's grief, I felt ashamed when I compared my own paltry feelings for Helmut with hers. But I cannot recall that she acknowledged my existence at that point. Perhaps as an only child, she was not used to dealing with siblings. Or she simply had no use for me.

In anticipation of the deportation that we knew was ahead of us also, I often tried to imagine what the places to which our community members had been deported months ago could hold for us. Occasionally a card would arrive from somewhere in Poland with a few penciled words on it. But these cards were either dictated to the writer, or written in fear of discovery, and they did not tell us anything. The appearance of such a card, months after it had been written, gave us no reassurance, and there was no way of knowing whether the writer was still alive by the time that card arrived.

One day early in June, Father came out to us in the field where we were planting the new crop of cabbage. He asked us to come indoors with him. Back in the apartment, we found several Gestapo men waiting for us. "You are under arrest," they told us. Then we were transported to a prison in Hannover. I seem to recall that it was the *Polzeigefängnis* (police prison). Orders had been received from the RSHA, Himmler's domain in Berlin, to deport the remaining officials and workers of the Reichsvereinigung der Juden in Deutschland; this, in effect, constituted the dissolution of its major branches in Germany. Father was its last official in Hannover. Some Jewish men with Christian spouses, such as the lawyer, Dr. Horst Berkowitz, seem to have been appointed to be "spokesmen" for the Jews living in mixed marriages, either just before or after we left. Dr. Berkowitz had been severely disabled in World War I, but this did not help him save his own family. His brother, our last choral leader and Grete's piano teacher, was sent to Riga with his wife and small daughter. Their elderly mother perished in Theresienstadt. Another brother, who had been our physician in recent years, had managed to emigrate to Britain.

We four women spent two weeks in one small room in prison. It included a washbasin and a bucket on which we learned to relieve ourselves. During that time, Father and Mania were once or twice taken back to Ahlem, where, watched by the Gestapo, they were allowed to pack. Mania brought us back some books to read. One, a book about Palestine at the turn of the century, had beautiful photographs of the land and its people. Its heroine, Rachel, a Russian Jewish student, was one of the first women pioneers. While she suffered many severe deprivations, these were temporary. At least her life had a purpose and her sufferings were not inflicted by an implacable and inscrutable enemy. Her story showed us that it was possible to live, surrounded by enemies, under the most primitive conditions.

While we were in prison, we met another prisoner: a young woman, a Miss Ferche, who was half-Jewish (a *Mischling*). Her name was familiar to me because her family had occasionally been part of the Kaunitz circle. She had been jailed for the crime of miscegenation (*Rassenschande*). Actually, she was engaged to be married to a non-Jew. She told us that she had an indefinite sentence. She longed, she said, to be with us Jews.

My mother's family. Mother is glued in above her father with flowers in front.

Cilly Grün, my father's mother.

My parents' wedding photo, 1920.

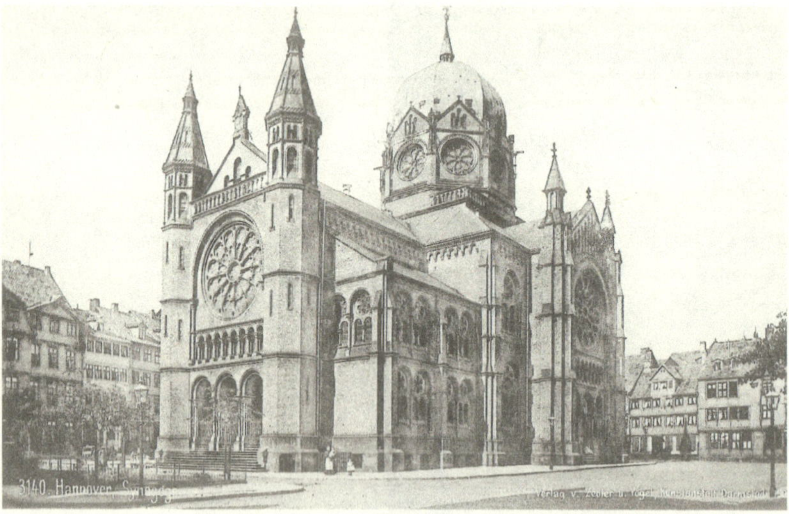

Our synagogue in Hannover before its destruction in 1938. Courtesy of the Historisches Museum, Hannover.

The interior of the synagogue with the desk (dark rectangle) where Father prayed. Courtesy of the Historisches Museum, Hannover.

Klärchen on the Island of Norderney. She was cared for by a non-Jewish family until the 1930s.

My family before Eva and I were sent to Holland, January 3, 1939.

My father at his desk, 1939.

My father and Mania's wedding, June 1939.

Mania's daughter, Lotte, when she was approximately fourteen years old.

The Bloemkoper children and I, 1941. They and their parents were killed in Sobibor in March of 1943.

n 480

Geheime Staatspolizei
Staatspolizeileitstelle Hannover

B.-Nr. II B 4 - ./.

Bitte in der Antwort vorstehendes Geschäftszeichen und Datum anzugeben.

Hannover, den 27.Oktober 1941.
Schlägerstraße 55
Fernsprecher: Nr. 86181

1980

Der Oberfinanzpräsident Hannover
28 OKT. 1941
/ Anlagen.

An den

Herrn Oberfinanzpräsidenten -Devisenstelle-

in H a n n o v e r
-.-.-.-.-.-.-.-.-.-.-

Betrifft: Juden Samuel H e r s k o v i t s, geboren am 3.3.1881 in Oberzsuk, dessen Ehefrau Machle Marjem H., verw. Münzer, geborene Montag, geboren am 3.2.1898 in Jareslau, und Kinder Charlotte-Sara M ü n z e r, geboren am 11.12.1925 in Hannover, Eva-Sara Herskovits, geboren am 8.3.1928 in Hannover und Ruth-Sara Herskovits, geboren am 8.3.1928 in Hannover, sämtlich wohnhaft in Hannover, Lützowstrasse 3.

Vorgang : Fernmündliche Unterredung Reichsbankinspektor Bungenstock - Krim.-Sekr.Bremer.

Die obengenannten Juden wandern Anfang November dieses Jahres nach Cuba aus.

Für die Bezahlung der Passage usw. sollen die inländischen Vermögenswerte der obengenannten Charlotte-Sara M ü n z e r verwandt werden.

Die schnelle Auswanderung wird von hieraus aus staatspolizeilichen Gründen gefördert. Ich bitte daher um die sofortige Freigabe des bei der Dresdner Bank -Filiale Hannover - in Hannover befindlichen Wertpapierdepots und Barguthabens, um die Auswanderung nicht in Frage zu stellen.

Im Auftrage:
[signature]

Geheime Staatspolizei
Staatspolizeileitstelle Hannover

Dated October 27, 1941, this letter from the Gestapo in Hannover informs the Foreign Currency Office of the *Oberfinanzamt* that my father was permitted to use his stepdaughter's funds for his and his family's emigration to Cuba. This memo was sent four days *after* emigration was to have ceased. If the emigration to Cuba had been permitted instead of being "temporarily postponed," my father would have been physically and morally saved. Instead the Gestapo decided to use his exceptional knowledge of the Jewish community's demographics to facilitate the deportations.

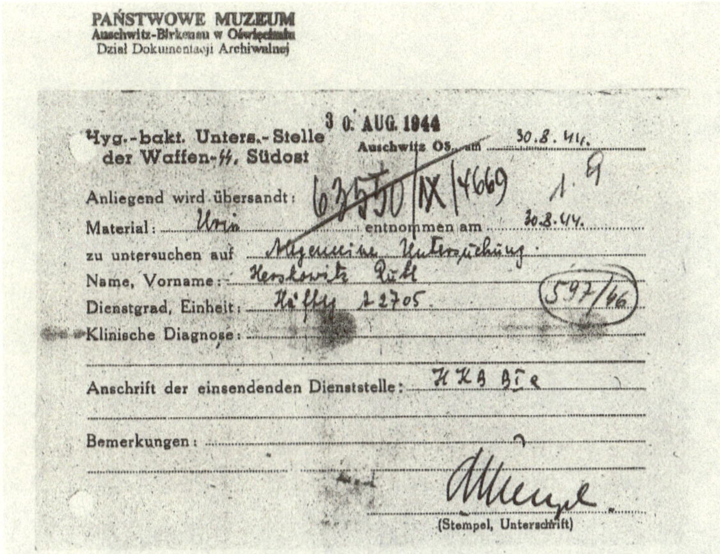

PAŃSTWOWE MUZEUM
Auschwitz-Birkenau w Oświęcimiu
Dział Dokumentacji Archiwalnej

Hyg.-bakt. Unters.-Stelle der Waffen-SS, Südost — 30. AUG. 1944 — Auschwitz OS., am 30.8.44.

Anliegend wird übersandt: 63550 | IX | 4669 1.9

Material: Urin entnommen am 30.8.44.

zu untersuchen auf: Allgemeine Untersuchung

Name, Vorname: Herskowitz Ruth

Dienstgrad, Einheit: Häftling A 2705. (597/46)

Klinische Diagnose:

Anschrift der einsendenden Dienststelle: HKB BIe

Bemerkungen:

Mengele
(Stempel, Unterschrift)

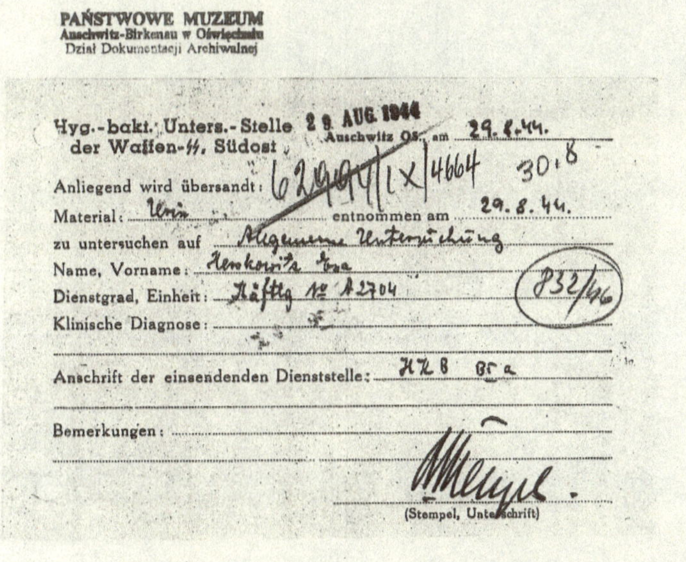

PAŃSTWOWE MUZEUM
Auschwitz-Birkenau w Oświęcimiu
Dział Dokumentacji Archiwalnej

Hyg.-bakt. Unters.-Stelle der Waffen-SS, Südost — 29. AUG. 1944 — Auschwitz OS., am 29.8.44.

Anliegend wird übersandt: 62994 | IX | 4664 30.8

Material: Urin entnommen am 29.8.44.

zu untersuchen auf: Allgemeine Untersuchung

Name, Vorname: Herskowitz Eva

Dienstgrad, Einheit: Häftling Nr A 2704 (832/46)

Klinische Diagnose:

Anschrift der einsendenden Dienststelle: HKB BIa

Bemerkungen:

Mengele
(Stempel, Unterschrift)

Dated August 30, 1944, these laboratory slips provide my and my sister Eva's names (misspelled) and tattoo numbers, and request the examination of our urine as a routine check. Such slips were evidently used for specimens of sick soldiers. They came from the Hygienic Bacterial Examination Lab, of the Waffen-SS South-East, and ask for the rank and division of the soldier, and the clinical diagnosis. Eva and I are identified as prisoners. Both are signed by Mengele. By this time both Eva and I were in the women's camp and, I assume, no longer subjects of the twin research. Courtesy of Gedenkstätte Auschwitz.

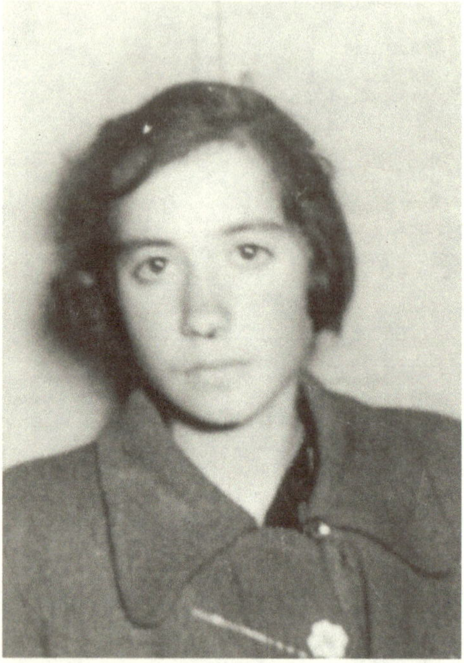

Myself three days after Liberation, May 3, 1945.

Eva, in the dark blouse, on a visit with me in front of the sanatorium, 1946.

Self-portrait of Dr. Victor Steffen, head physician at the Fagereds Sanatorium in Sweden, with holiday "prescription," circa 1956.

Our son, Sam; his wife, Nancy; their adopted daughter, A; and Nancy's sons, David and Eric, circa 2000.

Our daughter, Hannah, 2012.

Hannah's sons, Raffi (standing) and Ben (sitting), with Alfred and myself, 2009.

6

Theresienstadt

On June 30, 1943, after two (or three) weeks in one of Hannover's prisons, we were brought to a small railroad station and put into a freight train. Father told us that we had been imprisoned because the Gestapo thought that he might flee. Nothing could have been further from his capability or intent. Perhaps a single, unattached man, such as Dr. Hans Meyer, could disappear from Ahlem—if he had the means and the courage, and Dr. Meyer must have had both.

A family of five could not just disappear. Father was not about to leave us at the worst moment of our life. He had managed to bring Eva and me back from Holland, and as he assured us in his letters to Holland and later in person: "I am determined to keep us together." I sensed that he had suffered as much by our separation as Eva and I.

We knew that we were being deported to Theresienstadt although I do not know who told us. Aside from our own family of five, there were Fritzi and Edgar Baum, a young, deaf-dumb Jewish couple who were dental technicians. Until now they had been exempted from deportation because of their exceptional skill in "rebuilding" the faces of German soldiers who were coming back from the Eastern front with severely wounded or frostbitten faces. I do not know whether their skill had suddenly been devalued. They may have had to teach it to their German colleagues and were no longer indispensable. There was Ingeborg Ferche, the young woman whom we had met in prison. She had been released for deportation, possibly because, at her request, Father interceded for her. She survived the war, not least because Dr. Leo Baeck, who had considerable influence on some events during the last years of Theresienstadt, protected "mixed breeds" (descendants of a marriage between a Jew and a non-Jew) from further deportation to the "East." Apparently for Dr. Baeck, like for so many other German Jews, the law was the law, no matter whose. (Seen from today's perspective, this sounds like a generalization, but at the time it was a widespread attitude, a mixture of the old habit of obedience and the all-pervasive fear.) The ninth person was Frau Regina Engel, the seventy-four-year-old Hungarian woman whom we girls had met at our Ohestrasse seder. Father had continued to show his respect for her, perhaps even a kind of filial protection. As far as I know, the freight train that took us to Theresienstadt, with all of us sitting together on the floor, was not hooked up to any other transport.

Lotte did not feel well on the trip. Shaken by fierce retching, she stuck her head out of the open sliding door of the freight car. This picture puzzles me. Did the Gestapo leave that door only partially secured? Perhaps that open door was a whim of the Hannover Gestapo that was deporting us? There was no place for us to escape to on June 30, 1943. Too many Germans still believed they would win the war, and they would not have given us shelter. Our group of nine people was in this one freight car. When Lotte reappeared, her face was white. But when we asked her how she felt, she only shook her head. We were too preoccupied with our own anxieties and fears to ask why Lotte, a healthy, sturdy girl who always seemed so calm, should be the one among us who was feeling so ill.

Even if we could have done so, we had no wish to watch the passing scenery. The trip took more than one day, but the shock of our deportation had made me apathetic since leaving Ahlem. Our ominously hostile reception by Czech Jewish ghetto workers on our arrival in Theresienstadt rudely shook us awake. I could only wonder what awaited us here. Rudely, first our baggage, then we were searched; without ceremony, stuff these men liked or wanted was taken out of our rucksacks and "confiscated." It was immediately obvious that from now on, Father and we would be lowly inhabitants of this place—in contrast to what I had seen as the somewhat special position that he, and we because of him, occupied in Hannover.

When the ghetto workers had finally finished with us, we walked with them into the ghetto. We were put up in the attic of one of the many small houses, set in an enclosed courtyard. Exhausted, our family dropped down in a corner by a small mansard window, and the other people of our transport also found space for themselves. After a day or so, we tried to fix up the space assigned to us, cleaned the splintering and dirty wooden floor planks of the attic, and hung up a sheet, which we used intermittently to close off our corner to give us some privacy. We had brought some of the tins of vegetables and fruit that Mania had managed to conserve the summer before. She also had brought a bag of *Einbrenne* (roux), flour that had been mixed with margarine and then roasted in a pan. Occasionally, when I was hungry and there was no one around, I would take a pinch with my fingers and hold it in my mouth as long as I could before swallowing it. Mania did not seem to notice that it was getting less—probably because there was no opportunity to use it. In addition to those tins, we had a rucksack of clothes each and some bed linens. These were our earthly possessions.

A short time after we got to the ghetto, Father quietly told Eva and me the reason for Lotte's sickness during our trip: Lotte was expecting a baby. She was such a tall, well-built girl that no one had even suspected that she might be pregnant. The only rebuke—and it sounded more like regret—I heard from Father when he spoke with Lotte was that she had not confided in her mother or him. He gave Lotte to understand that if she and Helmut Bloch, the young gardener whom she first met on December 11, 1941, had been married, he might have been able to come to Theresienstadt with her. Perhaps Lotte did not want to be married to him—what is certain is that she had not known how to confide in her mother or stepfather. Always quiet and self-contained, she had seemed to accept, stoically and without protest, the events if not the demands of her environment. This was true not only in Ahlem, but equally true here in Theresienstadt. For a while Mania wrung her hands in almost mute despair. Father tried to comfort her by pointing out the futility of her agonizing: There was nothing anyone could do. Eva and I discussed with each other what we could do to help Lotte. We decided to share with her the *Buchtel* (yeast bun) that was distributed as the evening meal once a week to the younger children. At seventeen, Lotte was too old to be eligible for it. When we came back to the attic after having stood in line to be handed our buns, we placed the two rectangular pastries end to end, and measuring carefully, sliced off one third of each. Lotte graciously accepted this homage to her condition from us. The daily portion of soup, or a steamed yeast dumpling with a green dill sauce, or a *Buchtel* with an ersatz coffee sauce in which small particles of margarine floated, and a ration of bread with some inedible jam, made from indefinable sweetish roots, were wholly inadequate for young and old alike, and especially for a pregnant young woman.

Shortly after we came to Theresienstadt, Father located Dr. Schleisner, the last head of our Jewish community in Hannover. He found him ill in bed. Dr. Schleisner told him that for the first time in many years, he had been able to indulge an old hobby of his: bricklaying. Here in Theresienstadt he got his chance and more. Not surprisingly, Dr. Schleisner, a lawyer by profession, who was used neither to such hard physical labor nor to the prevailing unhygienic conditions, fell ill with pneumonia. Father brought him a tin of Mania's precious conserved fruit and promised to return. Before Father could keep his promise, Dr. Schleisner had died.

Hardly had we "settled" into our attic corner when the ghetto police came to search our meager possessions. They told us that they were acting on the information they received from someone who had been on our transport: We were alleged to have brought food or other items with us that did not belong to us. When the ghetto police were finished going through our things, they left with some words that sounded almost like an apology: They did not find anything special and judged that what we had brought with us really belonged to us. While we never found out who had complained about us, it was our first lesson in how quickly the behavior of human beings could change under conditions of extreme stress and scarcity such as we were now experiencing.

In a small shed in the courtyard of our house lived two young agricultural laborers who came from the southeastern region of Slovakia, bordering on Hungary, where Hungarian was also spoken. Father did his best to befriend them. He seemed to enjoy speaking Hungarian again. It embarrassed me when I heard him sing for them—although they seemed to enjoy it. Then I fell ill with acute dysentery, and we had no medication. Father asked the two young men for help. They gave him a precious commodity, a small green apple, and some blueberry tea. Mania grated the apple for me and brewed the tea. Whether or not it was due to these simple remedies, I recovered.

Mania became very silent. I thought there was reproach in her voice when she spoke to Father—as if she was disappointed that he had been unable to protect her from this misery . . . But her persistent feeling of malaise must have been aggravated by her worry for Lotte. Mania also had the misfortune of bleeding every two weeks, while Eva and I stopped menstruating immediately after our arrival. These two patterns, we were told, were common, if not the norm, in Theresienstadt. The only exception to this rule were women who, because of their privileged positions or jobs in the food chain of the ghetto—such as being a baker or his helper—had better, or simply more food.

On October 2, 1943, Lotte gave birth to a boy. She called him Daniel, which was a popular name for boys born in the ghetto. (While he was called Danny for short, the Czechs spelled the name Denny.) When I visited her in the hospital, she asked me to bring the news to a new girlfriend of hers. Although they had taken a walk together the day before Danny's birth, this friend was unaware that Lotte was expecting a baby! It took me a while to convince her that my story was true. Father built a little buggy for Danny. He enjoyed being with the blond, blue-eyed infant. Perhaps it reminded him of the time when we were little and he took care of us. I myself was suddenly reminded of my little Abrammetje. There he was before my eyes, toddling toward me, dark eyes shining and wispy dark brown hair sticking up every which way on his head. Danny was quite frail at first. He had jaundice, quite common in newborns, and his circumcision was delayed for a short time. Mania must have feared what was in store for him and us, for she could barely conceal her wish that he not survive those early weeks.

Even before Danny's birth, Eva and I were moved to the *Jugendheim* (youth home) for the younger German Jewish girls. Czech girls (and boys) lived in another residence next door. The Austrian girls lived either with the Czechs or with us. Why we should have been separated in this way, I do not know. The ghetto leaders tried to impose some structure on our lives. But they struggled with intractable conditions, and our new surroundings were only a slight improvement over the attic in which we had lived with our family. Lotte now lived with other young mothers and their infants. In the *Jugendheim*, the wooden bunk beds on which we slept were infested with bed bugs—round, bloodthirsty vermin that had an awfully nasty odor when we hunted them down and killed them. It was considered "good" for us to be with other youngsters our age, but it reminded me of our earlier separation from Father when we were in Holland, and as often as I could, I went back to our family in the attic.

We were assigned to a group of kids who were sent outside the ghetto to work in the vegetable gardens. Occasionally we tried to bring some vegetables for Danny into the ghetto. But one day we were searched and caught with spinach hidden in our clothes. We were petrified when we were pulled out of the line of returning children. In Czech, the gendarmes screamed at us. We had no idea what they said to us; we only knew we had lost our precious spinach. Czech girls later told us that the gendarmes had threatened us with arrest. But they let us get back in line. (Some of the Czech gendarmes were known to be quite sympathetic, especially toward their compatriots.)

Most of the leaders of the youth homes were staunch Zionists, and they organized all kinds of lessons for us although all teaching was forbidden by the SS commandant. We were taught biology by a young Czech physician, and I became very interested in the subject. Walter Freund—he let us call him by his first name—was gentle and courteous, and he was in charge of the health needs of our group home. He, his wife, and his infant son had a room in the same house, and when we needed attention, he was never far. I even did not mind when I got a bout of bronchitis, although I was reluctant to submit to an examination. At fifteen, I was extremely skinny and Walter diagnosed me as being "pretubercular." That diagnosis entitled me to an occasional small portion of a sardine-like fish.

There was a striking difference between the ghetto life of the German and Austrian Jews and that of the Czechs. By and large, the Czech Jews were young. They adjusted much better to their imprisonment than either of the other groups. Knowing the language of the country enabled them to find the occasional Czech gendarme or other non-Jew who was willing, for some payment or because he was decent, to risk his life to help with some provisions or even mail intended for the outside world. The Czechs were resourceful, and many of the positions that gave access to the food stocks of the ghetto were in their hands. We were impressed by how many of them had the practical skills to shape their temporary environment into a more livable space. They made bunk beds and shelving to utilize the tiny space everyone had, regardless of whether they lived in the large garrisons or in small houses. But for the majority of Czech Jews, as for the other nationalities except possibly the Danish Jews, Theresienstadt was to be no more than a way station to Auschwitz and other extermination camps farther east. Later when I was in Birkenau, I heard that Walter Freund and his young family had also been deported.

The German and many of the Austrian Jews were mostly very old or disabled veterans of the First World War. Many were ailing. They looked back on their past lives with regret and pain and mourned their immense losses. Some denied their disillusionment with the German nation's actions toward them while others were still engaged in finding excuses for what had happened to the Jews. This further incapacitated them and made their daily struggle to survive even more difficult. Many lost their will to live or their ability to care for themselves. To make matters worse, regardless of their former occupations and skills, they were almost invariably assigned the most menial and even demeaning tasks. If they had "protection" or advocates who spoke up for them, it was, except for a few instances, quite ineffective. Nevertheless many of these old people strove to maintain a certain dignity, a way of life that was deeply ingrained in them. They would not have been able to shed it, even though it, too, came at a cost. Already weakened by the terrible conditions and the extremely inadequate nutrition, the old people got even fewer calories than working people. This was a calculated decision by some of the ghetto elders to which not all of the ghetto's inhabitants agreed, and it was eventually revoked. Thus there was little chance that such individuals would want to learn to fight "for their rights" or to seek work more suited to their age or station. They were recruited to watch toilets and clean them if necessary. The purpose for these "toilet watchers" may have been important: to uphold a minimum of hygiene and cleanliness by those using the toilet. But I do not know whether that consoled the watchers. And it fell to the old people to have to clean up. Death was rampant among them.

I probably noticed these things because I was more an observer of the scene around me than a self-centered, feeling person. I was starting to slip back into an earlier, childish state in which I relied on Eva to ask all questions, a state that was to become even more pronounced later.

Many of the German Jews insisted on their continued pride to have served their—ungrateful—fatherland well. This attitude did not exactly endear them to the average Czech Jew or those in charge of the ghetto administration. Many German Jews continued to deny the terrible realities confronting them. They blamed the conditions in the ghetto on its Jewish "self-administration" rather than where it ultimately belonged: on the Nazis. In Prague, the Nazis had told the young Czech Jews that this ghetto was being especially established for them—while in Germany the old Jews were fooled into believing that Theresienstadt would be a comfortable old age home (*Altersheim*) for them.

After a while, Father found a place in one of the attics where he could serve as cantor at Sabbath services. I do not recall ever attending such a service myself. (However, a rabbi I briefly knew in New York said he had heard Father in Theresienstadt.) Father seemed to have "adjusted." He changed with his drastically changed circumstances. He became quieter and no longer exerted control over every aspect of our lives. Sometimes I thought that he felt a sense of relief. Perhaps it was relief to have lost the dubious "authority" he had held in Hannover. At the same time, it was painful to see him so changed and stripped of the effectiveness and strength we associated with him and on which all of us had always relied.

The ghetto was a revelation to me. I saw the gulf that separated us from the Czech Jews regardless of when these had arrived in the ghetto, because even late arrivals found their way quickly, sharing the language and finding friends and relatives to help them. Even among the younger German Jews, few had "connections," "protection," or skills at "organizing" (called *Schleusen*). To lack these advantages and skills was a handicap we could not overcome.

One day, Mania told me that Father had been called to the *Ghetto Commandantur* (headquarters of the Nazi in charge of the ghetto). A Gestapo official from Hannover had arrived in Theresienstadt and requested to see Father. This man asked Father to return with him, ostensibly for the purpose of restoring the information in the card files of Jews who had emigrated to America. The Gestapo wished to be ready for the eventual conquest of America and, with it, its Jews. Father, of whose exceptionally good memory they may have been aware, was to help in this work. The loss of the card files most likely dates to the time of the first major bombardment of Hannover in October 1943, when the Gestapo headquarters and with it a large part of their archives were destroyed. While it is now ludicrous to think that the Nazis could have made such plans, it was not improbable then. I do not know how Father phrased his response. According to Mania, he told the Gestapo official that he would not go back to Hannover without us. He pleaded not to be separated from us and was "allowed" to resume his ghetto existence. When some years ago I visited Hannover while we were preparing the German version of this book, I got at least a hint that confirmed my memory. Professor H. D. Schmid of the University of Hannover, a historian who studied the Hannover Gestapo, told me that Wilhelm Butterbrodt, one of their officials, was known to have visited Theresienstadt around that time. The purpose of his visit has not been ascertained although there was some talk about "repairing a card file." Most likely it was not the card file but its content for which they had wanted Father back in Hannover. Father had not shed his habit of keeping secrets. He did not speak with us about this event. Years later, reading about Theresienstadt, I learned how the Nazis in Theresienstadt would punish Jewish leaders for thwarting them or being insubordinate. It was a form of revenge and could be exacted days or many months later. Regardless of the circumstances of the Jewish "crime," or how long it took the Germans to deal with it, it always ended in the violent death of the Jewish leader. Jakob Edelstein, the first ghetto elder of the Jews when the ghetto was established in Theresienstadt, and his family were a case in point. Paul Epstein, a German Jewish ghetto elder sometime later, was another. I think there is no way of knowing whether Father's refusal to cooperate with the Hannover Gestapo on that occasion resulted in our deportation to Auschwitz in May 1944. All I do know is that about seven months after the Gestapo's visit our time had run out, and we joined a transport of largely old people to the family camp in Birkenau.

What little food we had brought was long since gone. There were people who could actually afford to exchange bread for toys and other luxuries. Eva knitted several sweaters with wool she was given for that purpose, and I made stuffed toy elephants, using scraps of red-dotted white oilcloth. The bread we earned with these activities we proudly took to Father and Mania to share with them.

While there was little food for people like us in the ghetto, there was music. In the youth home we learned a canon of which I can still sing the final line: "*Dona nobis pacem*" (Give us peace). Operas were performed and string quartets played. Eva and I attended concert versions of *Tosca* and *The Magic Flute* in one of the big garrisons, and in a different location, we heard Haydn's *The Seasons* (*Die Jahreszeiten*). That was also how I realized that I had long known two arias of *The Magic Flute*, "In diesen heil'gen Hallen kennt man die Rache nicht" (Vengeance is unknown in these hallowed halls), and "Oh Isis und Osiris." Both arias were for the bass voice, and Father had sung them many years ago. The room into which we squeezed with the other standees to hear the Mozart opera was so overcrowded and stuffy that I had to go outside for air because I was about to faint.

Theresienstadt had its own fashions. Many young girls wore their hair as short as boys, and I had mine cut the same way. I did not know that this kind of cut had originally been mandated by the ghetto authorities to cope with head lice. Somewhere—I think still in Hannover—I had got hold of an olive green knitted suit with short pants. These clothes I wore all the time. One day Father and I were walking together when he met one of his new acquaintances. This man exclaimed in surprise: "I had no idea you had such a handsome young son." Father thought this funnier than I. Another time when Eva and I stood in line to enter the public baths, the guard was about to refuse me entrance to the women's section. My face must have turned crimson, and he let me in.

Life in the ghetto had a veneer of normalcy, its reality often too terrible to bear. Many rumors and stories made the rounds, but regardless of their content or purpose, the ending invariably was punishment and death. One day, in the fall of 1943, the Germans marched every last person, regardless of their condition, out of the ghetto onto a large field. We spent a whole day "camping" on that field. We did not have the slightest idea whether we were going to be alive by nightfall. This action allegedly took place to conduct a body count because a couple of young men had escaped from the ghetto. The Jewish leadership had tried to fudge the periodic count of prisoners to hide the men's escape. There must have been fifty thousand people on that field. Wherever we looked on that large field, human beings were huddling together in tight clusters; the adults visibly anxious and afraid to be separated from their children; old people huddled under blankets if they were lucky enough to have brought them; everyone hungry and thirsty, and the younger children, despite the general misery and commotion, skipping about. Night had fallen by the time we were allowed to return. We had hours of struggle to get back because everyone had to enter through one gate. There was a terrible commotion and people panicked. When we finally entered the ghetto exhausted but relieved, it almost seemed like home to us. The next day we heard that some old people had been trampled to death in the stampede.

One day we saw a large contingent of Jewish children arriving. We were forbidden to go near them, but it became quickly known that they were from Bialystok. They were brought to an isolated building and no one, except for a group of nurses, among them Kafka's favorite sister, Ottla, and physicians who volunteered to take care of them, were allowed to mix with them. The children were malnourished and starved, dressed in rags, and full of vermin. When they were led to be cleaned up in the bath house, they resisted with all their strength, crying: "No, please, please, no gas." They had to be forced into the showers. The people who took care of them could not—or would not—understand the meaning of their fear. It was said that these twelve hundred or so children were to be exchanged for German prisoners of war. We thought: How lucky they are! For a moment I was reminded that there was a war on. Since coming to Theresienstadt, the needs and experiences of our day-to-day existence had wiped away all thought of the outside world for me. I had long since stopped wondering about the progress of the war or its possible outcome. The real fate of these children was to be quite different. Much later a few details of their story emerged: These children, who had witnessed and survived the murder of their parents in the Bialystok ghetto, a center of Jewish resistance, were eventually sent to Birkenau together with their voluntary caretakers. All were killed there.

That was how we clung to false hope, refusing to acknowledge the evidence that was before our eyes because it was nothing less than a portent of the evil that was still in store for us. Many of us preferred to fabricate, or at least believe, a constant stream of reassuring rumors. Nevertheless, originally a plan may have existed to exchange the children—or they would not have been saved at the time of the murder of their parents.

Less than a year after our arrival in Theresienstadt, Father was notified that we were scheduled to be deported. Although it was probably not made explicit, I believe that there was no doubt that we were being sent to Auschwitz. Lotte, whose little Daniel was now a toddler with blond curly hair, was not included in the transport. Father thought it would be better for her to stay in Theresienstadt with Danny and advised her not to volunteer for inclusion in our transport. She had come to know a young Czech baker, and both Father and Mania thought well of him. Father went to see him to ask that he take good care of her and Danny. Then he told Eva and me to come for a walk with him.

We went to the Magdeburger Kaserne (the garrison in which the Jewish administration of the ghetto had their rooms) to see Rabbi Leo Baeck. Father told us that he was going to ask Rabbi Baeck, the spiritual leader of the ghetto, to help prevent or postpone our impending deportation. He did this, I assume, on the strength of his former position in the Jewish community of Hannover. Father asked us to wait for him in front of the house. It seemed to me that he did not want to use Eva and me to gain the sympathy from Rabbi Baeck that might have helped to sway him in our favor. And ever protective of us, neither did he want us to witness Rabbi Baeck's possible refusal. Their conversation must have been very brief. In no time at all, Father came downstairs. Rabbi Baeck had denied his request. Father took our hands and told us we were going back to the attic to pack our rucksacks.

Did Rabbi Baeck deny Father's request on principle? Was he powerless to prevent our deportation? I have since learned that he did grant such requests to some individuals, and automatically to offspring of mixed marriages. To this day, whenever I hear Rabbi Baeck's name or see it in print, I am reminded of my father's request and Rabbi Baeck's response.

No more than a day or two later, we were to assemble on a railway platform that had been extended to reach the entrance of the ghetto, making both arrivals and deportations that much easier. There was a large crowd and a lot of agitation. Three transports that totaled 7,500 mostly elderly Jews were being sent away. Ostensibly the decision to deport in excess of 7 percent of the inmates to Birkenau was a visit by the Swiss Red Cross. Theresienstadt was being "beautified," and crowds of old people would disturb the image that the Nazis had given the ghetto dwellers orders to create.

Now there were only four of us. I do not remember saying good-bye to Lotte and Danny. Between eighty and one hundred men, women, and children were pushed, carried, and loaded into our freight car. Only a few seemed to have the strength to want to resist. Each of us had a rucksack, suitcase, or other bundle. A small pail was handed to us—it was meant to serve our toilet needs. No one wanted to stand or sit next to it. The sliding door was pulled shut and bolted. It was almost totally dark inside. Although it was early morning, I felt exhausted. To sit down was to risk being trampled on. I tried to lean against my father, but it was Eva and she complained. It was difficult to distinguish anything. A few rays of light came through a narrow strip just below the roof. Father told us to try to remain calm; complaining would only make us feel worse.

Now I truly knew what it was like to be *abgeschoben* (deported). Theresienstadt had only been the beginning. This journey—a wholly inappropriate term—was filled with fear and foreboding, and I could not picture what was in store for us. I thought it took several days—but since we left on the morning of the fifteenth and arrived when it was dark on the sixteenth, it must have taken two days and one night. One moment was memorable: Over the din and wailing we heard a man moaning. Raising his own voice, Father called for quiet and asked what was wrong. The answer came back that the man was having trouble with his hernia. He was in great pain. Father, who himself had a double hernia, knew that pain and how to relieve it. He fastened his belt to a hook he found on the ceiling of the freight car and used it to hold on to while he pressed past the almost inert bodies of the other people to get to the suffering man. He massaged the man's abdomen and that helped him. After staying by his side for a while, he returned to his spot next to us.

It was night when our freight train came to a halt in Birkenau.

7

Birkenau

The Family Camp

We heard the sound of loud voices outside and dogs barking. Someone was working to unbolt the door of our freight car. A voice commanded: "*Raus, schnell.*" (Get out, fast.) In the dark, awkwardly stumbling over strangely unresisting limbs, we found our way to the outside. Only when my feet touched solid ground did I realize that those limbs belonged to someone who had died during our journey. This person had sat or lain not far from us, but we were too numb to notice what was happening. Was it the man with the painful hernia? Or one of the old women who made up a large part of our transport? On the ramp we were met by shadowy figures in loose, striped, pajama-like clothes. They moved among us. SS guards shouted: "Hurry. Get moving." People hesitated. They remembered that they had left their rucksacks and other belongings behind. Someone loudly assured us that these would be delivered to us "later." Our possessions were the least of our worries. Father, Mania, Eva, and I merged with an untidy column of men, women, and a few children straggling in the direction of blinding floodlights. I was sure those lights would kill us once we got close to them. But the prisoners who kept urging us to move toward the lights said that we were headed for a camp. In much lower tones, I heard them ask for our rings and watches. They promised to keep them safe for us and to return everything "tomorrow." Our family had nothing left to give them. Whenever one of the armed guards came near, the prisoners fell silent.

Driven on by prisoners and guards, our procession finally reached its destination. It was called the family camp, but it was too dark to see anything. The men were told to go to the left. Father disappeared with them. Women and children were to go to the right. We were shown into a barracks. Since the lower levels of the bunks were occupied, Mania, Eva, and I climb to the top of a three-tiered bunk, and totally exhausted, we tried to find a little space next to the two women who already lay there. The wooden boards were covered with a sack of straw. The two women hardly stirred as we settled in the space next to them. The next morning when I went outside the barracks, I saw that we were in a rectangular enclosure, a barren gray strip of ground with a center "walk" with barracks on either side. The whole area was enclosed by barbed wire. Beyond that barbed wire on both sides of the family camp, there were similar barracks as far as I could see. Soon we were ordered to stand in line. Someone told us that we were to be tattooed. Eva, in front of me, cried out in pain when the needle penetrated the skin of her arm. (It looked like what we called a *Tintenkuli*, a fountain pen with a cylinder-shaped tip.) I felt almost nothing. Our numbers were in sequence: Mania, A-2703; Eva, A-2704; and I, A-2705.

It must have been a few days after our arrival when one of the women in charge of our barracks asked if there were any twins among us. Eva and I stepped forward and were immediately taken to another barracks. This separated us from our stepmother. The new place was in no way different from the first one. Not everyone there was a twin. Father finally found us. His tattoo was number A-253. Someone must have taken one of his shoes. He had not realized that he would have to protect his shoes by sleeping on them. Instead of his missing shoe, he had wound a piece of cloth around his foot. All belts seemed to have been confiscated, and he held up his trousers with a piece of string. What looked worse still, his head had been shaved. He looked so strange that it took us a little while to realize that he was our father. His face looked drawn, and deep folds ran from his nose to his chin. But he listened patiently to our repeated questions: "Vati, where are we? What is this place?" He reminded us that this was only the first day. Things would "improve" once we "settle down." "*Der liebe Gott wird schon helfen*" (The dear Lod will provide) or "*mit Gottes Hilfe*" (with God's help), he assured us. Although Father always used these expressions when he hoped to comfort us, it seems to me that he really believed this.

Soon Father assigned himself a job: With a shovel he had found somewhere, he pretended to scrape and clean the ground in front of our barracks. No one questioned him, and he was able to stay near us. Then he discovered that the washroom was for both men and women, who stripped without apparent shame to wash in the stinking, rusty brown water. When we told Father that we also had gone there to wash, he brought us water in a dish. He wanted us to wash ourselves in the barracks instead.

The prisoners who were incarcerated in the family camp when we got there the middle of May 1944 were mostly young Czech Jews who were deported from Theresienstadt at the end of December 1943, about five months earlier. During the early morning roll call, they treated us with extreme harshness. They shouted orders and slapped those who were too slow or bewildered to obey. Many on our transport were elderly women, who simply did not understand what they were being ordered to do. Now that I am an old woman myself, I realize just how confused they must have been. If German guards approached, our tormentors sprang to attention. They were obviously fearful themselves. This did not stop us from fearing them, but Eva and I told each other that these Jewish prisoners had been brutalized here. One of the younger Czech women from our transport managed to speak to the *Block Älteste* (barracks elder) whom she had known in Theresienstadt. Her story surpassed our worst imaginings:

When she arrived in Birkenau, an earlier group of Jews deported from Theresienstadt had been in the family camp for almost six months. To make room for the new arrivals, everyone in the original group was gassed. The new group "simply" supplanted the old. There was no selection; no one was spared or given a chance to work. "Because of your arrival," the Block Älteste said accusingly, her face contorted by something we are only beginning to grasp, "it is now our turn to end up in those chimneys." Their own six months were almost up. She did not care if her friend believed her. She was certain that our arrival in the family camp doomed her to the same fate that had doomed the first group of prisoners from Theresienstadt when she and her transport had arrived five months ago.

We had the same jailers, and not one of us chose to come to this place, but we were for all time divided into "them" and "us." At the very least, these young Czechs' expectation of imminent death and their hatred of us had to be welcomed by our SS guards. While it was their superiors and not the lowly guards who devised this scheme to limit the life span of each arriving transport in this so-called "privileged" family camp to an arbitrary period of six months, it made controlling us that much easier. Part and parcel of the vaunted "preferential treatment" of the Jews of Theresienstadt, it was our initiation into the real purpose of Birkenau: the eventual extermination of all those brought here.

The old people of our transport suffered the most. Some never got up again from their bunks. Women whom I saw alive when I left the barracks showed no sign of life when I returned an hour later. This happened so often that I was soon able to tell when a woman was near death. I had seen death in Theresienstadt, but here in Birkenau, Eva and I were surrounded by it. Even so, I thought that these old women were much better off dead. Some of the women were too weak to find (or fight for) space on any bunk and lay on the brick elevation in the center of the barracks, called the *Kamin*. One day, while we were waiting in line for our daily portion of soup, I saw the young woman in front of me dip her finger into her wet metal soup dish to drop water into the open mouth of an old woman lying on the *Kamin* alongside which we were lined up. The old woman's breath came and went in irregular, audible gasps. She had only moments left to live. I asked the woman to stop giving her water. "Can't you see that you are only prolonging the old woman's agony?" Surprised, she turned to me. She didn't answer, but she stopped. I had never reacted so vocally and decisively. Then I wondered what made me so sure.

Within days of our arrival, we found out why we had been singled out as twins. Dr. Josef Mengele, the camp's Nazi physician who conducted many of the selections, had been interested in twin "research" in civilian life. And Auschwitz gave him an exceptional opportunity to carry this research project beyond all acceptable limits. We were sent to the *Revier* (sick bay), where a prisoner-physician weighed and measured us and recorded all data relating to our lives and physiques. He took note of minute variations in our skin color and took blood tests and urine specimens on several occasions. As fraternal twins, we may have been somewhat less interesting to Dr. Mengele and his mentor, Dr. Othmar von Verschuer in Berlin-Dahlem. Von Verschuer headed the Kaiser Wilhelm Institute of Anthropology, Human Heredity, and Eugenics, and Dr. Mengele had the specimens of sets of twins of different ages, which he was "harvesting" so freely in Auschwitz, sent to him by his prisoner-pathologist, Dr. Miclos Nyiszli. Mengele's favorites were said to be young twin boys with whom he was known to have played before personally killing them.[1]

The young Czech woman prisoner who was the clerk of our barracks had instructions to give us an extra helping of the daily rutabaga soup. This was the standard rule for twins. We thought she dipped the serving spoon a little deeper into that huge kettle to get hold of some solid matter for us. There was both kindness and concern in her slightly freckled face. When Eva and I looked at the woman a little more closely, we noticed that she was pregnant.

Father tried to meet with us after he got his soup. Once in a while he found a lump in it that, he thought, might be meat. He would fish it out and give it to us. In Ahlem, when Mania persuaded him to allow her to use nonkosher meat if she could obtain it, he refused to touch any food that might have been prepared with meat or had even a drop of meat sauce on it. And he became very upset if he thought that Mania tried to serve it to him disguised in some dish anyway. Later we were told that those whitish lumps we were finding in the soup were bromide. According to German historians, no proof was ever found that bromides were added to any of the food we got. The "privileged" veterans among longtime prisoners had not eaten that soup in years, having been concerned about the possible effects of that alleged additive. If that story is true, it would just be further proof that they were not dependent on camp food.

Within a short time I again got diarrhea. At night a bucket just inside the back entrance to the barracks served as the latrine. On both sides of that bucket corpses were stacked up. They accumulated faster than they could be removed. Climbing down from the top of the bunk and squatting over the bucket next to those stacks of naked corpses was almost more than I could bear. It took all my willpower. But I saw others helplessly soil themselves, and I was determined to stay clean. Again Father tried to help me. He brought me a piece of white(!) bread for which he must have swapped his own ration of camp bread.

During the day we used a latrine for men and women. Two boards on opposite sides of the rectangular structure were the seats. There was no separation of the sexes except for the cesspool itself. We learned to relieve ourselves back to back, without actually sitting down and, just as importantly, without turning around. A large part of the day was spent looking for a little cloth, or even more precious, a little paper, to clean ourselves with.

If there were trees in the camp, I did not see them. Not a blade of grass or a lowly weed seemed to have taken root where we had been brought. Dust and pebbles covered everything. The sun continued to shine, and the oppressive heat and stench of decomposing bodies reminded us that it was summer.

Father wanted to take us on a "walk" around the various barracks. With little success, he tried to skirt the large piles of bizarrely spread-eagle corpses. Eva and I tried to reassure him and told him not to worry about us. Again and again we encountered prisoners and kapos as they busily undressed the bodies and extracted gold teeth and crowns from mouths left gaping in death. I thought it was the spectacle of these activities from which Father tried so hard to shield us. There were few places where we could walk. At another corner around which Father led us, we came upon prisoners who were supervised by a stick-swinging kapo. From what we could see, they were near exhaustion. They were lugging heavy stones back and forth. Except for the amusement it may have afforded the kapo, the activity was totally useless.

I began to develop my own ways of protecting myself from what I saw: Somehow I managed to persuade myself that these sights could not be true; they were "not real." I also occupied myself with adding numbers, those on our and other people's arms, birth dates, and whatever other strings of numbers occurred to me. I decided that some of the totals I derived from these "games" were "good omens." Another strategy was betting: If something could get done at a certain speed, or I managed to walk over a long ridge, or obstacle, "all would be well." These bets occurred to me in a flash, and I did not dwell on what might happen if I could not carry out my self-imposed "task" and lost my bet.

One day a van came to take us to the central camp of Auschwitz, where longtime political prisoners were held. They were called *Ehrenhäftlinge* (honor prisoners or, a better description, privileged prisoners). They were mostly non-Jewish Poles. One of these, a young student, photographed the twins for Dr. Mengele. His blond hair had been allowed to grow, and his clean, well-pressed white shirt contrasted sharply with the look of the men we saw in the family camp. He spoke fluent German, and once we lost our apprehension, we talked quite freely with him. The young man gave us a gift of several cigarettes when we said good-bye to him before we were taken back to Birkenau. We told Father about our trip and gave him the cigarettes, and he anxiously admonished us "to be good." "Don't do anything for a little food. You would regret it later." We understood what he meant, and we told him that these cigarettes were a real gift from that young Polish prisoner.

Some of the prisoners had fewer scruples. The top tier of the bunk bed next to ours was occupied by a Czech mother and her two daughters. The older daughter's black hair had recently been shaved when she was caught in some "illegal" activity. Now it was just beginning to grow back. Her younger sister, who was at most eighteen, was an exceptionally beautiful girl with very pale skin and Titian red hair. She was regularly visited by the most feared prisoner in the family camp, its chief kapo, Fischer. A middle-aged man, he had the reputation of treating his fellow prisoners with absolute ruthlessness. We could see him from afar, pacing along the barbed wire that divided us from a camp of Roma and Sinti (Gypsies). The kapo's large shaved head and upper body were always thrust forward while he was menacingly swinging his stick. Everyone was petrified when he came near, although I heard that he also expressed concern for some of the young Czech women he knew and actually gave them some food—he may have noticed that they were pregnant. We tried to stay out of his way. We were told that this kapo was a Czech Jew whose two sons the Nazis had hanged—in his presence. His own dehumanized behavior was ascribed to that experience. H. G. Adler, the historian of Theresienstadt, has another story: Fischer had volunteered to serve as hangman in January 1942, during the early months of the existence of Theresienstadt. The German commander wanted the Jewish head of the ghetto to execute sixteen young Jews who were to be punished for having communicated with their families in Prague or committed other "heinous crimes," such as having tried to buy a roll from a Czech bakery. (When the ghetto was established late in 1941, a small contingent of the original Czech population still lived in the garrison town.) The SS commander threatened them with their own deaths if they failed to kill the young men. The Jewish elders frantically conferred about what to do. They were given a deadline. That was when Mr. Fischer stepped forward. He explained that he had worked in the Anatomical Institute of Prague and, according to Adler, had at times assisted in the execution of death sentences. He had some knowledge of physiology, which would help to minimize the victims' suffering. He found a seventeen-year-old to help him in his gruesome task, assuring the boy that he, Fischer, would bear the main burden.

While H. G. Adler, who was never shy to comment and judge, tells this story without comment, I, strange as it may seem, feel that Mr. Fischer deserved the gratitude of the Jewish leadership and that of the ghetto.

One Friday night, Father climbed on the *Kamin.* He sang some of the familiar prayers of our Friday night service. He began with the *Lecho Dodi* (possibly written by S. H. Alkabetz in the sixteenth century):

> Come friend, to meet the bride,
> Let us greet the Sabbath . . .
> No longer shall you be downcast,
> For those who have tortured you
> Shall be defeated . . .

The women in the barracks, sitting or lying on their bunks, fell silent. I was very proud of Father—but minutes later my pride turned into embarrassment when, after his service, Father went around with a dish and asked for a contribution of bread. Surprisingly he received several pieces. Then Father offered these pieces of bread to Eva and me, but we shook our heads. Although I knew that Father desperately wanted to feed us and not himself, I felt terribly ashamed for him. He had fallen short of my image of him. I could not tell him—but Father must have understood. It was painful to see him standing there with that dish in his hand—wondering what to do with those few pieces of bread. I never thought to thank him for it.

There was one more time when we heard Father sing. He had "met" a Hungarian who was a prisoner in the adjoining "A" camp (BIIa) for men. This man had a violin, and one Sunday afternoon when, as usual, there were fewer guards around, he played some old Hungarian songs that Father knew. With the barbed wire between them, Father began to sing, and small audiences collected on either side of the electrified wire. While Father was singing, Mania spoke in Polish to a man on the other side of the wire in the "A" camp. He complimented her on her still fluent Polish. Then he disappeared for a moment, and when he returned, he handed her a whole loaf of bread! We were so glad that Eva and I teased Father and Mania about this windfall. We told them that there really was no way of knowing whether that Pole gave it to her because he liked Father's Hungarian songs or Mania's speaking Polish with him.

The Sinti and Roma held in the camp next to the family camp were in no better shape than we. German historians I told that the Roma and Sinti were located in BIIc, the camp next to us, would not believe me. Evidently, on May 15, a day before our arrival, they had rebelled, literally using sticks and stones collected for that purpose, on their guards, and were separated from their usual group location. We saw men, women, and children of all ages huddled together. Then, shortly after we came, during a succession of nights, the camp was emptied of all its prisoners. Day and night flames could be seen in the sky, rising high above the chimneys of the crematoria, which could not contain them. We were told that they had gassed all the Roma and Sinti and now were burning their bodies around the clock. It was the first time that we knew what we were witnessing: the gassing and killing of a group of human beings. The day before, they had been in the camp enclosure next to us; the next day, there was not a trace left of them.

It was early July 1944. While there were always rumors, one story became more and more persistent: The end of the family camp was near. Like the gypsy camp, we, too, would be liquidated. But this time, those fit for work were to be selected first. There were several weeks during which Mania, Eva, and I, but Eva ever more frantically, begged Father to stand for selection when the time came. "Otherwise you will be gassed," Eva told him plainly and repeatedly. Often Eva and I would sit with Father by the side of the barracks. That was when I noticed for the first time that Father's ankles were swollen. I had no idea why that should be. I remembered those hernias I knew he had on both sides. Many years ago, Mother told me that these were the result of Father carrying Grete's (or our?) baby carriage, including its contents, up the two flights of stairs to our apartment. Father's hair was beginning to grow back. It was white. He now had a shoe for his right foot to replace the cloth he had used. His trousers were hanging in folds around his legs. It was unlikely that they would consider this sixty-one-year-old man fit for work. Father answered our entreaties with: "*Seit doch keine Narren.*" (Don't be foolish.) It was another favorite saying of his. And we had always known what he meant. Now I was not sure why he thought our pleas and assertions so foolish.

We came face to face with Dr. Mengele when he examined Eva and me to check the accuracy of the physical data recorded by the prisoner-physician. I controlled every muscle in my body to be as calm as I could be, and Eva reacted similarly. But his tailored uniform and the cap he did not remove were the only reminders that he was no ordinary physician. He even made some small talk, commenting that my face was very deceiving: It was round although my body was very skinny. That was hardly news to me. All during my childhood my siblings had teased me about my moon face. Now even Dr. Mengele had noticed. Long after this encounter, we realized how fortunate his indifference toward us had been. It meant that he took little interest in experimenting on us, a set of fraternal twins. This has since been disputed by the researchers of the present Max-Planck-Institutes, who have, among other topics, investigated Dr. Mengele's research interests. He was also interested in fraternal twins, and if he had known that I was considered "pretubercular," it might have had lethal consequences for us. He liked to compare the dissections of his victims if one of the twins had tuberculosis while the other one was free of it.

We knew that Dr. Mengele was in charge of the selections. With a wave of his hand, whistling some aria from Verdi's *La Traviata*—apparently the opera was a favorite of his—he decided who was to live, and who to die. After Dr. Mengele had examined us, Eva was beginning to hope that she might have a chance to ask him to spare our father and to assign him some "light work." She asked me to come with her and help her in this attempt to save our father. One day when we saw Dr. Mengele and his entourage of SS men leave one of the barracks, Eva thrust herself in front of him and burst out: "Please, Dr. Mengele, save my father." She was simply brushed aside to make room for the men. No one reacted to her request, but neither was she punished. I stood next to her and did not even try to say a word. Ever after I was certain that she would always remember my failure to speak up. She had made an attempt to save Father while I remained silent.

Since our arrival in Birkenau, I was fearful and passive. I would not ask anyone for the simplest information or take any kind of initiative. Eva, despite her despair, routinely took a leading role in our existence. My fears persisted during our entire stay in camp and even beyond.

At the beginning of July, the first selection was held. First it was the women's turn, and they had to line up and march naked past Mengele and his team of SS men. Mania was chosen for work and immediately separated from us. For many days she was penned up with hundreds of women in another barracks at the other end of the family camp. Eva, who was good at ferreting out information, discovered where these selected women were held. We stood in front of that barracks and saw faces of women pressed against a small window. We thought we could see Mania. Actually I was never sure and am not sure now when I saw her for the last time. By the time we heard that Mania had been sent from Birkenau to Stutthof, near Danzig, she was no longer alive. Stutthof is not a camp about which much is known, except perhaps that there was typhus and, yes, a crematorium. Eva, who had become attached to Mania during our stay in Birkenau, was extremely upset by our parting. I remained silent and unmoved. I felt ashamed and guilty about my apparent indifference, but I could not react in any other way. I was beginning to think that I had no body at all, except a head with eyes. Although I took in everything, I moved about in an atmosphere of unreality, like a piece of wood.

In the family camp, the only prisoners left were those who, like Father, did not stand for selection either because they had "chosen" not to or because they were too old and had not been called. Others were special cases or sets of twins. We spent the few days remaining to him with Father, waiting anxiously for what was in store for us—but only Eva expressed what she felt. Bluntly, she spoke of her fear of what was going to happen to Father, while neither he nor I, certain though I was, and he had to be, could admit that in a few days, he would be killed. When I looked at Father, he appeared tranquil, without a spark of anger. He was intent only on trying to keep us calm, even consoled. He talked about the future and impressed on us to get in touch with Grete after the war. One day, without our asking for it, he gave us his *Kennkarte*, his German identity card, which he had managed to preserve. It had a good picture of him and a large "J" stamped on it. Now I was certain that he did not expect to live. Eva took the card, folded it, and put it into the breast pocket of her blouse. Vati asked us to take care of each other, adding: "*Seit schön brav.*" (Be good.)

We had been in the family camp for almost two months when, on July tenth, all the twins were called to come forward. It was another hot, cloudless day. Early in the morning we had to assemble and line up at the entrance to the family camp. We were to walk to the women's camp, situated perpendicular to the family camp, across the railway ramp. I do not know how many prisoners were waiting with Eva and me; I had eyes only for Father. He had heard that we had to leave and was standing there with us, waiting. Eva and I took turns embracing him. Then we had to march out of the family camp. On the road we kept turning back to try and get another glimpse of him. I could not see him very clearly. At fourteen, in a misbegotten fit of vanity, I had stopped wearing my glasses and promptly lost them. I begged Eva, who was more nearsighted than I, to let me—just for a moment—look through hers. She refused. Very soon there was a bend in the road. That faraway figure we thought was Father had vanished.

The Women's Camp

In the women's camp, Eva and I were assigned to a barracks in the *Krankenrevier* (*Revier*). We spent the first two days trying to get as close as we could to the barbed wire that separated us from the railway ramp. On the other side of the rail lines was the family camp, and we thought we might be able to see Vati there. We never did.

On July 11 and 12, every one of the family camp's elderly Jews, and mothers with small children, was transported to the crematorium and killed. The suffering they endured and the horror of that death for those who, like Father, knew what to expect would be unimaginable had it not been described by those in charge of these operations. But long before I read some of those accounts, I had my own picture of Father's last hours. It is with me still.

When we saw the flames in the sky, Eva and I were in despair. We stood crying on roll call, and wherever else we were sent. We took little notice of our new surroundings. Over and over Eva asserted that she did not want to go on living. To prove that she meant it, she walked toward the electrified barbed wire. She must have been deeply offended by my greater calm because she repeatedly accused me: "You don't care about Father's death." I could only tell her that

I did. Perhaps my old stubbornness reasserted itself, because something in me defiantly reminded me that I was alive. Unlike Eva, I wanted very much to go on living. I tried to persuade Eva that what Father expected of us was exactly the same: To go on living. It was the only coherent thought I was able to express during those days and weeks. And while we were in camp, my point of view prevailed. But whenever unusual difficulties arose—hardly an infrequent occurrence—she reiterated her wish that she would rather be dead. She was, at the age of sixteen, convinced that death was preferable to her unbearable pain. That conviction would remain with her for the rest of her life.

One evening when I was lying on my bunk, I found a piece of what I guessed was bacon under my straw sack. Eva and I shared it. It was the first time in our life we had eaten bacon. The next evening we found another piece. We could not imagine who had given us such precious food. For even though we had been taught that we Jews were not supposed to eat pork, we knew that in camp such special foods were rare and costly. But before long my stomach rebelled, and I was doubled up in pain. Next morning after roll call, I sneaked back into the barracks to lie down on my bunk. That was when the puzzle was solved, and I discovered who had been so generous toward us. A young Polish girl, the clerk of our barracks, must have observed our unhappiness. It was she who had slipped the bacon under our straw sack. Wanda, a blond and blue-eyed Polish girl, and I exchanged only a few words. In halting German, she explained that she was receiving packages from her parents in Kraków. She was a Catholic student who had been incarcerated together with a younger sister. They had been members of a resistance group at their university.

A few days later, Eva and I and other sets of twins were called before the female Nazi guard, either Mandel or Drechsler by name, who was in charge of the women's camp. A thin, buck-toothed, middle-aged woman, she was known to us by her derisive laugh. She was never without her whip, which she cracked against her riding boots. She looked at the row of twins that had been assembled before her. When she came to me, she looked me over from top to bottom, and then she laughed. I was still wearing the dark green short pants, the only clothes I had. Perhaps I looked funny to her. She gave orders that I was to get a dress, probably from "Canada," the place where the arriving prisoners' luggage was unpacked and sorted for reuse in Germany. She had chosen me to be a *Läuferin* (running messenger). From then on, from early morning until evening, dressed in a black felt dress—embroidered with pansies of different colors—I stood at the gate of the women's camp near the guardhouse and delivered messages from the guards at the gate, running from one end of the women's camp to the other. Very soon my shoes wore out and I ran barefoot, but I discovered that if I ran very fast, I hardly felt the pebbles of the camp road on the soles of my feet. I felt so light-headed, it confirmed my notion that I had no body. It felt as if I were flying above the ground.

Eva was assigned a similar position inside the camp. She was stationed in the *Schreibstube*, the office of the *Lagerälteste* (camp elder), where the records of arriving and departing transports were kept. The Germans had intentionally chosen twins to do this work, because the prior *Läuferin*, Mala Zimetbaum, had managed, if only briefly, to escape with her Polish boyfriend, Edek Galinski. The story of Mala's extraordinary flight and recapture has been told by others. After she was recaptured, we were ordered to line up outside to witness her punishment. Eva went, but I hid in the barracks. Eva later told me that the guards twisted Mala's arms until they came out of their sockets and broke. She endured her pain without uttering a sound. Finally she fainted. At that point they threw her inert body into a wheelbarrow and carted her off to the gas chambers.

One of the German SS guards—as many others, he was a *Volksdeutscher* from either Slovakia or the Ukraine—some days took me along when he went outside the women's camp to the central mess hall to get his midday meal for himself and the other guards on duty. Without saying a word, firmly holding me by the hand, he walked with me down the road until we got to the hall crowded with Nazi guards, who were noisily waiting in line for their turn to get their food. I felt acutely uneasy during that walk, and standing in line with a crowd of Nazi SS guards did little to lessen my discomfort. Relief came on the return trip because I was carrying the canteens in both hands. Occasionally, after they had finished their meal, the guards called me into the guardhouse and told me to scrape out the leftovers for myself. Years later I thought I could still taste that food.

Near the entrance of the camp, a space was reserved for the orchestra. Every morning while the columns marched out of the camp to work, the musician-prisoners were required to play. I think it was military music, even American Sousa marches among them. Eva and I got to know Anita Lasker, the cellist, who was a tall, good-looking girl with dark curly hair. Her older sister, Renate, usually was somewhere near the orchestra. She served as an interpreter and *Läuferin*. These two Jewish girls had been deported from Breslau many months earlier. They had worked in a factory in Breslau with some French POWs, but were caught when they fabricated false papers for them. They were put on trial and landed in prison. Possibly being sent to Birkenau was fortunate under the circumstances! Like us, they had an older sister in England whom they were hoping to see again. Their father's brother was the famous chess player Edward Lasker, who, years ago, had gone to live in the United States. They understood what we were going through because their parents were deported from Breslau even before them. They, too, had given up hope to see them again. Their father had been a well-known lawyer, one of whose clients was a foreign aristocrat. The family hoped that he would exert his influence with the authorities to allow them to emigrate. While he may indeed have tried to do so, the Gestapo got the better of him. It was a lesson of the uncertainty of life's promises that, in different guises, all of us had been taught, whether we accepted it or not. The Lasker sisters seemed, nevertheless, to manage to keep up their courage. The members of the orchestra were among the prisoners who had some special privileges. Their clothes were somewhat better and so was the barracks in which they were staying.

We were also getting to know several young girls from Slovakia who had been in this place for more than two years. Slovakia had split off from the western Czech part and become an ally of the Nazis. They proved their loyalty by readily agreeing to deport the Jews from their country. At least ten thousand young Jewish girls were sent to an unfinished Lager that lacked the simplest amenities. They had to build Birkenau, the wooden barracks, the paths running between them, and the roads. They told us of their hunger and thirst and how they had lost their mothers and sisters to the diseases that were rampant among them, experiences that were exceeded only by the terrible cruelty of their guards. We thought we had become quite familiar with such situations, but as they repeatedly told us, their own experiences had been immeasurably worse. The numbers tattooed on their left arms, like ours, had four digits. But theirs were the very start of the count, ours a new series beginning with an "A." Sometimes this was pointed out to us, and there was nothing we could say to counter their fierce resentment. Of the ten thousand young Jewish women and girls who came to Auschwitz in the spring of 1942, perhaps two hundred to two hundred fifty were still alive when we got to know them in the summer of 1944. Most had positions of responsibility and some "privileges." At roll call or in the daily block routines, whenever they had to deal with large numbers of prisoners, their harshness could degenerate into plain physical cruelty. Eva and I never doubted that their survival was the result of their toughness and loyalty to each other. We were handicapped in our relations with them because German was the only language we had in common, a language that was useful but also hated. (Our ability to speak German may have been a point in our favor when we were chosen to be *Läuferinnen* from among several sets of twins.) But understandably, the Slovak girls had no great love for the German language. So when we spoke with them, we always assured them that our parents had, in fact, been Hungarians—and to convince them, we came up with the few Hungarian words and phrases we knew.

We knew what the differently colored triangles on prisoners' uniforms meant and, by looking at their numbers, could estimate how long they had been in Birkenau. Instinctively we were more cautious when we were confronted by a prisoner with a black or green triangle, which stood for different criminal offenses, but we also knew that red meant "political" and purple, "religious crimes." The latter were mostly Jehovah's Witnesses, people who were counted to be among the best Germans at the time. Some of the German political prisoners, such as Orli Reichert, the young woman who headed the *Revier*, seemed quite compassionate, at least to us. Others, looking at our numbers, would treat us with contempt and even hatred because we had been fortunate to arrive later than they.

It may have been sometime in August, about one month after we had lost Father, when Eva told me that she was sure she had seen the kind, freckled-faced woman who served soup in our barracks in the family camp. Bertha Reich was in the *Revier*, where she and her friend, Ruth Elias, another Czech Jewish woman, had given birth to their babies. We went to see her, and she told us that after the selections in the family camp in early July, they had been sent to a camp near Hamburg. During the selections, Mengele had actually failed to notice that these two women were in the last trimester of their pregnancies, but in the camp in Germany, one of the prisoners in charge had reported them to the SS guards, and they were returned to Birkenau. They pretended not to be Jewish. But both "lost" their babies. Even then Eva and I were given to understand that the death of Ruth Elias's girl and Bertha Reich's boy had not been due to "natural causes."[2]

Mengele had forbidden Ruth Elias to nurse her baby—perhaps he had another experiment in mind. But he was said to be really annoyed that the two small bodies could not be found among the large stacks of bodies waiting for space in the crematorium. In 1991, I met Bertha Reich in Prague on a special visit to Theresienstadt.

Among men in a road gang, Eva recognized a young man that was one of the leaders in our youth home in Theresienstadt, and she managed to slip some bread to him. Both Eva and I became aware that we had a knack for recognizing the faces of people we had seen only rarely or months earlier.

Another Polish girl befriended us. Halina, who told us that she was not Jewish, was in charge of the *Krätzeblock*, the barracks that housed the women who had scabies. The barracks actually had a shower stall, and she let us use it. She warned us not to touch its walls because we might become infected. As we walked through the barracks, we saw the horrible suffering of these sick prisoners. The barracks was overflowing with women and girls. Emaciated, barely able to remain upright, they were leaning against each other along the walls. Others who lacked even that strength were crowded together on their bunks or lying next to the bunk on the bare floor.

Halina said that she was imprisoned because she had smuggled Jewish babies out of a ghetto (Warsaw?). One day she took us aside and sang several Zionist songs for us. After that we guessed that she must have been in Birkenau under an assumed name.

In the evenings when the agricultural work details came back from the fields, utterly exhausted and dragging themselves through the camp gate, they were often searched for vegetables they might have brought with them. If they noticed that a search was going on in the column ahead of them, they dropped their precious booty—usually carrots and potatoes—for fear of getting whipped or even killed. I was standing at the gate. Next to me a female German camp guard was shouting at the exhausted prisoners, who were trying not to call attention to themselves, "Hurry, move, hurry." As soon as the column of women prisoners had passed, the guard told me to pick up the vegetables. I had to carry them into the guardhouse. Sometimes the guard would let me keep some of the carrots and potatoes. I took them to the barracks of the orchestra. The next Sunday, Eva and I went to Renate and Anita. Renate suggested that we cook the vegetables in large quantities of water. That way, she said, there would be more of it. We shared this watery mush and felt—for a moment—fortunate and uncomfortably full. Almost unable to move, we had to laugh at our own discomfort as we fell back onto Anita's bunk. I don't think I gave any thought to the women who had tried to bring these vegetables into camp and who would have eaten them raw if they had been able to hold on to them, but I do remember becoming strangely aware of the sound of our laughter.

Some of the young Slovak and Polish girls we knew had male friends. They came into the women's camp on real or pretended errands. There were sexual encounters, and the girls received food, silk stockings, and sundry other usually unobtainable "goods." And we learned a Polish song that spelled it all out. It started with a common curse and ended with the statement: "For a piece of margarine I am willing to kiss for half an hour." Eva and I, at sixteen, were very young and very scrawny; we scarcely inhabited our own bodies. We seemed to exist, both physically and mentally, on some other plane.

During those summer months, even before we had had to leave the family camp, thousands upon thousands of Hungarian Jews arrived and were immediately gassed. Almost hourly their trains pulled in. We saw endless streams of men, women, and children, carrying smaller children and bundles, walking in the direction of the gas chambers. The crematoria worked day and night, obliterating the sky in stinking smoke. Very few were selected for work details. Among those who were spared—perhaps because they were an internationally known curiosity—and, I recall, brought to the family camp, was a family of Jewish vaudevillians called Opitz, some of whom were midgets while others were of normal height. We occasionally spoke with them. They impressed us with being both courageous and fatalistic. They survived the war.

In late September or early October, Eva learned in the office of the *Lagerälteste* that new transports were expected from Theresienstadt. We thought that since there no longer was a family camp, these transports would either undergo selection at the ramp or all would be killed immediately upon arrival as had happened to the Hungarians. We were totally certain that these were the only alternatives. In the space of a couple of months, the Nazis had taught us to think in such life-or-death categories. Our first thought was of Lotte and Danny. When we were deported in May, Father hoped that Lotte and her little boy would remain in Theresienstadt. Now we knew that if she had come with us in May, Lotte would have had a chance to be selected for work with Mania although there was not even a remote chance for Danny to be spared. Eva asked the women who were working at the ramp if there was a way to intercept Lotte. They thought that there might be, and Eva, trying to find Lotte in the confusion of arriving transports, mingled with the prisoners working on the ramp. While she never did see Lotte, she briefly saw Gisela Zamora, a roommate of ours from the youth home, and gave her a scarf. (Forty years later I saw Gisela's name on a sheet on which she and other survivors listed the names of people they were trying to find. She was looking for us because she wanted to thank us for that scarf. Eva was no longer alive.)

Eventually, a woman we knew from Theresienstadt told us that she had actually seen Lotte and Danny on the ramp and had briefly spoken with her. She urged her to give up her little boy. Lotte emphatically shook her head. Lotte was not quite nineteen when she and one-year-old Danny were killed.

In early October 1944, several crematoria crews—mostly Jewish prisoners—attempted a rebellion. Young Polish Jewish women prisoners who were working in a munitions factory had over a period of months brought them the explosives they would need to blow up one of the crematoria. Birkenau was shortly to be dismantled, and the crew had been ordered to begin hiding the evidence of the crematoria from the advancing Soviet armies. Daily gassing of incoming transports and of longtime prisoners was nevertheless continuing unabated. The crews' days were numbered; they had long known that the SS guards would not let them survive to tell of their experiences. We heard shots and saw the confused running hither and thither of the SS guards. It felt as if we were suddenly plunged into a darkness that enveloped everything. A thunderstorm threatened. For a fraction of a moment I felt glad. We were ordered inside our barracks. Almost instantly a rumor of what was happening had reached the women's camp. We knew those crematoria crews had little to lose by their revolt. They were filled with despair and degraded by the inhuman task the Germans had first invented and then forced them to perform . . . Even life after the Nazis could hold little hope of redemption for them. All those involved in the revolt, including those brave women who had brought them the munitions, were caught and killed by the Nazis.

It was beginning to get cold; Eva brought me an orange-colored wool coat and a pair of good, though slightly small, work boots. She herself had got a pair of high boots. She must have gotten these clothes from girls who worked in "Canada," the place where the personal luggage of arriving prisoners, which their real owners never saw again, was sorted for shipment to Germany. Transports of young women were leaving Birkenau for work in Germany, or so it was said. Wanda, the Polish student who had so generously given us some of her bacon, and her sister were sent on one of these transports. The office in which Eva worked was routinely notified when transports arrived at their destination. Check marks were placed against the lists of names of the women on these transports. But in this instance, no such notification was received. Although we had little doubt at the time that they had not arrived at their destination, but had met with a terrible fate instead, we never learned what had become of them. Occasionally good-looking, blond girls who personified the "Aryan ideal" (they were usually Polish) were selected for breeding as Germans in a place that Himmler had set up specifically for that purpose.

At the beginning of November 1944, we, too, left Birkenau. Eva and I were put on a transport on which many, if not most, of the surviving young Jewish Slovak girls were being shipped to a place in Silesia. I recall that Eva told me she thought it was a good thing that we were on the same transport as these girls. She may even have "volunteered" us for it. Reichenbach was not far from Breslau. We were to work in a Telefunken factory. Since this was indoors and involved precision work rather than heavy labor, it was considered a favorable assignment.

8

Reichenbach and Four Other Lagers

Reichenbach, also called Langenbielau, the camp to which we were brought, was a satellite camp of Gross-Rosen. Bleak, deserted brick barracks looked uninhabited, but we discovered that we shared them with some Dutch women and girls who were already working for Telefunken. These women were originally employed by the electronics firm Philips in Holland. The barracks were extremely cold, and while there were inside washrooms, the latrines were some distance away in the open. A day after our arrival, we were marched to the Telefunken factory, where we were first tested and then divided into work groups and shifts. Eva worked day shifts in a room together with just one somewhat older girl from Slovakia. The two of them had to monitor the temperature of several ovens in which glass tubes were heated and pressurized. They were continuously on the run, apparently because if an oven got overheated, the tubes would explode. As soon as they had checked and adjusted one oven, they hurried to the next. According to Eva, this had to be accomplished at a very fast pace. It is interesting to think that the tests the Telefunken people gave us—whose content I cannot recall—must have revealed Eva's quickness and mental alertness. I got work in a quality-control section and alternated weekly between day and night shifts. Sitting in a row at long tables, we had to check the filaments for newly manufactured (radio?) tubes. The filaments for these tubes were held in front of us on a special fixture. To be perfect, they had to run exactly parallel to each other. I tended to fall asleep at that task since I had trouble getting used to my weekly changing shift. When the German civilian supervisor passed my chair in the row of working prisoners, she thumped me on the back to get me to wake up.

Every other week when I worked the night shift, Eva and I saw each other only as our columns passed each other on the road, going in opposite directions. Exposed to the blustery winter weather, we walked what must have been several kilometers. We walked, not quite upright, huddled together. Not one of us was adequately dressed or shod. To defy the elements, some of the girls sang a song with the refrain: "*Durch die Hosen pfeift der Wind.*" (The wind blows through our pants.) To this day, there is nothing that reminds me of that time like when I happen to feel cold outdoors in winter.

We shared our bunk bed with Gisa, one of the young Slovak Jewish women. Dark blond, she was a tall woman with a large angular frame. Most important, she was a very patient person. In Birkenau, she had been in charge of the "sauna" and was housed in a small room adjacent to it. Eva and I thought that the prisoners herded into those shower rooms were not taken there to shower but to be gassed. But Gisa said that she had to stoke the ovens, presumably for warm water. That sauna may have been a delousing facility. (At that time the SS guards worried about the lice that infested the prisoners' clothes because the typhus this vermin carried could spread to them also. Later in the war they were less fastidious because we were all covered with lice during the final months.) Gisa was a girl whose age I could not even guess; she spoke so little. She made the impression of a very quiet, resigned person. We did not ever discover her last name. She had been in Birkenau for more than two years, and we could not come close to know how she must have suffered during that time. In Reichenbach, Gisa and Eva worked the same day shift, so that I had the bunk to myself when I worked nights. I had more space, but I was colder, and I felt alone.

After about a month of work, I felt a bad pain in my right side. I thought I had a fever. I went to the sickroom to speak to the woman physician in charge. She took one look at me and decided that I had jaundice. Apparently I was yellow. I hadn't known because there were no mirrors; neither Eva nor Gisa had noticed, probably because we rarely saw each other in daylight. There was no thought of the special diet doctors prescribe in normal times. But the doctor decided that I should stay in the sickroom so that I would not have to go to work. The sickroom was, if anything, colder and less inviting than the rest of the building. The bunks in that room were occupied by young girls who coughed, sighed, and, sometimes, cried. For four weeks I shared my bunk with another girl; both of us had a fever, but it was probably due to different causes. During that time another girl, lying in the bunk next to mine, died. Just before her death, she made what looked like a last, valiant effort to get out of her bed. For a moment she stood there, tall and thin, her uncombed blond hair framing her narrow face. Then she collapsed. The woman physician, herself a prisoner, was reluctant to say so, but somehow we knew that this girl had died of an advanced case of tuberculosis. After work, whenever Eva could, she slipped into the sickroom and begged me to get better. As soon as I could, I returned to her and went back to the factory.

But before long, I fell sick with a bad cold and cough. I had a lot of pain just trying to breathe. I went back to the doctor. Now she briefly listened to my chest and told me: "There might be something wrong with your heart." I do not know why she thought that diagnosis preferable to bronchitis or pneumonia. Somehow I did not believe her. I had a fever, and with each breath, my left side hurt. I suspected that there was something wrong with my lungs. The doctor did give me some pills to lower my fever. She warned me to use them sparingly because they were in very short supply.

Our bunk bed was extremely narrow, and the three of us always slept facing in the same direction. We turned in unison. I asked Eva and Gisa to lie as much as possible on their left side since I was very uncomfortable lying on my right. I could not allow my left side to expand fully, and lying on it helped. They agreed to try. During the day whenever Eva asked how I felt, I denied that I had pain; I even denied it to myself.

We only stripped to wash in the washroom. But it was ice-cold in there. And to keep a semblance of civilized behavior, we went outside to the latrine even during the bitter cold nights although quite a few girls simply relieved themselves in the hallway near the washroom.

Despite my denials, I was having quite a bit of pain, and going to work was starting to be difficult. I did not think it would help to go back to the sickroom, where conditions had not gotten any better. Instead of getting better, the sick rarely returned to us. So I continued to go to work at Telefunken although the long march to the factory was exhausting. Neither did I expect any help from the civilian Germans with whom I worked. My only contact with them continued to be their thumps on my back to wake me and remind me to pay attention to my work.

In the beginning of 1945, we heard rumors that Russian troops were advancing toward Breslau (now Wroclaw). We would have to move so that we would not "fall into their hands." Another Telefunken factory would make use of us. This became the pattern for the next five months. On February 18, very early in the morning when it was still pitch black outside, we were woken for roll call. I was still feeling ill, but comforted myself with the thought that the date was a good omen for me. (In Hebrew, numbers are indicated by letters. And eighteen spells "Chai," i.e., "life"). We were given a small loaf of bread to be shared by several girls and told it would have to last us several days. Then we marched out of the camp.

Our march took us south over winding, snow-covered mountain passes of the Riesengebirge. The road overlooked a valley dotted with clusters of villages. A mixture of bare trees and firs could be seen on the horizon. The snow glistened in the cold sun. That first day of our march I was amazed to see the undisturbed beauty of the land. We spent the night huddled together in some barns just off the main road. The next morning the guards and their dogs drove us on. When one of us fell by the wayside, we tried to help her up at once. We knew that those who stayed behind were shot. On the second day, Eva gave way to her exhaustion and refused to go on. She sat down by the side of the road and insisted that she would rather die than take another step. Gisa and I pulled her up, but her legs in those high boots were buckling under her. For some distance she resisted us as we half dragged, half carried her between us. First we begged her to hold out, but then we got worried and angry with her and scolded her. Finally she came to her senses; perhaps she realized that she had made us extremely anxious. She promised to try and go on.

There was one young girl who always walked flanked by two older girls who supported her. She looked extremely frail. We heard that she was not yet fourteen. Eva and I were almost seventeen; we were sorry for her and felt like veterans compared to her.

The second night of the march, we were put up in the loft of another barn. There was too little space even for those such as we, who were used to inhuman conditions. Our group was exhausted and irritable. Fights broke out among us for some space and some straw. A sleepless night would make for even greater exhaustion the next day. Most of us tried to settle down somehow. Eva and I discovered a farm cart and squeezed ourselves into the space underneath and lay unexpectedly snugly between its front and back wheels. All of a sudden, drowning out most of the bickering, we heard singing by what seemed to be a number of men. They sounded like a practiced choir, singing song after song. The fighting subsided as everyone strained to listen. Looking into the barn below us, we saw perhaps fifty men, lying in neat, ascending rows in the straw. It was an odd spectacle: They were singing, lying on a stage of straw, and we, the "audience," lay and crouched in the loft well above them among all kinds of farm implements. The barn resounded with their voices. These Russian men were slave laborers or prisoners of war. We listened to them for what seemed like hours, and their songs made us forget our discomfort and quarrels. I noticed that before morning some of the Slovak girls had a chance to speak with them, but they did not tell us what they found out.

The final day of the march was the worst. By now everyone was exhausted. Before we left Reichenbach, the doctor had given Eva a few more of those pills to control my recurring fever. She carried them in the same pocket of her blouse where she kept father's identity card, and she was guarding both with her life. She herself had developed an infected finger, and the cold made the pain even worse. It was evening before we arrived in a camp in Trautenau. We had crossed the German border into Czechoslovakia.

Eva's finger was badly swollen. She was told to go to the sick bay to have it looked at. She would probably have to lose her nail. When she refused to go, a German guard yelled at her: "Do you want me to shoot it off?" At that Eva went to the sick bay. Without benefit of an anesthetic, the infection was lanced and the nail removed.

There were both Jewish men and women in this camp. Behind the barbed wire the unshaved, gaunt faces of these ragged men looked both terrible and pitiful. These men were the first male prisoners we had seen since leaving Birkenau. My first thought was of Father and that men must have an even harder time surviving in camp than women; they were treated worse by the guards and may have treated each other worse. Some found it difficult to take care of their own needs. I imagined how Father would have suffered under these conditions. It did not occur to me to wonder how we looked to these men. We women did not look very closely at each other and took it for granted that we were decrepit.

Whenever we happened to be outside and got near the men's camp, they would come as close to the barbed wire as they possibly could. They stared at us as if they were seeing ghosts; then, scanning our faces, they called out different names: "Rifka, Soorele, Rosy?" If only for an instant, they seemed to be hoping to find, or get news of, their wives and daughters. They said that they had been separated from them months ago when they arrived in Birkenau. I think they were Hungarians, and we knew what had probably happened. What could we say to them? We said we did not know.

We did not stop long in Trautenau. Within a week we were being loaded into an open coal freight train with low side walls. It was still February and bitter cold. The train had no engine, and until one arrived several days later, we stayed on the railroad siding. The nights especially were hard to bear. Eva's infected finger was still very painful, and it made her extremely restless. Several times she attempted to jump out of the wagon. It would have been quite easy for her, and Gisa and I had to hold her down to stop her. All along this long freight train, we heard moaning and whimpering. Gradually I became aware that similar sounds were coming out of our own throats. When the engine finally arrived, we had no idea in what direction we were being taken.

Several times while we were traveling, Allied sorties flew over our open wagons. They dropped leaflets over the countryside but not close enough for us to obtain one. Once bombs began raining down all around us. Our train stopped so that the SS guards could run for cover in the nearby woods. We stayed on the open road in the open wagons. But those bombs left me, and probably the other girls also, quite undisturbed—we had little to lose. After about one week of stop-and-go travel, on March 1, 1945, we arrived in Porta Westfalica. It was one of several satellite camps of Neuengamme, built underground by slave labor very late in the war in an attempt to protect Germany's war production from Allied bombing raids.

Until then I had not realized that we were back in Germany. The camp was completely new and even unfinished, built to serve an equally new underground Telefunken factory some distance away. The barracks were huge, made of new wood, inside and out. My fever came back. I tried, nonetheless, to go to work with Eva. The very first day in the underground factory, I fainted, and Eva and I decided that I would have to go to the sick bay, at least for a while. But we were more and more afraid of being separated and wanted to avoid it at all cost. For several days I stayed in the barracks, but eventually I had to go to the sick bay. At night we could hear airplanes overhead and the responding flak. The girls hoped that the Allies were advancing, and they sang a number of Yiddish songs: "Es brennt, Städtele, es brennt" (It burns, the little town is burning); "Mein Stadtele Belz" (My little town, Belz, it is burning); and "Koift schoin Papirossi, trockene fun Regen nit vergossen" (Buy these cigarettes, they are dry, the rain has not made them wet). Porta Westfalica was the last camp in which we were together with our original group from Birkenau.

My fever seemed to be quite high. Once I was lying down, I felt as if I were floating just below the ceiling. Bombing raids became more frequent, but I heard the sirens as if the sound came from a great distance. One evening when Eva came on her daily visits to see me, she tried to rouse me. I heard her beg me: "*Rutchen, Rutchen, bitte, bitte sterbe nicht*" (Rutchen, Rutchen, please, please don't die). I wondered why she was repeating every word. When I finally managed to ask her what she wanted, she burst out: "You weren't listening, and though you did not look asleep, I could not get you to pay attention to me!" Her anxiety almost overwhelmed both of us. I promised I would not die. We talked of our sister in England—but even more we talked about the beet roots that, awake for a moment, I had seen someone bring into the kitchen. Eva, relieved to have brought me around, said she would try and "organize" one for me. The next day she came back and reported sadly that she had been caught with her beet. A German guard had taken the beet away from her and slapped her face to boot.

Rumors made the rounds that we would be leaving this camp also. Eva went to the person in charge of the sick bay and asked to get me released. Even though Eva promised to take responsibility for me, I was not allowed to leave the sickroom. At that, her ever-present anxiety went into high gear. She could do little but watch as we sick girls left Porta Westfalica ahead of the remainder of the camp inmates. We were loaded onto a V-shaped horse-drawn cart. There was no room for anyone to lie, so the sickest among us were put on the very narrow strip on the bottom, and we had to stand on top of these moribund, inert women. At a railroad siding we were loaded into a separate freight wagon, but we were on the same train as Eva. It was April 1. We had been in Porta Westfalica for exactly one month.

This trip began very badly. Although there was more room for the sick than in the other freight cars, doors and windows were sealed, and the air was stifling, permeated by a smell of excrement. The sick women were moaning much of the time. Within hours of the start of the journey, one of the women died. Somewhere along the route, the train stopped. I managed to get out and find my way to Eva. Surprised and relieved to see me, she helped me up into the freight car.

After perhaps a day in the freight train, we arrived at a railroad siding in front of Bergen-Belsen. We stayed on that siding for some days but were not "allowed" into the camp. While our train was standing there, a German Red Cross train arrived across the platform. It was packed with badly wounded German soldiers. They stared at us, and we stared at them. They must have known that we were concentration camp prisoners. Although I could not bear to look at their bloody bandages, I felt little compassion for them. And I wondered how they felt about us. A German historian whom I told about this encounter was the first person to believe my story: Apparently there was indeed a military hospital near Bergen-Belsen. But few civilians had been near there to be aware of it.

As Bergen-Belsen would not have us, we were taken to a camp called Beendorf. It was not known how long we would be staying. We were assigned a top bunk in a barracks, but I was totally unable to hoist myself up. Eva and I again decided that I would have to go back to the sick bay.

Conditions in that sickroom were not to be endured. I shared my bunk with a dying girl. When I tried to get space on another bunk, the emaciated woman who occupied it demanded my soup ration. I decided I would rather sleep on the floor in front of Eva's bunk than stay in that sickroom. The next morning I left and looked for Eva. She was glad to see me standing in front of her bunk. Several girls had gotten to know Eva while I was sick, and they offered to help me climb up. In addition to her still infected finger, Eva had developed several deep, festering sores on her right calf. With each step she took, the shaft of her boot rubbed against these open wounds. There were no bandages, and there was no one who could treat her wounds.

Beendorf was in a very poor, neglected condition, and its prisoners were covered in lice. These were both head and body lice. (The latter can be carriers of typhus baccili.) When Eva discovered the first lice in the seams of her own cardigan, she threw it away. The only clothes we had were those we wore. Soon enough we realized that we would be left without any clothes if we threw away all those infested with vermin. By the time we left Beendorf, at most a week after our arrival, we were totally infested with lice. Eva begged me, before we left, to examine her hair to see if she had any lice. She had been so good to me, I could not very well refuse although I hated to do it. She felt no different when I asked her to return the favor.

Our convoy had grown with the addition of the prisoners from Beendorf. (I do not know if all Beendorf was emptied out at that time.) We lost what little cohesion our original group from Reichenbach seemed to have had. Several freight cars in which male Jewish prisoners were held had also been hitched to our train. There may have been as many as one thousand of us prisoners.

One day we stopped on the Lüneburger Heide (heath), not far from our hometown of Hannover. To our surprise, we were let out of our freight cars into a beautiful spring day. Some of the male prisoners thought that the wooded terrain offered a chance for escape. They may have assumed that the Germans no longer possessed the will to control them. Everyone understood that the Allies were quite near because we could hear what we thought were sounds of battle. But the men trying to escape were shot before they could get very far. While we were happy to think that what we were hearing were the rumblings of the Allies coming closer, it was actually the SS guards who were shooting the escaped prisoners. In their striped prisoners' clothes, there was nowhere they could possibly hide. And even if someone would have been willing to shelter them, such a person would have been hard to find on the sparsely populated heath.

This event forced us to realize how precarious our situation really was: It was by no means certain that the SS guards would allow us to go free. They had now spent months transporting us from the east to the south, then to the west and from there to the north of Germany to evade the approaching Allies. Who or what was to prevent our guards from shooting the lot of us? Indeed, some of the older girls asserted that this was exactly what was going to be our fate.

Several large kettles of soup had been prepared outside on the heath. Eva and I stood in what looked like an interminable line waiting to get our helping. When I chanced to look up at the sky, I saw large threatening clouds. It was sure to rain before long. Instantly, I took Eva by the hand and we raced to the front of the line as if we were embarked on some urgent errand. Before anyone could question us or protest our temerity, we had our soup and ran back to our wagon. We dropped down, careful to protect that precious soup. Rain was pelting everyone outside. We escaped the downpour, but not the dripping women who eventually returned to our wagon with their soup.

There were about one hundred prisoners in each freight car. I could feel my temperature rising. The sliding door in the center of the car was kept slightly ajar. A German woman guard sat there. Eva and I had first seen this young woman in Birkenau. Eva and I called her *Die Puppe* (the doll) because she was so young and pretty. I was feeling so much in need of air, it made me whimper. As my father used to say: "Do not carry on. If anything, it will make you feel worse." But I needed to be heard and allowed to get near the opening of the car to get some air. I was lucky. The other women actually helped me to move to the front. The German guard told me to sit down. She handed me her flask and told me to drink: "Here, take a sip." I did. It was brandy or some other strong alcoholic drink. And not being used to alcohol, I began to sweat profusely. But as a result of this drastic thirst quencher, my fever dropped and I actually began to feel better.

After we left the Lüneburger Heide, we traveled north in the direction of Hamburg. For the last three days of this journey, we had neither food nor drink. It was the longest hunger spell we had to endure. On the third day some of the women, unable to bear their thirst any longer, asked for and got some water from the locomotive. It could be used for washing one's hands and face, but was hardly potable. Eva and I also got some of this rather brackish water and decided to use it to wash our very dirty hands. This did not prevent some of the girls from asking for our water and drinking what we had washed our hands in.

It must have been the third week of April when we arrived in a camp near Hamburg. Most likely it was Wandsbek, another camp administered by Neuengamme. By now all of us were totally emaciated, starved, and full of hair and body lice. We had truly come to the end of our endurance. There was very little food in the camp, and we spent most of our time in a kind of stupor, apathetically sitting or lying on our bunk beds. We had to be up for roll calls, and I found it hard to stand upright for any length of time. One day as Eva was walking behind me, I heard her sobbing. Worried, I turned around and asked her what had happened. "Nothing," she said. She had looked at my legs and seen how thin they were. She was sure they were going to break! Unlike me, Eva kept some of her emotional responsiveness all during camp. Sometimes that resulted in her imagination creating fears that even exceeded our reality . . . She seemed to have few if any means for self-protection, no escape hatch. My own reactions were so different that it was difficult for us to understand each other. Even in camp that made us at times very irritable, and then we quarreled with each other much as we had done at home.

In the early morning of May 1, 1945, we had our usual roll call. We heard that we would be leaving this camp again. As usual we were not told where we were going to be shipped next. By the time we were loaded onto the train, it was early afternoon. For the first time, no more than fifty of us women occupied each freight car so that we could actually sit down. More unusual still, the floor was covered with straw. All this greatly surprised but also frightened us. Some of the girls again asserted that it was entirely possible that we were about to be shot and the straw had been put there to absorb our blood! These somewhat more tolerable conditions were intended solely to fool us, they said.

As our train began to move, someone said that we were going in the direction of Denmark. Perhaps, for once, our pessimism was not warranted? But we did not know where this information came from. What did all this mean? Eva and I looked at each other. We were too tired to talk, and it was so long since we last dared to think that our ordeal might one day come to an end. Then, somewhere in the countryside, the train was stopped for us to relieve ourselves. Even such permission was a rare event, worthy of wonder. While we were squatting between two freight cars, we heard some shouting: "Hitler is dead. He committed suicide." There was no longer any reason to doubt it: For us, the war was over.

Eva looked for Father's identity card. She wanted to look at his picture. It was no longer in the breast pocket of her blouse. She found it on the ground not far from us. Someone had used Father's identity card for her toilet needs. Eva was inconsolable. Finally I thought of a way to comfort her. I reminded her that we were sure to get pictures of Father once we were in touch with Grete again. That made sense to her and she brightened up.

In the evening of the same day, we crossed the German-Danish border at Padborg. We had really left Germany behind us. We were exhausted and hungry, dressed in filthy rags that were full of lice. But we were free.

9

Liberation

The men and women who opened our freight cars were dressed in white and wore armbands with Red Cross insignia. They brought low ladders to help us climb down. Cheerfully, repeatedly, they reassured us that we had indeed arrived in Denmark. We no longer needed to doubt that we were safe. Still, a few feet away from us, by a fence on the other side of the railway platform, our former SS guards lingered, watching these proceedings. And then, some of our fellow prisoners, now as free as we were, walked over to them. They shook hands with those who, only moments earlier, had been their and our unpredictable and implacable tormentors. Just a few weeks ago, they killed those desperate, brave men who tried to find their freedom on the heath. Eva and I looked at each other in disbelief. We had not the slightest wish to shake hands with those people, and no regret to see them finally disappear on the German side of the border.

On heavy white pottery plates, the Danish Red Cross workers handed us steaming oatmeal over which they ladled cold milk. It looked and tasted delicious to us. Most of the Danes knew German, but even those who talked to us in Danish were not difficult to understand. They wanted to explain why they had decided to serve us such simple fare. When the first group of prisoners arrived, they fed them a meal of meat, potatoes, and spinach. Few were able to tolerate such substantial food, and many got ill. Eva and I enjoyed our oatmeal. I felt so well, I told Eva that I was sure my fever had disappeared, and with it whatever it was that had made me sick all these months.

By bus we were moved to a reception center. There were bunk beds that looked as if they had just been built, and they were covered with white sheets and blankets. We touched the sheets and looked around us, and then we hugged each other. Everything was clean and light and inviting, and every word spoken to us was kind and intended to reassure us. We had come to a different world.

Very early the next morning, we assembled to be taken by train and ferry to Copenhagen and from there by a second ferry to Sweden. Eva and I enjoyed the train ride and stood at the window to watch the countryside with its flowering fruit trees. We thought that we had never seen anything quite so beautiful. In the fields that passed before our train window, men and women put down their hoes and rakes when they saw our train, straightened their backs, and waved to us. They must have thought us a strange-looking, tattered lot waving to them from the train windows. We were still itching and dirty, but it did not worry us very much. For the trip, the Danes had given us packages of cold cuts or cheese sandwiches, and it all tasted wonderful. Once we were on the ferry to Sweden, we were encouraged to shed our outer garments and to toss them overboard because we would be receiving new, clean clothes upon our arrival. But few of us could quite believe those promises.

The dining room on the ferry was furnished with round tables and easy chairs upholstered in dark red plush. I hesitated before sitting down at the table to be served still another breakfast, because my clothes were crawling with lice, and I could foresee the result on those plush chairs. A waiter told me, "Don't you worry, miss(!)," and I sat down to enjoy my meal.

After a short trip on the second ferry, we reached Malmö at the southern tip of Sweden. As we entered the harbor, I discovered that I no longer had the card we were given in Denmark on which we had to record our name, the place we came from, and other information. Eva, annoyed and as always worried about the consequences of my carelessness, scolded me severely. I refused to believe that this loss was irreparable. We were still arguing when our pictures were taken. I still have that picture, and while it shows some of the hardships I had undergone, it also registers my quarrel with Eva. The loss of the card turned out to be quite unimportant. Knowing when fear was warranted, and when it was not, was going to be extremely difficult to learn for both Eva and me.

From Malmö, we immediately went to Hälsingborg. A school had been converted into temporary quarters for us. On the evening of our arrival, nurses and physicians bathed and disinfected us. I experienced a moment of real happiness when I got a cake of fragrant light green Palmolive soap. Gladly I gave up every shred of my old, lice-infested clothes, which I had worn day and night for almost ten months. I wanted to keep the leather belt I had worn on my black felt dress since Birkenau, but the nurse who supervised the proceedings dissuaded me. Clad only in nightgowns, we were shown to our beds. I was disappointed when it turned out that these were covered with paper sheets. I had already been spoiled by the Danes' cotton sheets.

But for the first time in two years, we had our own bed! For one or two days I felt so well, I was sure that I was over whatever ailed me, until I found it almost impossible to walk upstairs—a weight in my lungs was dragging me down. I was put into a sickroom. Soon all of us were x-rayed.

Within days, without too much ceremony, a young Swedish physician sat down on my bed and told me that I had pleurisy on both sides. There was a great deal of fluid in my lungs. He suspected it was caused by tuberculosis. The extent of my lesions could not be determined from the x-ray because the fluid appeared white on the film and obscured all the details underneath. My temperature had risen again. Eva, told of this diagnosis, reacted with deep anxiety. Again she begged me not to die. I tried not to show her how unhappy I was myself while some voice in me, sounding like a broken record, kept repeating: "You have TB." It was a disease I knew from novels I had read. Those suffering from it usually were poets or other artists. I was neither. Our bedmate, Gisa, also had a mild case of tuberculosis. I soon found out it was the most prevalent disease among us. Then Eva fell ill. She had a very painful sore throat and high temperature that was later diagnosed as scarlet fever. When we were weighed more than a week after our liberation, Eva weighed forty and I thirty-four kilograms (eighty-eight and seventy-five pounds, respectively).

While I was trying to get used to the idea of having been diagnosed with tuberculosis, Eva was looking for Mania and making contact with Grete and our friends, the Karo family in Zurich. Three weeks after we were liberated, she wrote them a long letter about our experiences in the concentration camps. It may have been an attempt to unburden herself as much from the load she was still carrying as to tell these friends in Switzerland what had really happened to us. She was still very worried about me, a worry that had hounded her for the last six months or so.

As a very early document, written by a seventeen-year-old girl so soon after her liberation, it is quite remarkable. It is actually, considering Eva's usual way of describing her experiences in rather stark terms, quite restrained. But since Eva worked in the *Schreibstube* (office) she may have heard these details of the gassing and separate burning pits from the people working with her. The details ring true to the actual procedure. Much of this was confirmed after the war.

At the time I had no idea about her activities, being much too busy with myself. The Karo family—parents and a daughter of around twenty or so—typed her letter and sent it to the Wiener Library in London, which then sent it to Yad Vashem in Jerusalem. It was shown to me when I visited Yad Vashem in 1989. Eva was no longer alive. She took her life in July 1973.

This is what Eva wrote them:

May 21–23, 1945
Dearest Family Karo:

You can imagine our joy when we received your kind telegram yesterday. We have already sent a telegram and air letter to Grete, but have no news from her yet. We addressed it to the Victoria Memorial Hospital. You asked how it is with Ruth's illness. Well, I do not want to anticipate, but report to you in proper order. I shall be brief and tell you only the main points. I will tell you the details next time. As you know, we were deported to Theresienstadt in June 1943. Prior to our deportation we had been in prison in Hannover for two weeks. We were the last Jews from the town. Nine people. We went by cattle car to Theresienstadt. We had a decent amount of luggage. Bed linens, mattresses, clothing, a few dishes. When we arrived in Theresienstadt, we were received by Czech gendarmes. Luggage was searched and plundered by Jews. We were brought to an old, ramshackle house. That is where we spent the summer, in a stifling hot attic. In winter Ruth and I stayed in the youth home. Vati and Mutti were in the same house, but downstairs. For the first few months we still had some supplemental food which we had brought from home. Then Mutti sold bed linens for bread. Of the parcels from Lisbon we received only three. In May 1944 we came to Auschwitz with a transport that included 7,500 people. Sixty-five people per freight car and a great deal of luggage. Most people on our transport were old people. One hundred seventy died on the way. Luggage had to be left. We were assigned to a family camp for those from Theresienstadt. That is: transports from Theresienstadt were given preferential treatment. 1) Men and women in one camp. 2) Transports did not undergo selections at the railway ramp. (More about that below.) 3) Women on the transports did not get their head shaved, but hair was cut short above the ear. The next day we were tatooed. A number on the left arm. Those two months were the worst in our lives. We almost died of hunger. At half past nine, a half liter water soup, which can really only be eaten by one who, because of hunger, can no longer stand on his legs. Shortly thereafter we were given the daily ration of bread, one kilogram for four or five people. But how often that bread was moldy. With it a tiny piece of margarine, or salami or a spoonful of jam. That was our total nourishment. A woman may just about manage on that, but a man cannot exist on that nourishment. So one would save a little of this food for the other. Everyone suffered more because of the other's hunger than because of his own.

The image of the Lagerstrasse: men, shabbily dressed, heads shaved, carry heavy rocks, behind them (other) men with whips. These beat down continuously on their poor limbs. Behind the barracks lie stacks of the dead and daily more die of typhus. No one had looked after them while there was still a spark of life in them. All this is framed by barbed wire as far as the eye can see. The wire is electrified. Beyond that wire there are other camps. As far as the eye can see: one huge hell, a concentration camp such as never existed before. How can I describe it all? When we see each other, I shall tell you everything. One more thing: To pass the time, the SS-camp doctor has elected (*auserkoren*) to do twin research. What he did with us is hard to believe. We were examined, measured, weighed a hundred times. How much blood did he draw from us? We were brought to Auschwitz by car to be photographed (we were in Birkenau). X-rays were also not forgotten. For these hardships we received an extra portion of soup. That was very welcome because we could help Vati and Mutti.

Now I want to write something about the selections. Then you will understand the remainder better. Every arriving transport was unloaded, men to the right, women to the left. In the center, legs astride, stood the Lagerkommandant and the Lager physician. First the women. Every single one must file past while, with a playful gesture, he points to the left or the right. To the left all young women with small children—up to approximately fourteen years. As well as all older women over forty. But girls are also going there who are perhaps a little too fat or a little too thin, or have some other minor disability. Mothers are being separated from daughters and they are told that they will soon see each other again. Many a young daughter does not want to leave her old mother and is magnanimously allowed to go with her. Men are sorted in the same way; here only the few strong ones are chosen.

How arbitrary these doings are. How many young people look a little heavier because for the transport they have put on double clothing. Why is a woman or man old when he has a few gray hairs on his head. Well, the left side is led to the gas. A few steps and that long line is near the crematorium. On the outside nothing tells of the murderous work that is being conducted on the inside. It is built of red brick and looks like a bath house A few steps lead downstairs. Soon these poor ones find themselves in a splendid dressing room. Large mirrors on the walls. They undress and the mothers are told that they should tie up their children's clothing so that they will not have to look for them later when they get dressed. Then they go to the "showers." This room too is beautifully appointed. When one hundred persons are assembled in the room, the door shuts. In the wall there is a hole, and now an SS-man throws a gas bomb through it. This bomb was originally intended for 1,300 persons. But because the Germans had to save gas, and besides intended to annihilate many more human beings, they now use one gas bomb for 3,000 persons. Now the unhappy ones notice the hoax that has been perpetrated on them. By their gradually subsiding cries one realizes that they have lost consciousness. The door opens and prisoners, clad in striped clothes with tattoos on their forehead, enter. They are Jewish men, and it has happened more than once that they have recognized their parents or wife with a child among the lifeless. The task of these men is to free the gas chamber for the next load because many thousands are waiting outside to be "bathed." "It is assembly line work [*sic*]." Once all are "taken care of," the burning begins. Through the wide, square chimney an indescribably high flame can be seen miles away. That is the kind of "bath houses" these were.

Just at the time we came to Auschwitz, the Hungarian Jews were arriving. Many of them had large families, and the work soon became impossible to accomplish. The following solution was found: Deep pits were dug into which calcium chloride was scattered. Then the children—living!—were thrown into the pits and set aflame. The corpses of the adults were layered: one layer humans, one layer wood. This (structure) also was set aflame. This is only a small glimpse into the methods the Germans used against the Jews.

After we were two months in the camp and already knew all of this, orders came one day for the family camp to be dissolved. The doctor came and soon a big selection began. Naked, everyone had to walk past those "gentlemen." This did not take one day. No, for more than three weeks we still had time to tear our hearts out because we knew that Vati, who had greatly deteriorated in those two months, would not be considered capable of work. Mutti was sent with a work transport to Stutthof (Danzig). Ruth and I went with the other twins into the large women's camp. During the night of July 11 (there may have been two nights, the eleventh and the twelfth of July), Vati and (about) 8,000 others went to a martyr's death. During the night I stood outside and looked at the closed cars that went, without letup, to the crematorium. [I feel that Eva might have wished she could have done that, but being outside at night was not possible.] I knew that in one of these cars Vati sat and thought of us for the last time. The flames blazed high in the chimney, and as usual in Birkenau, it smelled of burned bones. But this night too came to an end, and despite all the horror, we did not lose our reason. Neither did we act as if we were in total despair. No the horror was so overwhelming that we became apathetic. The bromide we got in our soup also stupefied us. (Some researchers maintain there is no evidence that we had bromide in our food.)

Because we were twins (and knew German well), we were used as messengers. We were at the beck and call of the SS guards, we had to listen to their wishes and to carry them out. As a result our clothes were slightly better and we lived in a better block and had a little more bread. In October everyone from Theresienstadt arrived. I was eyewitness as many of my acquaintances passed by me on their way to the gas chamber, but I could not help, my hands were tied. It was a quirk of fate that I did not see Lotte who arrived one Saturday morning. Only later did a friend of hers tell me that Lotte also went to the left! Whether I could have saved her I do not know, because we had begged the Lager physician to save my father, and he said then that he would see that he got "light" work.

In November we reported for a transport, we were four months near Breslau and worked for Telefunken. Here Ruth fell ill. She had jaundice. Of course there was no diet food. For weeks she ate nothing and got terribly thin. As soon as she got better she got pleurisy for the first time. She was three days out of the sick room when we had to flee from the Russians, and for three days on foot we crossed the Riesengebirge (a mountain range at the border of Germany and Czechoslovakia). This was the middle of February. Our food was one loaf of bread. We stayed for three days in Trautenau, then we were put in open coal cars. We were about sixty-five in each wagon. This transport took seven days. It rained, snowed and hailed and there were some bomb attacks by the allies. Again we had one loaf of bread for the seven day journey. When we arrived in Porta Westfalica Ruth's pleurisy was worse again. I worked in a subterranean factory that made radio tubes. After four weeks we again were transported to another camp. This time Ruth had high fever and could not walk one step. After a trip of several days we arrived in Beendorf. I put Ruth in the sick room, thinking that she would be taken care of there. The next day she came back to me in the barracks. She had run away from that "sick room." People were full of lice and boils and wanted her bread to give her space on one of the bunks. After five days in this completely neglected camp we left again. Now as many people as "possible" were packed into each wagon. We were 105. Some wagons had 140 people. We were together with gypsies, German asocials [German term for deviants]. Ruth had a high fever. At night there were fights for space and food. But there were more lice than food! This unbearable state of affairs lasted 14 days. The allies bombed our locomotive. But a new one was ready for use. A hundred times we were five minutes away from being liberated, but at the last moment there was still another train to carry us away. We seemed to criss-cross Germany and had an opportunity to see how damaged everything was. One large mountain of ruins! These pictures were our only comfort during this difficult time. After two days without any food or drink whatsoever, we were brought to yet another camp near Hamburg. Here we were tormented for another week. Then we went to Schleswig-Holstein.

Here the Swedish Red Cross took charge of us. It was like a dream when we were liberated on May 1, 1945. The Danish population rejoiced over us and showered us with the most delicious sweets. After a one day stay, we went to Sweden. You may have seen the pictures in the newspapers of the condition in which we arrived and how the good Swedes made human beings out of us again. Our rags were burned, and we were freed from our lice. Then we were a fortnight in quarantine in Hälsingborg. Here we were weighed, Ruth lost 13 kilo and only

> weighed 34 kilo. And how she has grown! I only lost 10 kilo and grew 5 cm. My chest X-ray was negative, while Ruth of course has all kinds of lung damage. I gained 2 kilo and Ruth 6 kilo. But you cannot tell on Ruth because she was so emaciated. For the last three days we have been in Halmstad, in a wonderful hospital with first rate food. Unfortunately Ruth is seriously ill. She still has pleurisy. There is also water on her lungs. She withstood all those hardships with an energy which shows that she is father's daughter. I have just recovered from a mild flu—later thought to have been scarlet fever. I believe that I shall have to stay in bed a few more days. How long I will remain here I do not know. Ruth will go to a sanatorium. I shall look for light work as other girls are doing. It is better to work, there is not so much time to think. Also I want to make money, because up to now we have only one coat, one dress, a pair of shoes and a little underwear, and then we can buy additional clothes . . .
>
> Have you heard nothing from Mutti? She is not in Sweden, I believe, but with the Russians. Hope very much that she is alive.
>
> —Eva Herskovits

Some of our fellow camp mates had a very difficult time believing in the reality of their liberation. They feared that somehow their suffering and hunger would return sooner or later. It was as if their current life were a pleasant but strange interlude from which they would wake up to find themselves in their old familiar nightmare. At mealtime, they took more than they could eat, and they stored the leftover food under and in their beds. When crowds of curious Swedes congregated outside the windows of our temporary housing, some of our camp mates pointed to themselves, like us, still clad only in nightgowns, and asked the Swedes for clothing. In response, the Swedes would bring both new and used clothing. Eva and I reoriented ourselves quite quickly. We readily believed that we would no longer have to starve and that, eventually, we would receive clothes and other necessities.

Around the third week of May, all those who had been diagnosed as having TB were transferred to another temporary hospital in Halmstad. Unlike siblings of other patients, Eva was allowed to stay with me. Only later was I to learn why. She had been told that the doctors were not so sure I would recover. But some weeks later, when a probe was inserted into my left lung to extract the accumulated fluid, most of it had dried or been reabsorbed. The nurses told me that this was very good news. My appetite was excellent, and I had every intention to go on living. In fact, I began to reflect that I had been patient much too long. It was time I let them know that I was occasionally in pain. Now, whenever it hurt me to breathe, I complained loudly. This only made the pain worse. Apparently this pleurisy came with quite a bit of pain.

One day, a middle-aged woman physician sat herself down on my bed. Brusquely she told me that I could expect to have some pain breathing "for the rest of your life. You might as well get used to it." It was hardly a pleasant prospect—although I had trouble understanding what she meant by "the rest of my life." But I stopped complaining.

At the beginning of July, the physician in charge of the Halmstad facility, Dr. Citron from Danzig, chose eight patients for transfer to a Swedish sanatorium. The head physician, Dr. Victor Steffen, had offered us a place in his sanatorium. I was lucky to be among those eight whose prognosis, while uncertain, was not considered hopeless. And so, just about two months after our arrival in Sweden, on July 3, I began my life in the only Swedish setting I came to know well, the Fagereds Sanatorium near Falkenberg. However, while several of us girls recuperated well, at least one third of the girls of our first group died during the first year despite our physicians' best efforts. At that time there were not many treatments available that held out any promise for a lasting cure. Good air, good food, and a fairly reasonable way of life offered as good a chance for success as pneumothorax and lung resections.

Eva meanwhile received an invitation from a family in Stockholm, the Weingartens, who had known our family in Hannover, where they had owned a raincoat factory. Eva accepted their offer to join them and discovered, not unlike Grete in 1939, that her new hosts' motives were, at best, mixed. Eva performed the duties of a maid in their household. Although she was only seventeen, she was not encouraged or helped to resume her schooling. The family had two young adult sons. One, perhaps mentally unstable, spent his time at home while the other was in business with his father. At times these two young men made life very unpleasant for her. Eva and I were no longer living together—the sanatorium in Lia was in the south of Sweden, and Stockholm was a day's train journey north of Lia. Thus I did not really know what was happening to her, and why she might have been reluctant, or too timid, to complain. If there was a central agency responsible for the refugees—as we who had been brought to Sweden were called—she did not know of its existence. Eva was quite alone with her difficulties and had no idea how to go about changing her unpleasant situation.

Eva's first effort after our arrival in Sweden was to find out whether Mania, our stepmother, had survived. After months of fruitless inquiries, she wrote me that Mania had probably died sometime between February and May 1945. Mania was last seen in February by a fellow Hannoveranian, Klaus Becher, in Stutthof, a camp near Danzig. When the Riga ghetto and the camps in its surroundings were being evacuated ahead of the approaching Soviet troops, some of the surviving German Jews were sent to Stutthof. While not much is known about the conditions that prevailed in Stutthof, as in many other concentration camps there was typhus. Mania was forty-seven years old. She had been a healthy, stately, and very resourceful woman. Aside from the physical deprivations and hardships she must have suffered in Stutthof, the separation from her husband, daughter, and stepdaughters may have undermined both her health and will to live. I have seen a document showing her arrival in Stutthof. Below her name, and date and place of birth, it reads: "Married. Children: 4. Arrival: 20.7.44. Via: Concentration camp Auschwitz. To concentration camp: Stutthof. Reason for imprisonment: Unknown. Prior infractions: None. Special marks: l. underarm tattoo, A-2703." That she thought not only of her own daughter Lotte, but even of Margaret, safely in England, as one of her four daughters speaks of her loving kindness and sincerity. It still moves me.

A few months later there was more terrible news. The war never "passed" for little Abrammetje. He, his brothers and sister, and their young parents had all been killed. The precise dates I learned only recently: According to the Dutch Red Cross, they were deported to Sobibor on March 10, 1943. There Jeanette, thirty-three; Jacob, nine; Elie, eight; Roosje, not yet seven; and Abrammetje, four and a half years old, perished on March 13, 1943, while Victor, thirty-four, "was apparently shot" on April 30, 1943. Eva's host family, the Meijers, went underground in Holland. It was, however, much more complicated and dangerous than this terse statement can convey. To live "underground" required being constantly on the move. Their younger son, Benny, was betrayed and arrested. He was sent to Auschwitz. In January 1945, with the Soviet troops approaching, the prisoners were marched out of Auschwitz. Benny, together with some other prisoners, escaped en route. But they were caught and incarcerated in Mauthausen, one of the worst camps at that time, where prisoners were worked to death in a quarry. It was the Meijers' good fortune to have had three older children and only one small girl, who was five when they managed to hide her. Their oldest daughter, Gerda, joined in the work of the resistance, but when the Nazis discovered her group, she went to prison and endured lengthy interrogations. Family Meijer also had the requisite courage and self-reliance, and some financial means and friends among non-Jewish farmers and Dutch cattle dealers who were willing to help them. Although they lost many of their extended family and underwent many trials, they emerged from the war with their immediate family intact.[1]

Grete received a notification from the Swedish Red Cross that we had been rescued, and we started writing each other immediately. Eva also began an active correspondence with our family in Palestine and our uncle in New York. To our delight, our maternal grandmother, Charlotte Kiss, was alive. She was still living in the same area of tiny houses called Siebenbürger Häuser (Transylvanian houses) in Jerusalem with a widowed, childless daughter, our Aunt Blanca. We were hoping to join them eventually, and they encouraged us in that hope. Mother's favorite brother, Bela (Ben), was living in Haifa with his wife, Rachel, and two sons. While we had never actually met any of our mother's family, except for Uncle Iszo, we were happy to be in touch with them again.

Eva even made contact with people in Hannover. She heard from Frau Nyszli that she had used the few things she had received from our father and Mania for safekeeping to pay for medical treatment for her son, Geza, who had fallen ill with rheumatic fever. Frau Nyszli also related that only hours after we were deported, Mania's Persian carpet was carried out of our apartment in Ahlem by one of the remaining Jewish men (whose marriage to a non-Jewish woman protected him from being deported). Of course, she did not know if he had acted on the orders of the German authorities who were in charge of confiscating, or robbing, Jewish possessions!

Fritz and Erika Blankenburg survived the war in Hannover, although Fritz Blankenburg was sent to Theresienstadt in early 1945 together with other Jewish partners living in "mixed marriages."

10

Time to Reflect

The Fagereds Sanatorium

At first, my illness was a fortunate circumstance for me. It gave me a much-needed breathing spell, a time for thought and recuperation that Eva, and many other former prisoners of the Nazis, never had.

I know that it was July 3 when we refugees came to the Fagereds Sanatorium. We were eight girls and young women, and all of us had recently come to Sweden after being liberated from concentration camps near the northern border with Denmark. We were chosen on the basis of a physician's prognosis that the Fagereds Sanatorium would give us our best chance to recover from our tuberculosis.

I was still quite weak and sleepy when we arrived. I have no memory of my first impression of that very stately place with the big driveway and the impressive entrance hall. The building stood on a slight hill and could have been a hotel or even a large mansion. It was white and its two wings were totally symmetrical. It looked as if an area of virgin forest had been cleared for the building and much of it still remained at the back and on both sides of the building. In front, on a downward slope, there was a large croquet field embedded in a park with benches and flowers. Later, I read Mann's *Magic Mountain* and found that, despite the many superficial differences, our elementary fears and hopes at this more prosaic place were quite similar to those of the patients at that "magical" Swiss sanatorium.

As soon as my fever dropped, I was allowed to get up for a few hours. Gradually those hours became days. The physicians making their daily rounds were amused by the drawings on my chart with which I celebrated fever-free days, weight gains, and other notable events in my physical recuperation. I also decorated the headboard of my bed with sayings and aphorisms that I was gathering from my reading. By the time I was allowed to go outdoors, it was late autumn. An early snow covered everything in sight. Dark green pines and firs contrasted with the overwhelming whiteness of the landscape. It reminded me of another snow-covered landscape I had seen on our march into Czechoslovakia. Though only six months had passed, it was an unimaginably long time and distance away . . . I enjoyed my walks and almost lost my fear of freezing.

Indoors, in the large sitting rooms where we spent a good part of our day, I learned to speak Swedish with the patients and nurses. The sanatorium had a good library, and the librarian, a theology student who had been a seriously ill patient with several operations on his lungs behind him, hauled out all the books, in Swedish, I wanted to read. For the next two and a half years in Fagereds, I had a chance to orient myself in the adult world by reading everything in sight, and I eagerly read a mixture of philosophy, fiction, and social science. Gunnar Myrdal's *American Dilemma*, a problem that President Roosevelt had asked the Swedish political scientist and his wife, Alva, to investigate, introduced me to the central problem of the America of that time and to this day: that of the inequality of life's opportunities for the different "races." It was a subject I had no trouble understanding because of my own experience with irrational and eventually murderous racism.

The earphones at my bed were almost always tuned to a classical music station. I felt like crying when I heard Beethoven sonatas and Brahms intermezzi that I had last heard Grete play at home. When I wrote her that I had heard "*Yom Kippur ist vorbei*" (Yom Kippur is over), and remembered how John Mandelbrod had sung it when he came to give her weekly piano lessons, she answered that it was Beethoven's Tenth Piano Sonata. The Brahms piece I liked so much was an intermezzo, op. 117, no. 3. For the first time I heard Gershwin's music, even his folk opera, *Porgy and Bess.* But whenever I heard a male voice sing German lieder or the Mozart arias my father had sung, I took off my headset. It was to be years before I could listen to male voices singing familiar music.

We learned that our liberation and the asylum we had been given in Sweden were the result of Count Folke Bernadotte's negotiations with Himmler's Finnish masseur, Felix Kersten, or Himmler himself. Bernadotte, a nephew of the Swedish king, originally wanted to rescue Danish and Norwegian Jews, but by then the nervous Nazis offered him other Jews as well. In April 1945, Himmler or his masseur approached the count with a proposal to take over some of the prisoners still alive in the various camps in Northern Germany in addition to the Scandinavian group. Sweden, we were later told, actually welcomed the influx of a mixed population: We were from Germany, Poland, Hungary, the Balkans, Czechoslovakia, and the Baltic states. While many of us were sick, this was deemed the result of general deprivation and starvation. Our very survival—aside from sheer luck—seemed proof of a basically healthy constitution. Sweden had long coped with tuberculosis. It had a rather high incidence of the disease in its population. In fact, many of the Swedes I got to know had been in the sanatorium repeatedly and not a few were incurably ill.

At times our environment with its strict routine and the short days during the long winter months became quite depressing. Grave illness was a constant topic. We refugees nonetheless managed to be not only cheerful but also mischievous. We broke all the rules of the place, and our transgressions ran the gamut from missed rest periods or dancing the tango to an unwanted pregnancy. Lucky for us, the chief of the sanatorium, Dr. Victor Steffen, who painted and played the violin when he was not working as a physician, was an exceptionally tolerant and understanding man. Dr. Steffen's wife, Karin, also suffered from tuberculosis. When she, also a physician and the mother of five young daughters, became depressed, her husband asked me to their house to read Heine poems to her. That was why when, after a long hike in the woods, we girls arrived hours late for dinner, I had to speak for our group. Although I really was no better than the other girls at inventing excuses, he forgave us.

During the summer and fall of 1945, more groups of former prisoners came to the sanatorium. Among the newer arrivals was the fourteen-year-old girl whom we had so pitied on our three-day march to Trautenau. She was making arrangements to meet a cousin in Jerusalem who was said to be her fiancé. She was actually a couple of years older than I. She had pretended to be a child to get the sympathy of the other women imprisoned with us and succeeded in being helped by them. Gisa, who had always been very good to us when we shared our bunk with her in Reichenbach, briefly stayed in Fagereds but soon left to return to her surviving sister in Czechoslovakia. She even sent me a photo from a vacation in the Tatra Mountains but neglected to put her last name and address on it. I always regretted to have lost touch with her.

At that time we refugees were no longer living in the large, beautiful main building of the sanatorium. A pavilion had been specially built for us on the grounds. A simple rectangular structure, it was furnished with light stained furniture and beautiful home-woven fabrics, a craft of which the Swedes were very proud. We had breakfast in the pavilion and learned to use an electric dishwasher. Living in the pavilion may have isolated us somewhat from the other patients, but it gave us the freedom we craved without disturbing the Swedish patients. We could bathe to our heart's delight—a habit that had offended the Swedish patients who, compared to us, seemed water shy. For me, that bath and a cake of Palmolive soap daily re-created the marvels of our liberation.

I shared my room with a non-Jewish Polish woman. She was twice my age, thirty-four or thirty-five, but looked older because of a facial palsy. She had been arrested by the Nazis shortly after her officer-husband was killed at Katyn. Her young daughter was in Poland, living with relatives. Her only language was Polish and some French. Since I knew no French, I learned to speak a little Polish, enough to help her communicate with our doctors when they made their rounds. Later we traveled to the nearby town of Varberg together, where she was treated by a Swedish dentist, and I helped her to make herself understood. Zofia Stawiczka was an artistically gifted woman who appreciated the beauty of the surrounding landscape. When we walked together outdoors, she pointed out the fine details of flowers and plants to me that I would not have noticed. She continued to suffer a low-grade fever and spent most of her time creating dolls in Polish national dress. To me, she was very motherly, and she comforted me when she felt I needed to be comforted.

It was difficult not to be upset when girls whom I had gotten to know in the sanatorium got sicker and sicker and finally gave up their fight to stay alive. Most were young girls in their late teens or early twenties for whom liberation from years of incarceration and starvation had come too late. After months of illness and suffering, they died. Glickel had survived many years of "life" in the Lodz ghetto. Her pain threshold was rather low, and my friends and I were often impatient with her frequent complaints of aches and pains. Then she was stricken with tubercular meningitis. Now no one could doubt that she suffered excruciating headaches. She was isolated from the rest of us, but her cries could be heard through the wall that separated us from her. There were no antibiotics, and painkillers seemed to have little effect. The only member of a large family to have survived the war, Glickel, too, was finally claimed by death. Mentally I had refused to feel sorry for her when she was complaining of pain while she seemed to be recuperating with us. While I protected myself, I had failed her. My impatience with her many complaints had been terribly unjust, but my remorse came too late. Other young girls slipped away quietly and almost heroically.

Perhaps it was these girls' suffering and their eventual deaths that shamed me into questioning my general cheerfulness. At times I was downright optimistic although there was little reason for it. My childhood faith, jolted well before my incarceration, had long been replaced by a pervasive skepticism. I decided that I had inherited my optimistic attitude from my father, and like his, it defied reason. Nevertheless, Eva's and my survival encouraged me to be hopeful. Why had we been so lucky? When we were asked: "How come *you* survived?" I could only answer that it was luck that had enabled us to survive. Then why did I feel shame whenever I thought myself lucky? We had been neither particularly courageous nor particularly smart. Had we not behaved decently toward our fellow prisoners? Even if we had wanted to "sell" ourselves for food, as was occasionally intimated by our questioners, who would have found two skinny young girls attractive?

No one ever asked us that far more difficult question: How come you landed in a concentration camp? We ourselves hardly dared ask it. It was years before I was able to read contemporary history. While I found explanations verging on excuses and theories that contradicted each other, or worse still, denied the events or blamed the victims, I did not find an "overarching" explanation for the catastrophic events of the war years. In the 1940s, the study of the Second World War had, if anything, barely begun. There is no longer any paucity of general or specific histories of the Second World War, and since the opening of the archives in Moscow after the Soviet Union's collapse in 1989, additional documentation has become available. One historian has even complained to me of his holocaust fatigue.

I thought a lot about my past life and tried to understand what had happened, if only to find some meaning for my feelings. I did not want to hate the Germans, and I did not want to blame my father for having been too trusting or too obedient. I only rarely used the phrase "If only," but I could not believe that what happened to us had been inevitable or could not have been averted, or worse still, that somehow we had brought it upon ourselves.

Several factors were pivotal in our survival: Father's decision to bring us back to Hannover late in 1941; the relative lateness of our deportation in June 1943, and Eva and my way of compensating for each other's weaknesses during our time in camp; our inexplicable resilience and innate self-control. I often wondered what would have happened if Father's request to join the Riga transport had been granted. It would have spared him the agonies of the last two years in Hannover—but would Eva and I have survived? Not many of the original one thousand Jews from Hannover who were deported to the Riga ghetto from our congregation survived the almost four years of incarceration in various camps. Being twins, a condition Eva said she had always disliked, helped us to become *Läuferinnen* (messengers) in Auschwitz. And as a result, we may have gotten to Reichenbach (i.e., Langenbielau) in somewhat better condition. Even so, I fell sick soon thereafter. Finally I was fortunate to have been taken to Sweden the moment the war ended and put into the hands of competent physicians who were trying to help us and in many instances succeeded.

My future was shrouded in darkness. I was aware of the temptation my illness afforded me to be taken care of for the rest of my life. To reenter everyday life, I would have to overcome not only that temptation but also the power of this particular illness to stigmatize and exclude me from the rest of humanity.

Occasionally one of the mostly elderly nurses in the sanatorium would ask us to tell her about our life in the camps. We all reacted in the same way: We recalled an incident with some humorous implication and dissolved in uncontrollable laughter. To this day, I see Nurse Sigrid's white locks shake in surprise at our reactions, which must have been so strange to her. Thus we managed to evade the harsh facts. Despite this avoidance, I was certain that I would never forget my experiences. Holding on to my memories was a necessity, my means of preserving the brittle connection I felt with my former life. At times those memories, powerful and inconvenient, made the present appear unimportant and without significance. Then I recalled my mother's expressed wish for a less good memory. I was beginning to understand what she had meant.

Some help came in the form of books. Among many others, I read Plato's *Dialogues*, Descartes's *Meditations*, Spinoza's *Ethics*, and later, both Freud and C. G. Jung. Not surprisingly, I took from these tomes what suited my needs, not what they might have taught a better educated reader. I no longer know why Descartes confirmed for me the preeminence of mental functions and their separateness from those of the body. He enabled me to rationalize both my very deep-seated doubt and my very tenuous awareness of my body. After I read Jung, I decided that I had to categorize myself as "introspective." A coward in many respects, I had courage in abundance to read more than I could possibly have digested.

Very soon it was made clear to me that once I left the sanatorium, it would be very difficult for me to go to school. And as Dr. Steffen wrote to Grete, he was against my going to Stockholm in order to get an education. My solution at the time was to order a correspondence course in algebra—a decision that still makes me blush, since it was not a subject I had expected to be missing.

Both doctors and nurses reiterated that I would have to be "careful" all my life. Why should I fare any better than Eva or the other girls whom no one thought of giving an opportunity for an education? A few years later in England, when I dared voice my pain at lacking almost all formal education, I was told: "Don't be so ambitious. Be glad you survived." It became a refrain I was to hear from many quarters.

At home I had learned that worldly goods were of relatively little importance, and I had come to a similar conclusion. Among the many reasons why the Jews did not leave Germany in time, their fear of losing the security provided by their possessions played a not insignificant role. Ironically, the Nazis robbed the Jews of their possessions before they murdered them. Understandably, Jewish anxiety about emigration was reinforced by the additional fear of lacking the skills or not finding opportunities to support themselves in a strange country. They could not know that eventually they would be condemned to lose not only their last possessions but their lives. Perhaps if they had been less afraid of the hardships of poverty in a new country, a few more Jews could have saved themselves—provided that other countries would have offered them shelter. My judgments of the relative importance of events and material things were also based on criteria I had acquired during the previous few years. As a result, I found it difficult to sympathize with anyone's material concerns or losses, and for a long time I had real trouble understanding that for most people such financial issues were not simply trivial.

I looked for precepts that could guide me, but there were few I believed truly important. My attitude toward my fellow human beings became my most crucial concern: I knew that to be indifferent to the suffering of others was unforgivable. I wanted neither to inflict pain on others nor to be hurt myself. At the same time I expected little help or sympathy from others, and it surprised me when someone acted with greater considerateness than I had expected.

I had lost my faith in God but not my fear of Him. Now I thought of myself as a human being first, and as a Jew second. In the concentration camp, I had found repeatedly that when people were in great need, stripped of all pretense, their religion had played little or no role in their behavior toward others. I had experienced kindness and cruelty from Jew and non-Jew alike. What enabled some to act humanely while others forgot all human decency was truly inexplicable. Despite the fact that my whole life, in all its aspects, had been determined by my being a Jew, and I intended to remain a Jew, I could no longer consider the fact of being Jewish of prime importance in my relations with others. Religion, I had learned, added a dimension of divisiveness to an already belligerent humanity that possibly outweighed its undeniable civilizing benefits.

In themselves, these notions were not particularly troubling to me, and I might have come to the same conclusions if my experiences had been more ordinary. My reading of Plato strengthened my belief that some of my ideas were innate. But I had trouble sorting out which of my notions were due to those eventful years and which were not. Trying to imagine what kind of person I could have become if my life had taken a different turn was a futile exercise. I had to conclude that my experiences set me apart from much of humanity. Not even Eva or my fellow camp mates shared the lessons I had learned from our common experiences. While I would not have minded standing somewhat apart from others, there was a gulf of incomprehension between myself and others that I did not know how to bridge except by ignoring, if not denying, what I had experienced.

At times, my solution was to refuse to admit the centrality in my life of what had been done to us and to maintain that I was shaped as much, or more, by my early years as by my incarceration. More rarely I managed to *admit* my estrangement, but while I mocked my pain as a form of self-importance, I felt less insubstantial and less dishonest on those occasions.

Despite my generally optimistic attitude, I found it almost impossible to make plans or to undertake any initiative. I could not believe with any consistency that the future existed for me. Death was the only certainty. I was just fortunate that it had been deferred for a while. This inability to believe in a future for myself cast a pall on all effort. When life presented challenges or difficulties, a feeling of defeatism immediately beckoned and had to be fought before I could begin to make any plans at all. At times this defeatism became a crutch and at others an excuse for inaction. I found it easy to withdraw into myself or, worse still, to use the old gambit—"It can't be real"—when I came face-to-face with an unpalatable situation. I had the impression that my, mostly Hungarian, girlfriends and fellow patients had matured quicker than I. They were less afraid to meet life head-on. Perhaps they questioned it less. However, that ever-present reminder of the inevitability of death in the sanatorium offered quite another temptation as well: to get hold of life as I found it, and to live it unquestioningly. Sometimes I thought I could follow that path.

There was no one with whom I could discuss these thoughts. My Hungarian girlfriends teasingly told me that I looked eleven and talked like a seventy-year-old.

Perhaps my reading strengthened my tendency to detach myself from spontaneous encounters and physical experience. Slowly, with lots of backsliding, I was learning not to express my disagreements and opinions of everyone and to everyone with such frankness, especially if what I had to say was not flattering. But when I restrained my critical attitude toward my friends, I not only—silently—deemphasized the differences between us, but learned to stifle much of my spontaneity.

Eva visited me in Fagereds and was surprised to see me so well, bicycling with friends and generally acting like a strong, healthy young girl. Her surprise quickly turned to fear when Edith, one of my friends, told her that bicycling was totally against the sanatorium's rules. The exertion was apt to cause me to hemorrhage. Late one afternoon, Eva saw me cycling down the road with a boyfriend. She planted herself in the middle of the road and stopped me in my tracks. I fell and badly gashed my elbow. I was taken back to the sanatorium, and Dr. Steffen was called from his private residence to attend to my injured arm. The kindest of men, he pretended not to know what had caused my accident. While he was stitching the skin on my elbow, I heard him say repeatedly: "*Spitsa stoener, spitsa stoener!*" ("[Those must have been] sharp stones!") Only later did Eva realize that my friend Edith, who had so alarmed her, may have had motives other than the preservation of my health.

I may briefly have been the envy of some of my friends because I had acquired a boyfriend. By the time I was allowed to be up all day, Ingvar Olsson, a young Swedish student, had already made the acquaintance of some of the refugee girls. Ingvar planned to become a journalist. I thought he was quite intrigued by us, because we were so different in both looks and demeanor from the Swedish girls he knew. He was surprised that I knew the story of Alfred Dreyfus, and I had little trouble impressing him with other bits of information I had garnered from my reading. He gave me Rilke poems to read, and we shared our preference for "Ernste Stunde" (Solemn Hour), whose first line, "*Wer jetzt weint irgendwo in der Welt*" (Whoever weeps now somewhere in the world), set a tone of human connectedness that moved me and appealed to him. The poem was also easier to understand than some of Rilke's other works. Before long we were friends, and he taught me to cycle. One day, as we sat together in the park-like surroundings of the sanatorium, he talked about his plans for the future. I understood it to mean that he was, somehow, including me. As I was listening to him and doodling in the sand, the word "dilemma" emerged under my twig. He demanded to know what I meant. I had to tell him that I did not think I could marry a non-Jew—despite my ardent wish not to differentiate between people of different religions. Ingvar left the sanatorium, but not before he had left me and befriended the young Hungarian girl who had so worried Eva a few weeks earlier when I was cycling with him. Edith had fewer dilemmas than I. Some months later Ingvar came for a visit and took Zofia and me to an outdoor, evening performance by the sea of *Hamlet* in Swedish. It was a wonderful experience. I still cherish my paperback copy of that Swedish performance with Ingvar's (Swedish) dedication: Hamlet, III, ii: "And let those that play your clowns speak no more than is set down for them." It has been, at times, a useful admonition. That my left elbow still has thick scars from that 1946 wound is not surprising. Dr. Steffen rarely needed to practice his stitching skills.

Zofia tried to comfort me when I lost Ingvar, but her advice went against my grain: "Always keep something in reserve, Rutka, and don't be so honest. Did he ask you about marriage? You could have enjoyed just being with him." But I was deeply hurt and took a long time to admit that I might have pushed him away. In waves, my pain came and went. Zofia scolded me and reminded me to go on enjoying life and the beauty of my surroundings. A romantic, she never gave up hope of finding new love. She kept herself alive by writing to her young daughter in Poland and to a Polish artist she had befriended in Sweden but had never actually met. I was very fond of Zofia. But I could neither read nor write in Polish, and when I left Sweden, I lost touch with her forever. But to this day I can speak a few sentences in Polish, and I still call squirrels by their Polish name.

Two other Polish women whom I got to know did not manage to create lives for themselves as Zofia had. Jadwiga, who was around fifty, occasionally visited Zofia and me and chatted with us. She had no family at all, and although she seemed gradually to recover from her camp experience and her illness, her prospects for her future were very bleak. One day when she had ostensibly traveled to Varberg for some shopping, she walked into the ocean instead. Eva, a pretty young woman, suffered terrible psychological agonies. I felt very close to her and spent evenings in her room listening to her talk of her experiences in camp. But that only increased her pain. One night she became so agitated we were unable to soothe her. She was taken to a mental hospital, and we never saw her again.

In the fall of 1946, I received permission to visit Eva in Stockholm, almost a day's journey by train. It was my first train journey since my liberation, and I enjoyed every moment as keenly as if trains had never taken me to other, terrible places. Eva and I were glad to be together. She had bought opera tickets, and we heard Borodin's *Prince Igor.* We paid a visit to an elderly couple from Hannover, the Hummels. They were quite aware of Eva's unhappiness and dissatisfaction but, besides sympathy, gave her little help. We were talking with them about our parents and their memories of them when Frau Hummel commented that our mother had been a beautiful woman. This greatly surprised me. I had never thought of her in those terms. And instantly I was back in Ahlem and recalled Father's praise of Mother's intelligence and musicality. I loved her, but even when I was a small child, I felt critical of her tendency to dramatize and see disaster in minor events. I did not think of her very often. When I did, I thought that she had perhaps been fortunate to have died so young. She, whose life had more than its share of misfortune, would have appreciated the irony in that thought. If she had been lucky, that luck surely had been our misfortune. It was years before I surmised that she may have been the more realistic, down-to-earth one of our parents. Although her judgment, in the 1930s, that we ought to leave Germany may have originated in her intense desire to be reunited with her own parents and siblings, it had been no less correct for that.

In December 1946, Grete came to Sweden to visit us. She was now a full-fledged nurse. We hardly spoke about the past. Together we traveled to Göteborg, where Eva boarded the *Gripsholm* for her voyage to New York. Our Uncle Akos, Father's half-brother, and his married daughter had provided the necessary papers to enable Eva to join them in Brooklyn. That week of reunion was to be the only time since childhood that Grete and Eva would have together during our lifetime. Upon Grete's return to England, she asked her friends to write to me. She assumed that Eva's departure had left me lonely. One of Grete's friends, a young man named Alfred Gutmann, started writing to me. He had come to Manchester from Germany, having arrived in England on the very day the war had started. Now he would soon leave England for the United States. My correspondence with him, at first a pleasant diversion, soon became an all-consuming interest. He wrote me in English, which I had started to read, and after a few months, I was able to respond in English.

My health improved steadily. Despite the dire prediction by that physician in Halmstad, the pain in my chest lessened. In December 1947, I said good-bye to my friends. I was especially sad to part from my roommate, Zofia. We had become friends. For a short time our affection for each other had managed to bridge the language divide. Dr. Steffen and I exchanged greetings every year until 1956, when he sent me a "self-portrait" to announce his retirement. Now I had to leave the protective environment of the sanatorium to join Grete in England. My pen friend had meanwhile left Manchester to join his family in New York. In July 1948, after we had exchanged many letters dealing with many different subjects and our feelings about the world and for each other, Alfred and I decided to marry. In April 1949, I joined him in New York, and we celebrated our wedding in the apartment he shared with his mother and uncle. Eva and I were happy to be reunited and to be able to live in the same country again.

11

Then and Now

Father

When I think of my father, I am certain that he knew what lay ahead of him, but that he nevertheless held fast to his faith in God. This was evident to us in all his expressions and actions during our time together in Theresienstadt and in Birkenau until the day we were separated from him. He never stopped being helpful to those in need. In Theresienstadt, he found a place to hold weekly Sabbath services, and even in Birkenau, he sang a shortened version of a Friday night service. But more than anything, it was his complete lack of anger, remarkable in a man who had always been quick to anger. Father's quiet acceptance of his fate, and the composure he showed us, said to me that he was at peace.

Not until the summer of 1939 did my father seek help from members of our Jewish community who themselves had managed to emigrate. He had helped many families with his own means to find safety abroad over the previous six years. When Margaret wrote him from England that she worried about owing her employers for the postage she needed to write him, he answers her in a letter of August 1939, that since the 1920s, "your parents gave away . . . two-thirds of my salary. You can tell your employers that once I am abroad, I shall repay them with compound interest." While in the 1920s our parents' gifts served charitable purposes, during the next decade their funds helped mostly poor Eastern Jews with large families to immigrate to Palestine. Even during the summer of 1939, he refused no one his assistance. And as always, he reports in the same letter, almost everyone, especially those with limited means, "look me up at home"—

which he expresses by a pun—before they leave the country. Since the archives of the Jewish community of Hannover have not been found (actions against the Jews during *Kristallnacht* on November 10, 1938, were said to have been ordered to include the confiscation of the archives of the Jewish community), only Father's letters of 1939 and 1940 to his daughters have been preserved. Now only I am left to testify to his generosity. He evidently extended his help so discreetly that the recipient did not know its source. Perhaps that is the reason why I have not heard of a single individual who, in the postwar years, has acknowledged his exceptional generosity. As likely is that everyone was occupied with their own problems, and good deeds of long ago were simply forgotten.

Aside from his deep concern for Margaret's well-being in her new English surroundings, two themes recur in our father's letters: First, his desire to leave, his hope to find work to support himself and his new wife—he stresses that he is ready to do any kind of work, no matter how menial—and second, no less important, his realistic fear that he will not be able to leave because the Gestapo intends to hold him in Hannover.

In another letter of late August 1939, Father speaks of needing the consent (*Einverständnis*) of the Schlägerstrasse (site of the Gestapo offices in Hannover) to emigrate.

> My longing for you and the Little Ones is surely no less than yours for your father, especially since you are feeling the loss of your dear mother. But, dearest Gretel, there is something you must, at your age, think about and understand. There have to be men who are ready to look every danger in the eye when the interest of the larger community demands it. In addition, and regardless of any danger to myself, I also have to remain here in the interest of the State [*Staatsinteresse*]. And when such factors are in play, neither my love for you children, my instinct for life nor my own well-being can take the place of this higher law which must take precedence and even replace personal consideration . . .

This is a strange statement, which seems to contradict those letters to Grete in which he urges her to help him emigrate as quickly as possible. He wrote it because he assumed that his letters were being read by the Gestapo. Now, with the help of the newly declassified documents in the main archive of Lower Saxony, we know that his assumption was correct. The Gestapo did read his mail.

These sentences were written for their benefit. He still expected that the time would come when he was no longer needed in Hannover. At that point he would be allowed to emigrate, "not a moment sooner." He clearly visualizes that liberating moment: "The preparations will be made in every detail. Then, with the consent of the *Schl[äger]strasse*, I shall buy my ticket, get on the train and leave."

This letter tells me that our father knew that he was in a very precarious situation. He was aware that he was under close scrutiny by the Gestapo. War was imminent. It is possible that the phrase "the interest of the larger community" refers to the increasingly impoverished Jewish community remaining in Hannover and its difficulties, difficulties he shared and which he had mentioned in the letter quoted above. But he also twice plainly tells his daughter—who may have wondered what he meant—that if he is forced to remain in Germany, he will be facing (unspecified) dangers. And by invoking the Third Reich's mantra: "The interest of the State," he was reminding the Gestapo that he, a Jew, continued to be a conscientious civil servant. He knew that while Jews were expected to act in "the interest of the State," the anti-Semitic literature of the time considered Jews constitutionally incapable of acting honorably.

While he was seeing his chances for escape dwindle, and the Nazi regime was unveiling another series of anti-Semitic restrictions, he seems nevertheless to have clung to the hope that he still had a little breathing room left. But in February 1940, he again wrote to Margaret to ask our Uncle Iszo in Palestine and, if needed, Uncle Akos in the United States to help him and his wife emigrate: "To any country whatsoever" (*In irgendein Land*). As we were wont to do until the Germans invaded Holland in May 1940, Eva and I forwarded that letter of Father's to Margaret. We had caught his urgency and begged Margaret to get to work on his request. When in November 1941, despite all Father's efforts and those of the relatives that Margaret asked for help, we were unable to emigrate to Cuba, he must have lost his last hope of escape.

A month later, shortly before the first deportation train left, this seems to have prompted him to volunteer himself and his family to join the majority of the remnant of our Jewish community on this transport to Riga. The Gestapo had other ideas. Their refusal to let him go meant that they still intended to make use of him. If Father understood this, he bore it, as he always did, totally alone. He confided in no one. I have described how the years 1941 to 1943 turned into the worst years of our father's life. He did not complain. We only saw a strangely silent, haunted man. But for his family it meant two more years in Hannover before we were deported in the summer of 1943.

My Thoughts about Father and His Work

Shortly after our liberation in May 1945, I began to think about our father's death and the events of the last years of his life. All the joys of our childhood had emanated from him. His love and concern for his children had guided most of his actions. Even under the most terrible conditions, he sought to protect us. Our stepmother was a good, attentive woman, but it was Father who, in the last five years of his life, replaced our mother for Eva and me. It is very painful to confess that there was a time years ago when I felt, despite many reasons to think differently, that there was a kind of "justice" in Father's death. Now I think that even to have had this thought is, to put it mildly, unforgivable. This was before sociologists and historians began the debates of the 1960s of the alleged cooperation and collaboration by Jewish officials and Jewish Ghetto Councils with the Nazis. It was grounded solely in what I thought I had observed of my father's attitude and what appeared to be his role vis-à-vis the Gestapo at the time of our return from Holland.

But ever since I began working with my translator on the German version of this memoir, I have been rethinking many of the events I have described. And I have perhaps a somewhat better perspective. A book by J. Walk, *Das Sonderrecht für die Juden im NS-Staat* (The Special Laws for the Jews in the National Socialist State),[1] helped me to see, in great and relentless detail, the hardships caused by those laws and regulations the German Jews faced in the 1930s and 1940s. Moreover, documents that were put at our disposal in the summer of 2000 by the *Hauptstaatsarchiv* (main archive) of Lower Saxony provided information completely new to me, and I shall come back to that below. While these documents do not constitute a complete record, some preliminary conclusions can be drawn from them. These documents and the letters my father wrote to us when we were in Holland in 1939 point to a situation in which it became increasingly difficult for a Jewish official like my father to continue to do his duty to his Jewish community and simultaneously obey the onerous Nazi laws of Germany. Gradually these two objectives had to come into conflict. Three examples will suffice to show how these problems developed; in one case the seeds of the problem can, in hindsight, be said to be apparent in the 1920s, the time of the Weimar Republic.

1. After the promulgation of the Nuremberg Laws in September 1935, Father's work with the Gestapo to identify and catalog "mixed marriages" and their offspring may not have done these groups any harm. On the contrary, if he could prove that, at the cutoff date, someone was not a member of the

Jewish community, and their children did not receive religious instruction, it could actually help. Nevertheless researchers now hypothesize that eventually the Nazis would have sterilized the offspring of these marriages, the so-called "mixed breeds."

2. The Nazis wanted the Jews to leave Germany. My father helped especially those in need to emigrate, both by asking wealthier Jews for extra contributions and by using his own funds. While it was the goal of the Nazis to rid Germany of its Jews, the lives of those able to leave the country were saved. In a similar vein, after the Austrian *Anschluss* in March 1938, Jewish organizations, such as the American Joint Distribution Committee, helped fund Jewish emigration from Austria so that there was no need to use German foreign currency reserves. Thus while the Germans were helped, so were the Jews who were enabled to leave.
3. As early as the 1920s, at the behest of the president of the Jewish community, my father worked at the Finanzamt to record the incomes of its membership. The purpose was to accurately levy the church tax (*Kirchensteuer*), which was payable to the German State. Since part of that tax levy was returned to the Jewish community (as to other religious institutions), it helped shore up the finances of the Jewish community for its multifarious activities and its many needy members. The Jewish community had lost many of its resources because of the inflation after the war. The synagogue had actually been defaced and badly needed to be repaired. The Jewish community also saved the fee—a percentage of the total tax—they had previously paid to the Finanzamt when the financial officials provided the information to them. Members of the Jewish community were, quite naturally, not pleased by this development. They must have seen it as an invasion of their privacy, and a number actually canceled their membership. But in the 1930s, the Nazi regime did everything, by passing special laws, to make it easier, even "legal," to gradually rob their former Jewish citizens of all their property. And having precise financial information about the holdings of every member of the Jewish community must have made that robbery even easier. By then, the earlier and expected cooperation with the German authorities had been turned into a weapon used against Jewish citizens.

In 1938, the Nazis decreed that all Jewish organizations were to be folded into a Reichsvereinigung der Juden in Deutschland. Now Jews were no longer considered *deutsche Juden* (German Jews) but Jews who happened to be living in Germany. The consolidation of the Jewish organizations seems to have taken a year to fully implement. It was the first step to concentrate the Jews figuratively under "one roof." They lost their last vestige of independence, because their officials now were under the direct control and command of Himmler's SS Security Office, the rightly feared Reichssicherheitshauptamt.

The only escape from this trap was emigration. The Nazis were still asserting that this was their goal also. It had always been puzzling to me why Father did not come to the same conclusion sometime in 1938 at the latest. Now, having read some of the already mentioned documents, I must assume that this may well have been impossible for him. The dangerous legal difficulties he experienced because of the registered account he kept in Switzerland for the support of his mother consumed a whole year: from August 1937 until his final exoneration on September 1, 1938. (We children had thought that his release from prison was also the end of his troubles.) In the December 1937 decision to free him from prison, the *Sondergericht* (special court without possibility of appeal) twice stated specifically that there was "no danger that the accused would escape." That statement may well have served as a warning to my father: No matter how justified his effort to emigrate would have been, the Nazis would have suspected that he intended to escape from his legal problems. Instead, while the case against him was being considered by three different courts, he began the more than yearlong work on Margaret's emigration to England, and resumed his more and more arduous work in the Jewish community. Only after his final exoneration, just two months before Nazi persecution became sheer terror with the pogrom of *Kristallnacht*, did he begin to speak and write about his own emigration again.

If the documents in the archives are to be believed, in late October 1941, the Gestapo gave my father and us permission to leave for Cuba. They "put in a good word" with the *Oberfinanzamt* to grant Father's request to use his stepdaughter's funds for the trip because he had less than four thousand marks of his own left. But we do know that Himmler issued a secret edict on October 23, 1941, forbidding all further Jewish emigration. It is as likely that the Gestapo's cancellation of our emigration was as much connected with the plans for the start of the deportations. When our emigration failed, Father seems to have resigned himself to his fate. That was the man I saw when my twin and I returned from Holland.

Before our own deportation, during the years 1941 to 1943 when I observed Father in actual contact with the Gestapo, I felt critical of him because of what

I saw as his anxious compliance with their demands. Just watching my father in Ahlem, as he hurried to cut the lilacs they were demanding from him, was painful to witness, because the change in his behavior contrasted so strikingly with how I remembered him. His old-fashioned courtesy had served always to underline his natural dignity. Now I saw only his humiliation and compliance. Did my father's compliance constitute "cooperation"? Can one speak of cooperation when a choice of action does not exist? And if the term "cooperation" is applicable in my father's case and in those of other Jewish officials in similar situations, we do not know precisely what this "cooperation" entailed and how it was achieved. The unprecedented nature of the circumstances in which these Jewish officials found themselves is impossible to judge or even to re-create with historical accuracy and fairness. Despite all the research and the many studies of the catastrophe that befell us, the various methods used by the Nazis to intimidate the Jews and force them to their knees may not be the whole story. I recall too well when Father walked out backward when he and I left the Gestapo offices after planting their tomatoes! In my father's case, I have some hope that these questions may find at the very least partial answers in the just begun research in the newly opened files of the *Oberfinanzdirektion* in the main archives of Lower Saxony.

While it may be possible to quantify how much property and other possessions the Nazis stole from the Jews in what one Hannover newspaper, citing H. G. Adler, calls the *Finanztod* (financial death) of the Jews before their deportation and likely murder or death, how do we quantify their suffering before they met their end? I believe that the degradation and the terror these Jewish men and women had to suffer constitute another part of this tragedy in which Father and others like him were forced to play a role.

I do not know with any certainty to what extent, and in what direction, my father's work during those terrible years of 1941 to 1943 affected the fate of members of our community. The question of the deportation lists that has troubled me for close to sixty years could now be resolved, at least in the case of Hannover. At the moment of my writing, it is still not certain whether it was the Jewish officials or the Gestapo that compiled and handed out the deportation lists. It is known that different demands were made of the Jewish officials in different German cities. In Hannover it must have been my father who not only had to notify the hapless Jews that their turn had come to be deported (as Klemperer did in Dresden), but also had to write the actual circular that informed them, a sample of which I have included in this book. What is documented is that the

Gestapo had to give permission for any change in those lists. When I returned from Holland, not yet fourteen years old, I thought my father had to prepare those lists. I could not realize how powerless my father was to confront the evil that faced him.[2]

Even so, I saw how Father suffered: Today that picture has become even grimmer because I have an inkling of what must have been his predicament. At the time the fifteen (or sixteen, depending on the definition) *Judenhäuser* (Jew houses) were established in accord with *Aktion Lautenbacher*, a representative of the Reichsvereinigung briefly visited Hannover. But when the deportations began, there was little or no opportunity for consulting with Jewish officials in other cities. They must have received the same or similar orders from the Nazi officials. "To pick up the telephone" was impossible. The fear that the Gestapo or their spies might be listening must have accompanied all activities. This isolation, which was planned and maintained by the Nazis, created a nightmarish atmosphere and prevented the formulation of any kind of perspective. We know today that Jewish officials acted similarly in other German cities, from the largest communities such as Berlin to the smallest ones. The opinion of Rabbi Leo Baeck that Jewish officials would show more consideration than the Gestapo when they took the defenseless Berlin Jews to the collection points for deportation—a decision to "cooperate" since real resistance was impossible—is probably only the best known among many, no matter how wrong his assumption about the "compassionate" helpers turned out to be.

Would my father have had greater freedom of movement if he had not brought Eva and me back to Hannover? That decision was, of course, connected to our failed emigration to Cuba, but in the end our return improved Eva and my chances of survival. The young family and their four small children with whom I had been living in Leiden for two years was deported from Westerbork and killed in Sobibor in March 1943. Eva's family existed precariously underground. At the very least, our return to Hannover must have made life more difficult for Father since it multiplied his family responsibility. Besides, we were a constant reminder that, despite much effort, he had not succeeded in saving us, just as he had not succeeded in completing Lotte's hoped-for emigration to the United States.

It took many years until I managed to grapple with this story. Questions I did not even dare to think, I shunned the longest: my father's presumed "guilt" and my dreadful feelings of shame to harbor such thoughts. But these evasions did not help me. Nor did the passage of time provide the necessary distance. On the contrary, my struggle to find words for this story has, if anything, brought those events closer again. The pain of these conflicted feelings has always remained with me. Nevertheless, I can only say that I have never stopped respecting, loving, and mourning my father.

I, too, have at times doubted the value of my survival. To have survived in the close proximity to the death of so many has had a lasting effect on my life. It was a daily occurrence in the family camp of Birkenau for me to be witnessing an old woman in the throes of death. I seemed to know what it must be like to be that person struggling with death. Then, with a sense of relief, I was able to pull away and remind myself that I was, after all, alive. But before long my relief gave way to a feeling of shame. Did I feel such relief after our father was gassed? I ask myself this question because there were almost two weeks of torment while we were waiting to be separated from him. We knew that after our removal from the family camp, our father and all those remaining there would be gassed. And that is what happened.

Only a year later, in the sanatorium in Sweden, I felt I had new cause to feel such shame when the girls I knew, former prisoners like me and no older than I was, died of their tuberculosis. Only by reminding myself of the certainty of my own eventual death could I ward off my shame.

Not so long ago it occurred to me that on July 10, 1944, when the time came for us twins to be marched out of the family camp of Birkenau, neither Eva nor I made an attempt to stay with our father. We could have made a different choice: We could have refused to leave him. I hasten to add that the words I am using do not describe that reality: We were not given a choice but were told that we were to assemble at the entrance to the camp—which meant that the dreaded moment of separation had come. And we obeyed as we always did and left. At that point we might have refused to move and would possibly have been shot on the spot. I do not wish to speculate how our father would have felt. My point is that it never crossed my mind to stay. I do not know about Eva. Neither Father nor we had broached such a possibility during the last few weeks even though we knew that we would soon be separated and that Father would be gassed. Instead, Father spoke to us of our sister in England, whom we were to join after the war. It took forty-six years for me to wonder what would have happened if we had refused to leave our father . . .

Eva

In the winter of 1946, I got permission from Dr. Steffen to visit Eva in Stockholm. She told me that she had met two of our former camp mates. The younger one had been, at most, in her mid-twenties when she became second in command to the *Lagerälteste* (camp elder) in the large women's camp in Birkenau. It was a position of "power" and "privilege." (Again, these terms then connoted a different reality.) She was a thin, dark-haired woman whose features expressed utter determination. She showed little mercy for the women prisoners who failed to immediately understand what she meant when she yelled at them. She was one of the very few surviving Jewish girls from Slovakia who had built Birkenau in early 1942. Her experiences of hunger and total deprivation, coupled with the brutality of the guards, must have helped to harden and even brutalize her. In Stockholm she lived together with an older woman whom we knew from Reichenbach, and they supported themselves as seamstresses. This young woman, whose name I can no longer recall, was shunned by many former prisoners who had known her in Birkenau. Eva and I decided to visit her. We did not think we should judge her. She deserved our sympathy.

Over the years Eva became less tolerant. I found that, in many respects, our ideas and judgments evolved in very different directions. Her judgments of others were based on the high moral standards she set for herself, and I knew that I had not met them. I was certain she remembered my failure to speak up in Birkenau and judged me to have been a coward. Yet because she had not succeeded in saving Father, she seemed to derive no comfort from knowing that her courage did not fail her when she tried to speak up for him.

Eva insisted that fate itself owed her compensation for her suffering and that, at the very least, she ought to be spared further pain. She brooked no opposition when I tried to dispute and assuage her frequent dark fears. Thus even quite impersonal political developments threatened her with personal disaster. Years of psychological treatment gave Eva the tools to question her own motives and those of others. But instead of ameliorating her suffering, this treatment seems to have repeatedly evoked the traumas she had experienced. At the same time she lost much of the warmhearted generosity that had been so much a part of her. It was very difficult to speak about our common experiences. If we tried at all, we differed about almost all details. Neither could we agree in our judgments of what aspects had been meaningful or what we had learned from our experiences. If Eva had recorded her memories of our experiences, as I have done here, she would have described them very differently. A letter—now in the archives of Yad Vashem—that she wrote to friends in Switzerland three weeks after our liberation in May 1945 in which she summarized the two years of our incarceration and the process by which the arriving Jews were essentially tricked into going into the gas chamber and taking off their clothes—is testimony to her more dramatic way of seeing and feeling everything. (The translated letter appears in chapter 9.) The experiences of our incarceration, which could have brought us closer, instead created disagreement between us. I had my own problems. My struggle with my memories was not won easily, and I did not understand Eva's attempts to find peace by a different road.

Some of Eva's and my disagreements must have stemmed from, or harkened back to, our childhood strife. We never learned to talk about our past jealousies or rivalry for Father's affection. And yet these feelings were mirrored in our relations because seemingly trivial subjects led to highly charged, even absurd, conflicts. Although we continued, until near the end, to have our reconciliations, we drifted apart.

The subject of our father and his actions soon became taboo. Eva had loved and trusted our father absolutely. Her disillusionment and anger at his final failure to protect her seem to have been equaled only by her pain to have been unable to save him.

Fate had no sympathy for Eva's hope or even expectation for some surcease, and illness and other misfortunes came her way. Although she struggled mightily with inevitable and ordinary disappointments and pain, these often overwhelmed her. We long hoped that her pronounced sense of humor and her ever-ready repartee with which she negotiated her life would help to sustain her. Finally she, too, had two talented children. But these new joys could not outweigh either old or new pain. Ever since losing Father at sixteen, she had felt that death would be the solution to her suffering. It was almost like a secret drawer to which she had access and that she kept at the ready. Her first attempts to end her life began in the 1950s. After almost a year in a hospital with capable physicians and a very interesting group of patients, Eva emerged strengthened and newly hopeful. She loved our two children and felt ready to have her own. But in 1973, my husband and I were returning from a visit to Margaret when we met Eva's husband at London's Heathrow Airport. He told us that Eva had committed suicide on July 12, 1973, while her children were away for the summer and he was on one of his business trips. It was twenty-nine years to the day that Father had been gassed in Auschwitz. Her children were told by their father that she had died of a heart attack.

It was evidence of her own determination and strength that she managed to overcome her problems long enough to have a family at all, even though her pain eventually defeated her. Perhaps understandably, she poured her memories and all her thoughts and feelings into her older child, a boy for whom she had the highest hopes on every plane of achievement. On our birthday, less than nine years after his mother's suicide, David took his own life. He was twenty-four years old, a law student at Harvard University. I think that David, too, was a victim of the catastrophe that befell us Jews. There are still times when the deaths of Eva and David haunt my thoughts. I cannot accept that there was nothing we could do to prevent these deaths.

Today I know that Eva and I had more in common than we were able to acknowledge. Our striving for self-protection and healing took different forms, but sprung from similar roots. For a long time now, I have considered our inability to confide in each other, to seek and give comfort, at least in part, responsible for her death.

The years between 1949, when I came to New York, and 1973, when Eva committed suicide, were often difficult. To build a new life without the requisite education or practical skills, to raise small children despite frequent doubt and despair, required strengths that I was surprised to find in myself. It helped me that my husband stood by me as a faithful friend. It was a fortunate circumstance for me that he was a refugee who had managed to get to England days before the war broke out. His more "normal" past helped both of us. Eva's husband was a survivor who struggled with his own problems in addition to those Eva brought into the marriage. During much of that time, my own difficulties were overshadowed by those of Eva. But by the time my own son and daughter started school, I gradually learned that I had my own life to live.

Margaret

Faith did not die in our family. It lived on in the life of our sister Margaret. After some years of pursuing her career in several different branches of nursing, Margaret married a German Jewish refugee in London. Together they raised and educated two girls and two boys in strict Jewish Orthodoxy, and her children and many grandchildren continue to actively practice their faith. After Margaret was widowed, she resumed her nursing work until retiring some years ago. Then she became a licensed piano teacher and taught children the piano. Margaret died in London at the age of eighty.

Today it may be difficult for full-fledged members of a democratic society to understand the many differences between our society and the Third Reich. Then repression and fear of informants ruled almost all thought and behavior. Already in the early years of the twentieth century, ideas such as the "purity of the German race," the need to combat outsiders and to sterilize and then euthanize the mentally disabled, all those considered deleterious to the German community (*Volksgemeinschaft*), were prevalent. Later, during the Nazi regime, these ideas and theories became lethal because the German society was willing, even eager, to convert them into deeds. And although such ideas were widespread in other European countries as well as in the United States, they did not lead to the German result. These differences are indisputable. From today's perspective, regardless how large or small our focus may be, it is still difficult if not impossible to understand the decisions that made it possible to convert these fixed ideas into deeds of the worst brutality. As for the thoughts and suffering of the Nazis' victims, I can speak only from my own perspective, and I must confess that there are still times when it is difficult to believe that these inhumane actions could actually have been carried out.

Conclusion

It is now hard for me to believe that my experiences from 1939 onward were not crucial in shaping at least some aspects of my later life, such as my reactions to new challenges. I would have preferred to assume that while these experiences were difficult, I would have been who I became no matter what. And I maintained this posture of what I now see as denial most of the time. It was my daughter, Hannah, who told me that she understood this denial first and foremost as my attempt not to concede defeat. "You wanted to deny the Nazis that final victory." All I knew was that it was my aim to protect my children from the worst aspects of my experiences and my negative outlook, a task difficult at best and sometimes impossible. My refusal to regard these experiences decisive for my life helped me not to feel bitter and shielded me from the guilt I bear. At the same time, it placed the burden of real or perceived shortcomings and failings in my adult life strictly on myself rather than, at least in part, on the unusual and disruptive circumstances of my youth. It was hard for me to reconnect to ordinary life, and to admit my desire for a modest share in it, and what success I had was interspersed by many difficulties. Sometimes I felt that my present reality was little more than a garment that I could slip off with some ease. My old habit of detachment provided a haven that I had to struggle to forgo because close relationships were often threatened by fearful forebodings of separation and even death.

Only with my family could I find the consolation I needed—but it was my children who showed me, by their more wholesome approach to life, how flawed and incomplete the life I was leading had become. But while I learned from them, they, no doubt, absorbed some of what continues to trouble me.

There are still times when I, too, use the absolute moral yardsticks of my childhood instead of the more forbearing judgments that so many situations, and especially the Nazi era, call for. Faith and doubt continue to be at war in me although it is the temptation of my childhood faith with its unfulfilled promises I struggle against most.

I continue to brood about my father's life and to mourn his death and the deaths of those I have loved. My experiences as well as my reading about the period have convinced me that the majority of the murdered millions could not have averted their fate. That is not to say that their fate was inevitable or that they were responsible for it. The responsibility for the suffering and deaths lies with those whose maniacal ideas unleashed those deeds. But it must also be said that the guilt for these events must be shared by those who were too slow, reluctant, and miserly to avert them: the democratic countries of that era.

Afterword

Primo Levi's Last Book

> Before discussing separately the motives that impelled some prisoners to collaborate to some extent with the Lager authorities . . . it is necessary to declare the imprudence of issuing hasty moral judgment on such human cases. Certainly, the greatest responsibility lies with the system, the very structure of the totalitarian state; the concurrent guilt on the part of individual big and small collaborators (never likable, never transparent!) is always difficult to evaluate. It is a judgment that we would like to entrust only to those who found themselves in similar circumstances and had the opportunity to test for themselves what it means to act in a state of coercion. Alessandro Manzoni, the nineteenth-century novelist and poet knew this quite well: "Provocateurs, oppressors, all those who in some way injure others, are guilty, not only of the evil they commit, but also of the perversion in to which they lead the spirit of the offended." The condition of the offended does not exclude culpability, which is often objectively serious, but I know of no human tribunal to which one could delegate the judgment.
>
> –Primo Levy, "The Gray Zone"

Primo Levi warns us in the words of a much-revered writer of the nineteenth century not to judge others hastily, but it is a warning he himself finds difficult to follow. He also believes that: "To polemicize with a dead man is embarrassing and not very loyal, all the more so when the absent one is a potential friend and a most valuable interlocutor: but it can be an obligatory step."[1]

Primo Levi addresses his "potential friend" Jean Amery, survivor of Auschwitz and a writer like himself. Amery, whose name was Hans Maier, was born to a Catholic mother and a Jewish father. After the Nuremberg Laws were promulgated, he fled to Belgium and joined the anti-Fascist resistance. He was caught, tortured, and sent to Auschwitz. His 1966 book about his experiences was one of the first to describe Auschwitz. Only a few years earlier, before Primo Levi "engaged" Amery, Amery ended his own tortured life. Shortly after the appearance of the Italian edition of *The Drowned and the Saved*, Levi, too, committed suicide. When corresponding with Amery, he had argued against such an act. Interestingly, he had used the title for this collection of essays as his working title for his first book, *If This Is a Man*—his autobiographical report about Auschwitz. Eventually it became, in slightly modified form, the heading for one of the most important chapters of that first book. In that chapter, Levi critically scrutinizes the behavior of his fellow prisoners. One who catches his eye is the young man he calls Henri, about whom he is still thinking years later.

Many years have passed since I read Primo Levi's *The Drowned and the Saved* for the first time. I have reread it many times, and as I am still finding it a painful task, I have given it a good deal of thought. Levi has long since become an icon. The precision with which he, a young man, recorded his experiences in Auschwitz and the ability with which he spoke for all survivors has earned him, together with his later writings, well-deserved recognition and influence. Levi never hesitated to describe even his worst experiences calmly and with scientific clarity. Despite his palpable despair, this holds equally true for the chapter "The Gray Zone." Here his main subject is that special group of prisoners, the prisoner-functionaries (*Funktionshäftlinge*), kapos, among them. These prisoner-functionaries were mostly longtime prisoners who were coerced by the SS guards to help run and administer the Lagers. There were not only many different Lagers, but many different prisoner-functionaries. According to Primo Levi, regardless of the circumstances, all shared two attributes: power and privilege. While both terms have their problems, and they are difficult to separate, "privilege" is even more difficult to define in the Lager situation. One should not forget that not all prisoner-functionaries used their privileges for their own ends.

In "The Gray Zone," Primo Levi repeatedly crosses the Auschwitz boundaries when he points out that undeserved privilege is by no means confined to the Lager; it exists everywhere in the outside world as well. Levi actually crosses eleven times into the outside world in this essay. To my knowledge, this has not been sufficiently analyzed. "The ascent of the privileged, not only in the Lager, but in all human coexistence, is an anguishing but unfailing phenomenon. . . . It is the duty of righteous men to make war on all undeserved privilege, but one must not forget that this is a war without end."[2]

On the page before, Levi tells us that the meaning of privilege can be grasped, "if we only want to understand what takes place in a big industrial factory." I think that by comparing the privileged and powerful of the Lager with those having these advantages in the outside world, Levi blurs a crucial distinction: Unlike the privileged in the outside world, those "obscene and pathetic figures [in the Lager]", did not accept their functions freely. These functions were thrust upon them. Levi asks that only those who have lived in similar circumstances, and "had the opportunity to test for themselves what it means to act in a state of coercion", be allowed to judge these prisoners.[3] As these passages show, Levi wrote these essays, and this one in particular, in a state of despair. He negates his own knowledge. He knows that these prisoners did not perform their functions voluntarily but then describes them to us as evildoers. It is the same with his plea not to judge others.

It is generally agreed that life "on the outside" is as different from existence in the Lager as night is from day. And, I would submit, even within the Lager, the vantage point of the ordinary prisoner differed greatly from that of any prisoner-functionary. An ordinary prisoner, exposed to one or more of the many injustices perpetrated by a kapo—a particularly low and frequently vicious example of foreman—would lack the strength of body and mind to understand what was being done to him. I agree with Levi that this was especially true at the traumatic moment of arrival in the Lager. And Primo Levi, even if he could not at first comprehend the circumstances, seems for decades to have nursed his memory of the offenses done to him at the time of his own arrival. His first essay in this collection is appropriately called "The Memory of the Offense," in which Levi assures us that he has preserved his memories, contrary to the perpetrators who deny their misdeeds, or their many victims who try with more or less success to repress the worst of their memories. And even forty years later, Levi is unforgiving about the way "old-timers," mostly functionaries, treated the "newcomer" arriving on a transport. He was not being taken by the hand and eased into the misery that awaited him! Clearly to remember this offense is not sufficient. While memories need to be preserved, they must also be understood.

And the "old-timers" had reasons to resent those of us who came later. I knew young women from Slovakia, then the eastern part of Czechoslovakia. These young women, in their early twenties, had been deported to Birkenau when that camp was just a name. It was the spring of 1942. They built roads and barracks. They lost their mothers and sisters. Some died in a massacre.[4] When we arrived in May 1944, perhaps two hundred and fifty out of an original contingent of roughly ten thousand had survived. Most were in positions of that vaunted privilege.

In Birkenau, I gradually came to understand that the differently colored triangles of these prisoner-functionaries did not necessarily describe the character of such men and women while the colors told everyone why they had been incarcerated. I am speaking here mostly of non-Jewish Germans who had been Socialists or Communists, or accused of consorting with foreign nationals. Their mark was a red triangle. Or those with a green triangle: the convicted criminals who, after serving their sentences in a jail, were actually rearrested and thrown into the Lager; and those with the black triangles of the so-called asocials, and other assorted "undesirables" who might be sex offenders, prostitutes, or possibly Sinti and Roma (Gypsies). Among those marked with the black triangle, many came from the lowest strata of German society, whose poverty and unsettled family situations were likely contributing factors in their problems with the law. These functionaries' behavior differed greatly toward the ordinary prisoner, both when we arrived and later, and I was at the receiving end of both good deeds and vile misdeeds. What they did have in common were untold years of incarceration, which seem to have had different effects on their actions and reactions to us. It was only after the war, by thinking about such persons and reading about their inescapable situation, that it became more comprehensible to me just how horrible and tragic their own Lager existence must have been.

There were many different kinds of functionaries, running the gamut from those with "real" power to those, like myself, who as messengers had to run from one end of the Lager to another to deliver messages for the SS guards. And there was, I believe, another important difference among functionaries. There were those, and I think many longtime prisoners were in this group, who had begun to adapt to, and probably even accept, their existence in Auschwitz and other Lagers as the only life they had, or were likely to have. Other functionaries saw their existence in the Lager as an overwhelming, but hopefully only temporary, misfortune. I believe it was such differences in attitude that influenced and even dictated their behavior, aside from the SS guards, who always stood above them and to whose orders both groups succumbed. It was that ultimate, absolute force whose decisive role Levi unaccountably slights. This may be due to a peculiar circumstance in the Lager. While prisoner-functionaries were ever present, the SS guards were often invisible. But that did not alleviate the prisoner-functionary's fear of them, because the SS's behavior was unpredictable. They would suddenly appear and call the prisoner-functionary to account. It was probably the first group of prisoner-functionaries that was more likely to achieve, at any cost, some semblance of success, be it in the acquisition of privilege or power, or satisfaction of any kind. Levi dwells at length on that cruel reception he and other newly arrived prisoners were accorded by those old-time prisoners. It was probably that "adapted" group that could not tolerate being reminded of the outside world and, concomitantly, of the losses they had sustained. Those newcomers had enjoyed the outside world years longer than they, and the newcomers had no inkling of the turmoil their arrival must have caused in the functionaries. Not incidentally, no question was asked as frequently in Auschwitz as "How long have you been here?" Much revolved around our answer and determined the questioner's attitude toward us. But even though we soon learned what that question implied and might have wanted to lie, the numbers on our arms answered for us.

The second group of prisoner-functionaries tended to retain the value system of the outside world and with it a better perspective on their surroundings. It was this second group that was more likely to look for ways of resisting their jailers. They knew that this was an environment of total lawlessness in which personal ambitions could play only a dubious part. The prisoners' prior political experience and education may well have influenced this process of adaptation or resistance. Nevertheless it would be an oversimplification—and Primo Levi warns us repeatedly against simplifying the conditions in the camps—to sort these longtime prisoners into the usual political and criminal groups. Matters were never that simple in the Lager, and it would be a mistake to insist that there was only one morality and only one correct and one incorrect way to act in the camp. For the ordinary prisoner, these differences in the behavior of the various functionaries could have crucial consequences. Rarely did a prisoner know who the person was who confronted him, and he or she was at the mercy of the unpredictable mood of the functionary. But I have to stress that it makes little sense to judge the behavior of the prisoner-functionaries as an independent phenomenon since they were wholly dependent on those who had, always contingently and temporarily, ordered them to assume the power they wielded, namely, the SS guards.

No prisoner-functionary was more affected by the direct dictates of the SS guards than those chosen for the *Sonderkommandos*. It was mostly Jewish men who were forced to work in the crematoria. Often they were chosen for this work at the time of their arrival when they were confused and ignorant of the environment into which they had been thrust. Levi rightly emphasizes that "conceiving and organizing the squads [*Sonderkommandos*] was National Socialism's most demonic crime. . . . This institution represented an attempt to shift onto others—specifically the victims—the burden of guilt, so that they were deprived of even the solace of innocence. . . . In fact, the existence of the squads had a meaning, a message: 'We, the master race, are your destroyers, but you are no better than we are, if we so wish, and we do so wish, we can destroy not only your bodies but also your souls, just as we have destroyed ours.'"[5]

Despite Levi's evident, profound insight into the workings of Nazi thinking, and his repeated warnings about judging these men whom he calls "the crematorium ravens" in these extraordinary, inhuman circumstances, he himself does not refrain from making judgments. But his judgments are usually directed at the prisoner-functionary, much more rarely at the true villain: the Nazi perpetrator. Levi twice calls the *Sonderkommandos* "collaborators,"[6] and speaks of their "acquiescing" in performing their grisly work. He speaks of them, and the *Judenrat* of the Warsaw ghetto, moreover, in the same breath as the Quisling of Norway and Vichy France and the Salo Republic of Italy. Was this not the moment to pinpoint the central difference between the decision of a Quisling to betray his homeland to the Nazis and any person in a Lager, plucked from among the arriving masses at the ramp to perform any work whatsoever? I have asked myself over and over again, why did Primo Levi, scrupulously fair to even his Nazi tormentors, not see this? Did Levi fall victim to his own despair and shame? Indeed, "Shame" is the title of the next essay in the collection, in which he relates his failure to share with others some sips of water he and his friend had discovered, a failure that was to haunt him all his life. Levi asks that "we meditate on the story of the 'crematorium ravens' with pity and rigor, but that judgment of them be suspended," yet his own words reveal a recurring moral conflict.[7]

Some of Levi's readers believe that what afflicted Levi was his rage, not with these prisoner-functionaries, but with those who appointed them: the Nazi jailers of the Lager. Levi rarely bothers to distinguish between "Nazis" and "Germans": Mostly he speaks of the Germans. The last part of his book deals with his longtime and extensive correspondence with an assortment of Germans: those who had begun to comprehend what had happened during the Nazi era and those who never did. Levi never fails to be courteous and attentive, but one has to wonder whether he attends sufficiently to his own feelings toward "the Germans." That may be why he continued to show a kind of forbearance toward the perpetrators that he does not consistently grant that most tragic group of workers of that time: the *Sonderkommando.*

Levi starts his essay "The Gray Zone" with the question: "Have we—we who have returned—been able to understand and make others understand our experience?"[8] He does not answer that question except indirectly, and with evident bitterness. Those who survived, he believes, were the wily, who—to put it mildly—managed by hook and by crook to obtain more food than the others; the good were by necessity submerged. We, the survivors, all resemble Chaim Rumkowski, the compromised and compromising ghetto elder of Lodz, although Levi admits that, eventually, Rumkowski's attainment of temporary power and privilege could not save his life either. At the end of his essay, Levi reveals why in his analysis of the behavior of the prisoner-functionaries he has so frequently crossed the border between camp and outside world: He believes that it is our flawed human nature itself that is to a greater or lesser degree "provoked by oppression."[9] And that, he stresses, is valid not only for the past, but for the present and future of our civilization as well.

Why is it that "The Gray Zone" holds me captive? Levi and I lived different lives both before and after the war. Primo Levi was fortunate not to have lost any family members in Auschwitz although he had many friends among the thousands of Italian Jews who died or were gassed there. He was able to return to his country, to resume his profession, and to die in the house in which he had been born. In Auschwitz, too, where he eventually worked as a chemist, and I, being a twin, as a messenger, we had very different experiences. Even so, I, too, have had considerable difficulty dealing with my conflicts about the perpetrators and bystanders, the Germans of that time.

Over the years I have sometimes been told by a friend about a memory of a hurt or injustice inflicted in everyday experience by another human being that he or she has been unable to forget. By my yardsticks, these experiences were relatively trivial. Sometimes this has caused me to ask myself: Since this is how people react to an experience of fairly minor injustice, how do you truly feel about what happened in the Lager, and about those who perpetrated these deeds? While I have so far been unable to answer that question, I have long known that I prefer being a victim to being a perpetrator.

On the whole, it is much easier to reflect on the different behaviors of one's fellow prisoners: For example, the already mentioned Henri,[10] the young man who, according to Levi, after the death of his brother—actually his only friend—"does everything" to survive; he even "befriends one of the functionaries." And so one thinks about one's fellow prisoners' resilience or lack of it, their helpfulness, their indifference or cruelty vis-à-vis others or oneself, and most of all, their will to live. To think about oneself under those circumstances is much more difficult.

Under the extraordinary circumstances prevailing in the Nazi camps, both helpless prisoners and privileged functionaries acted, if they were still capable of something deserving that term, according to their understanding of any particular moment. Almost invariably, that meant that their own survival was uppermost in their mind. Even so, it is beyond question that there were women, like my stepsister, not quite nineteen-year-old Lotte, who, when she heard the warnings of friends on the ramp to leave her one-year-old boy, refused to part with him and went with the child to her death. But when she arrived in the chaos that was the ramp of Birkenau, did Lotte know what awaited her and her little boy? Precisely because of the circumstances in the Lager, such actions and reactions were rarely freely chosen. The coercive environment in which we existed puts into question the whole notion of the meaning and possibility of choice.

But the political structures that lay behind the invention of the Lager are another matter, and Levi's analysis breaks down when he compares aspects of it to the everyday injustices of our common world. What lay behind that failure can only be surmised. He may have seen the continuing conflicts and wars with their killings in numerous places of the world during the decades following the holocaust as proof of his personal failure to make the world understand what it had allowed to happen. That disappointment could have been the cause for his numerous allusions to the undeserved privilege and other injustices extant in the outside world. I, too, have in occasional despair thought that "the whole world is no better than a concentration camp." I, too, would have preferred to be able to say that the Allies, who, we learned, heard our cry for help, did have the will to save us. (Writing a review of the book that told us of the Allies' knowledge of events in "the east," a British historian made clear that "we did not fight the war to save the Jews.") Cries for help continue to be heard from many places. Often we fail to convert indignation at some slaughter in distant or not so distant countries into action. Occasionally the world shows its potential for good, and there is the will to do what is in our power to prevent or at least ameliorate disaster.

Appendix

Circular for Jewish Community Members Anticipating Deportation

From the Central Archive for the History of the Jewish People, Jerusalem

Translated from the German by Ruth Gutmann.

District Office Northwest Germany of the Reichsvereinigung of the Jews in Germany. Administrative Office, Hannover

Circular 1

Hannover, July 11, 1942
Bergstrasse 8
Telephone 4-01-92

Mr.
Mrs.
Miss

On orders of the authorities we are required to inform you that
You
Your wife
Your children

Have been included in a transport to migrate to Theresienstadt that will in all likelihood leave Hannover on the 23rd of this month. We are kindly asking you to complete the enclosed declaration of your resources. This is to be done separately for you, for your wife, and any person expected to be migrating with you. This is to be done carefully and returned to Bergstrasse 8 no later than midday of the 17th of this month. Keeping this date is absolutely necessary. A clear handwriting is essential.

Not to be included in the declaration:

1. Those items that people expect to take along when they migrate (50 kilogram). For this information compare Circular 2.
2. Those items that are intended as equipment for the whole transport (sewing machines, tools, cooking pans, etc.).

All documents relating to your possessions, such as proof of mortgages and savings bank accounts are to be attached to the declaration of your possessions. The amounts currently allowed for your limited use by the Finanzamt and Foreign Currency Division may be withdrawn to the extent of the permitted amount. Should you need your bank book, you may retain it for the time being, but it must be brought to the place of collection for the transport.

On orders of the authorities every participant of the transport must donate part of his available funds to the Reichsvereingung. The donation should not be less than 25% of your available funds. This should not include other possessions.

Your donation is to cover the amounts other participants are allowed to take along [but do not possess?] and cover the cost of equipment etc. Other uses are for the Welfare needs of the Reichsvereinigung. Besides the above, the usual fees for the Reichsvereinigung for all of 1942 and any outstanding debts to the RV of prior years, as well as the specially assessed amount for the year 1942 are to be paid now.

The enclosed donation form is to be completed for your donation that you will pay to the RV.

These donations and contributions are not to be included in the completed declaration. They are to be deposited at the

Dresdner Bank, Branch Hannover, Acct. 57158.

Or paid in cash to our office Bergstrasse 8.

Your donation is to be paid to the address in Hamburg as shown on the donation form.

We call your attention to the importance of completing the declaration of your resources with great care. Untrue or unclear information will be severely punished by the authorities issuing this order.

If you still have bicycles, cameras, light meters, enlargement equipment, binoculars, typewriters, calculators, electrical equipment and spare parts, these are to be brought to Bergstrasse 8 without delay, or for those outside Hannover on this transport, by mail.

Every item that is brought to the office must be carefully labeled with the owner's first and second name.

These items are not to be included on your list of resources either.

District Office Northwest Germany
of the Reichsvereinigung of the Jews of Germany
Administrative Office, Hannover.

Notes

Prologue

1. *Beiträge zum 300. Jahrestag der Errichtung des Landesrabbinate Hannover am 10. März 1987. Hrg. Vom Landesverband der Jüdischen Gemeinde von Niedersachsen, der Jüdischen Gemeinde Hannover und Peter Schulze, et al., Hannover, 1987* (Contributions in Observance of the Three-Hundredth Anniversary of Establishing the Rabbinate, March 10, 1987), issued by the Association of the Jewish Communities of Lower Saxony, the Jewish Community of Hannover and Peter Schulze et al. (Hannover, 1987).

2. David Sorkin, *The Transformation of German Jewry 1780–1840* (New York: Oxford University Press, 1987).

3. Ibid., 22.

4. Arnaldo Momigliano, "J. G. Droysen Between Greeks and Jews," in *Essays in Ancient and Modern Historiography* (Middletown, CT: Wesleyan University Press, 1977), 307.

5. Jacob Robinson, *And the Crooked Shall Be Made Straight: The Eichmann Trial, the Jewish Catastrophe, and Hannah Arendt's Narrative* (New York: Macmillan Co., 1965).

6. Hannah Arendt, *Eichmann in Jerusalem: A Report on the Banality of Evil*, revised and enlarged edition (New York: Viking Press, 1965).

7. Isaiah Trunk, *Judenrat: The Jewish Councils in Eastern Europe Under Nazi Occupation* (New York: Macmillan Co., 1972).

8. Birthe Kundrus and Beate Meyer, eds., *Die Deportation der Juden aus Deutschland: Pläne, Praxis, Reaktionen, 1938–1945* (The Deportation of the Jews from Germany: Plans, Actions, Reactions, 1938–1945), 2nd ed. (Göttingen: Wallstein, 2005), 20.

Chapter 1

1. Dovid Katz, *Words on Fire: The Unfinished Story of Yiddish* (New York: Basic Books, 2004), 243–53.

2. Bernhard Rust, who became minister of education, also was responsible for prohibiting the attendance of Jews at all German institutions of higher learning. He committed suicide at the end of World War II, May 1945.

3. Werner Weinberg, *Self-Portrait of a Holocaust Survivor* (Jefferson, NC: McFarland & Co., 1985). The Weinbergs succeeded in hiding their two toddler-age daughters in Holland during the Nazi occupation of Holland. However, one of the girls died during that period. The parents were deported to Bergen-Belsen, which, unbelievably, was considered a privileged destination. Dr. Weinberg, after his survival, became a professor of theology at Hebrew Union College—Jewish Institute of Religion in Cincinnati. I had the impression that he was uncomfortable in his role as witness and survivor. He sounded unreconciled to the suffering and survivors' guilt he and his family had endured.

4. Raul Hilberg, *The Destruction of the European Jews* (New York: Holmes & Meier, 1985), 1:53ff.

Chapter 2

1. Carol Herselle Krinsky, *Synagogues of Europe: Architecture, History, Meaning* (New York: The Architectural History Foundation; Cambridge, MA: MIT Press, 1985), 310–13.

Chapter 3

1. Martin Gilbert, *Churchill: A Life* (New York: Henry Holt & Co., 1991), 167.

Chapter 4

1. Martin Gilbert, *The Holocaust: A History of the Jews of Europe during the Second World War* (New York: Holt, Rinehart and Winston, 1985), 120.

2. Iszo's and Father's life had intersected in 1937 when Iszo sent funds to a Swiss account that Father held for his mother. Father's six weeks in prison were only the beginning of a long, drawn-out trial. In 1939, Iszo procured a permit for Father that would have enabled him to go to England. But his remarriage prevented Father's emigration. Of course, we do not know if the Gestapo would have let him leave.

3. Uncle Iszo may have arranged the emigration to Cuba that eventually failed.

Chapter 5

1. Despite Himmler's decree, a handful of Jews were able to leave Germany. Some eventually landed in Jamaica, others in the Dominican Republic, where traces of small Jewish refugee camps were discovered after the war.

2. Marlis Buchholz, *Die hannoverschen Judenhäuser: Zur Situation der Juden in der Zeit der Ghettoisierung und Verfolgung 1941–1945* (The Houses for the Jews at the Time of the Ghettoization and Persecution 1941–1945) (Hildesheim: August Lax, 1987). This study has still to be translated. It describes the period before the deportations in great detail, especially the so-called *Aktion Lauterbacher*, i.e., removing the Jews from their apartments and houses, and putting them into "Jew houses."

3. Uwe Dietrich Adam, "The Gas Chambers," in *Unanswered Questions: Nazi Germany and the Genocide of the Jews*, edited by Francois Furet (New York: Schocken Books, 1989), 134–54.

Years later I tried to find Cholm on a map of Poland. But Cholm was a fictitious asylum named on the notifications to the parents and relatives of the recently murdered disabled Jews and non-Jews. It was invented by T-4, the office in Berlin in charge of carrying out the euthanasia program set in motion with Hitler's signature in October 1939, backdated to September 1, 1939. The date of death, attributed to some disease, was also falsified in order to charge the relatives for a period of upkeep in Cholm. Klärchen's actual place of death was probably Hartheim.

H. Immenkötter, *Menschen aus unserer Mitte: Die Opfer von Zwangssterilisierungen und Euthanasie* (Human Beings Who Lived in Our Midst: Victims of Forced Sterilization and Euthanasia) (Donauwörth: Auer, 1992). This was the Catholic home for the mentally disabled where my sister lived from 1934 until she was euthanized in September 1940. The book includes a photograph of Klärchen and another Jewish boy.

4. We know that Father assigned the cash value of his life insurance for that purpose. Henry Friedländer mentions Father's action in his study, *The Origins of Nazi Genocide* (Chapel Hill: University of North Carolina Press, 1995), 265. I thank Dr. Bernhard Strebel, the German translator of my memoir, for this information.

5. Sometime around 2002, I learned from my German historian friends in Hannover that they had evidence that the District offices in Hannover of the Reichsvereinigung der Juden in Deutschland were ordered by the Gestapo to produce the deportation lists. The Reichsvereinigung was the last Jewish organization in Germany. It encompassed the remnants of all Jewish communities, and was under the control of the RSHA (Reichssicherheitshauptamt) by way of the Gestapo. My father must have been the author of Circular #1 (Rundschreiben). Headed by the words "On Order of the Authorities," it tells the recipients that they, their wives, and children have been ordered by the Authorities to be included in the next transport to be sent to Theresienstadt. There was also a detailed list of what the deportees might take along. They were requested to set aside 25 percent of their liquid funds for the Jewish community to help defray the transportation costs!

Little did they know that what they may have chosen to take along would be stolen from them on arrival at their destination. In Theresienstadt, they might have kept a few things. Nor did they know that the 25 percent for which the circular asks was actually taken by the Gestapo and put in a special account. Thus the local Gestapo cheated their superiors at the RSHA in Berlin out of these Jewish possessions. A translation of this circular is in the appendix.

6. Hans-Dieter Schmid et al., eds, *Ahlem: Die Geschichte einer jüdischen Gartenbauschule und ihres Einflusses auf Gartenbau und Landschaftsarchitektur in Deutschland und Israel* (Ahlem: The Story of a Jewish Horticultural School and Its Influence on Horticulture and Landscape Architecture in Germany and Israel) (Bremen: Edition Temmen, 2008).

7. I have not found the author of that song.

8. J. Brahms, op. 94, no. 5. The text is by Friedrich Halm (1806–1871). I thank Dr. Marlis Buchholz for her help in identifying one of Father's last songs.

9. Beate Meyer, "Handelsspielräume regionaler jüdischer Representanten (1941–1945): Die Reichsvereinigung der Juden in Deutschland und die Deportationen" (Possibility for Action by Jewish Representatives [1941–1945]: The Jewish Umbrella Organization [RV] in Germany and the Deportations), in *Die Deportation der Juden aus Deutschland* edited by Birthe Kundrus and Beate Meyer (Wallstein, Göttingen, 2005).

Chapter 7

1. In 1999, the president of the Max Planck Society established a commission to investigate the past activities of its predecessor, the Kaiser Wilhelm Institutes (KWI), during the Nazi era. The commission members were German as well as international scientists. Their task amounted to "bringing the whole truth of the role of the KWI to light." It was known that the Kaiser Wilhelm Institutes' research for the war effort had gone hand in hand with medical and so-called racial-hygiene research.

One of its members, Professor Robert N. Proctor, now of Stanford University, an American authority on German biological sciences, cautioned that "it cannot be the whole truth. It no longer exists." Professor Proctor had researched the activities of the German Nobel Prize winner Dr. Adolf Butenandt, who was not only informed about the activities of his colleagues such as Otmar von Verschuer, mentor of Josef Mengele, but asked a coworker, Dr. Günther Hillmann, shortly before the end of the war, to destroy specially marked files in his own office. Furthermore, as late as 1949, Professor Butenandt was a member of a committee that declared that Dr. Otmar von Verschuer was in no way unethical to have used human remains from Auschwitz for his important scientific studies.

Just as eminent scientists destroyed their files before Germany capitulated, so present-day German scientists have had conflicting feelings about this search for historical truth. There are files that are not accessible until 2025. One of the reasons is alleged to be concern for the privacy of the patients whose remains had been investigated!

A special symposium was held at the Max Planck Society in Berlin in 2001: "The Biological Sciences and Experiments on Humans at the Kaiser-Wilhelm Institutes. The Connection to Auschwitz." One of its themes was Josef Mengele's twin research with Dr. Otmar von Verschuer, who received the dissected human remains from Auschwitz, and Dr. Karin Magnussen, whose eye research was conducted on the eyes of twin prisoners. Wallstein Verlag has by now published more than fifteen volumes dealing with the activities of the KWI during the Nazi era, and if relevant, during the decades before.

2. Ruth Elias, *Triumph of Hope: From Theresienstadt and Auschwitz to Israel*, trans. Margot Bettauer Dembo (New York: John Wiley & Sons, 1998).

The newborn infants were killed by injections of morphine. This was supplied by a sympathetic female dentist in the Revier, where they had given birth. Mengele had forbidden Ruth Elias to nurse her infant, warning her that both would be gassed. He was annoyed that he was unable to find the small bodies among the stack of the dead waiting to be burned.

Chapter 9

1. I base this description of what happened to the Meijer family on information received in 2000 from Gerda Wijler–Meijer. The family emigrated to Israel after the war and were largely responsible for creating Dutch-type cheese in Israel.

Chapter 11

1. J. Walk, ed. *Das Sonderrecht für die Juden im NS-Staat* (The Special Laws for the Jews in the National Socialist State), 2nd ed. (Heidelberg: UTB für Wissenschaft, Hüthig C. F. Müller, 1996). The volume includes an introductory essay by Robert M. W. Kempner, chief prosecutor at the Nuremberg Trials of November 1945.

2. Birthe Kundrus and Beate Meyer, eds., *Die Deportation der Juden aus Deutschland: Pläne, Praxis, Reaktionen, 1938–1945* (The Deportation of the Jews from Germany: Plans, Actions, Reactions, 1938–1945), 2nd ed. (Göttingen: Wallstein, 2005). A recently published monograph by Beate Meyer on this subject is currently being translated for publication in the United States.

Afterword

Primo Levi, *The Drowned and the Saved*, trans. Raymond Rosenthal (New York: Summit Books, 1988), 43–44.

1. Ibid., 127.

2. Ibid., 42.

3. Ibid., 41, 44.

4. Deborah Dwork, "Agents, Contexts, Responsibilities: The Massacre at Budy," in *Catastrophe and Meaning*, edited by Moische Postone and Eric Santner (Chicago: University of Chicago Press, 2003), 154–69.

5. Levi, *The Drowned and the Saved*, 53.

6. Levi does not even use quotation marks around the term *collaborators*.

7. Levi, *The Drowned and the Saved*, 60.

8. Ibid., 36.

9. Ibid., 61.

10. Paul Steinberg, *Speak You Also: A Survivor's Reckoning*, trans. Linda Coverdale with Bill Ford (New York: Metropolitan Books, Henry Holt,). Levi mistakes Henri for a "highly cultivated twenty-two year old." Paul Steinberg was not quite seventeen when he got to Auschwitz. Born in Berlin to Russian Jewish parents and raised in France, he spoke all three languages of his background.

Appendix

The German term for "migrating" was *Abwanderung*.

References

Adam, Uwe Dietrich. "The Gas Chambers." In *Unanswered Questions: Nazi Germany and the Genocide of the Jews*, edited by Francois Furet, 134–54. New York: Schocken Books, 1989.

Arendt, Hannah. *Eichmann in Jerusalem: A Report on the Banality of Evil.* Revised and enlarged edition. New York: Viking Press, 1965.

Beiträge zum 300. Jahrestag der Errichtung des Landesrabbinate Hannover am 10. März 1987. Hrg. Vom Landesverband der Jüdischen Gemeinde von NiedersachSen, Der Jüdischen Gemeinde Hannover und Peter Schulze, et al., Hannover, 1987 [Contributions in Observance of the Three-Hundredth Anniversary of Establishing the Rabbinate, March 10, 1987]. Issued by the Association of the Jewish Communities of Lower Saxony, the Jewish Community of Hannover and Peter Schulze et al. Hannover, 1987.

Buchholz, Marlis. *Die Hannoverschen Judenhäuser: Zur Situation der Juden in der Zeit der Ghettoisierung und Verfolgung 1941–1945* [The Houses for the Jews in Hannover: The Situation of the Jews at the Time of the Ghettoization and Persecution 1941–1945]. Hildesheim: August Lax, 1987.

Dwork, Deborah. "Agents, Contexts, Responsibilities: The Massacre at Budy." In *Catastrophe and Meaning: The Holocaust and the Twentieth Century*, edited by Moische Postone and Eric Santner, 154–69. Chicago: University of Chicago Press, 2003.

Elias, Ruth. *Triumph of Hope: From Theresienstadt and Auschwitz to Israel.* Translated by Margot Bettauer Dembo. New York: John Wiley & Sons, 1998.

Friedländer, Henry. *The Origins of Nazi Genocide.* Chapel Hill: University of North Carolina Press, 1995.

Gilbert, Martin. *The Holocaust: A History of the Jews of Europe During the Second World War.* New York: Holt, Rinehart and Winston, 1985.

———. *Churchill: A Life.* New York: Henry Holt & Co., 1991).

Hilberg, Raul. *The Destruction of the European Jews.* Vol. 1. New York: Holmes & Meier, 1985.

Immenkötter, H. *Menschen aus unserer Mitte: Die Opfer von Zwangssterilisierung und Euthanasie* [Human Beings Who Lived in Our Midst: Victims of Forced Sterilization and Euthanasia]. Donauwörth: Auer, 1992.

Katz, Dovid. *Words on Fire: The Unfinished Story of Yiddish.* New York: Basic Books, 2004.

Krinsky, Carol Herselle. *Synagogues of Europe: Architecture, History, Meaning.* New York: The Architectural History Foundation; Cambridge, MA: MIT Press, 1985.

Kundrus, Birthe, and Beate Meyer, eds. *Die Deportation der Juden aus Deutschland: Pläne, Praxis, Reaktionen, 1938–1945.* [The Deportation of the Jews from Germany:

Plans, Actions, Reactions, 1938–1945]. Vol. 20 of *Beiträge zur Geschichte des Nationalsozialismus* [Contributions to the History of National Socialism]. 2nd ed. Göttingen: Wallstein, 2005.

Levi, Primo. *The Drowned and the Saved.* Translated by Raymond Rosenthal. New York: Summit Books, 1988.

Meyer, Beate. "Handlungsspielräume regionaler jüdischer Repräsentanten (1941–1945): Die Reichsvereinigung der Juden in Deutschland und die Deportationen" [Possibility for Action by Jewish Representatives (1941–1945): The Jewish Umbrella Organization (RV) in Germany and the Deportations]. In *Die Deportation der Juden aus Deutschland*, edited by Birthe Kundrus and Beate Meyer, 63–85. Göttingen: Wallstein, 2005.

Momigliano, Arnaldo. "J. G. Droysen Between Greeks and Jews." In *Essays in Ancient and Modern Historiography*, 307. Middletown, CT: Weslyan University Press, 1977.

Robinson, Jacob. *And the Crooked Shall Be Made Straight: The Eichmann Trial, the Jewish Catastrophe, and Hannah Arendt's Narrative.* New York: Macmillan Co., 1965.

Schmid, Hans-Dieter, et al., eds. *Ahlem: Die Geschichte einer jüdischen Gartenbauschule und ihres Einflusses auf Gartenbau und Landschafts-Architektur in Deutschland und Israel* [Ahlem: The Story of a Jewish Horticultural School and Its Influence on Horticulture and Landscaping in Germany and Israel]. Bremen: Edition Temmen, 2008.

Sorkin, David. *The Transformation of German Jewry 1780–1840.* New York: Oxford University Press, 1987.

Steinberg, Paul. *Speak You Also: A Survivor's Reckoning.* Translated by Linda Coverdale with Bill Ford. New York: Metropolitan Books, Henry Holt, 2000.

Trunk, Isaiah. *Judenrat: The Jewish Councils in Eastern Europe Under Nazi Occupation.* New York: Macmillan Co., 1972.

Walk, J., ed. *Das Sonderrecht für die Juden im NS-Staat* [The Special Laws for the Jews in the National Socialist State]. 2nd ed. Heidelberg: UTB für Wissenschaft, Hüthig C.F. Müller, 1996.

Weinberg, Werner. *Self-Portrait of a Holocaust Survivor.* Jefferson, NC: McFarland & Co., 1985.

Index

Page numbers in italics refer to illustrations